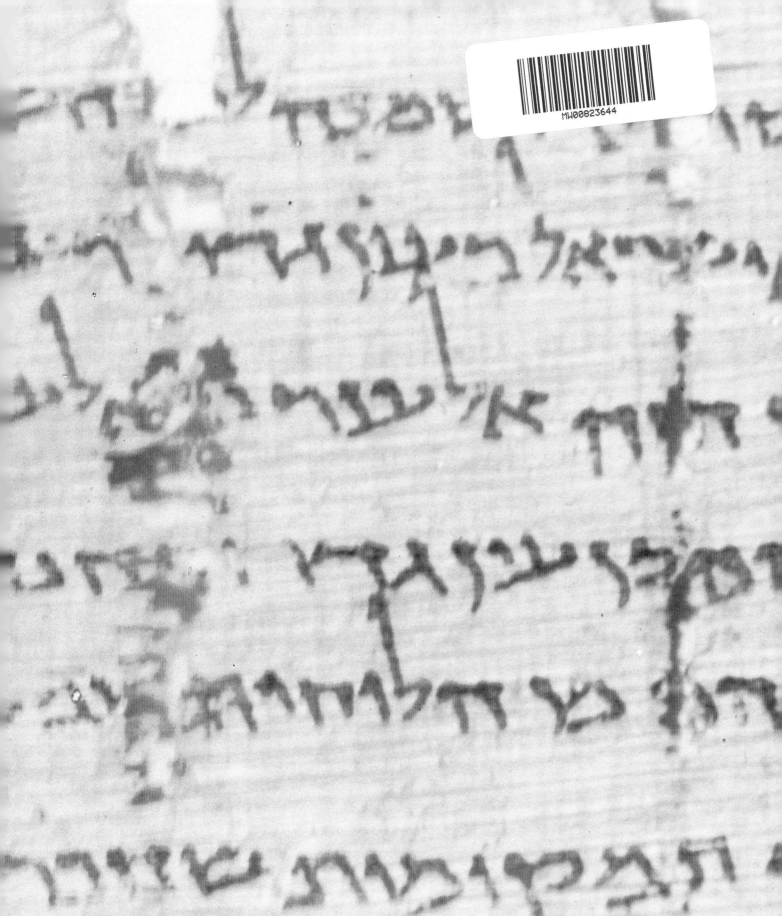

THE BIBLE

A People Listen to God

Design by
Ignasi Ricart

•

Text by
Joan Baró i Cerqueda

•

Illustration by
Maria Rius

•

Translation by
Carmen Aguinaco

A Liturgical Press Book

 THE LITURGICAL PRESS
Collegeville, Minnesota

To my father, Salvador Baró i Triquell: *the endeavour.*
To my mother, Carme Cerqueda i Balart: *the trustfulness.*
To their courage.

This book has been published in Spanish under the title *La Biblia: Un pueblo a la escucha de Dios* © 1995 by EDITORIAL CLARET, S.A., Barcelona, Spain. For the design, the introduction, and the notes © 1995 by Ignasi Ricart; for the original literary text © 1995 by Joan Baró i Cerqueda; for the illustrations © 1995 by Maria Rius; for the translation of *La Biblia: Un poble a l' escolta de Déu* © 1995 by Ana Muñoz Durán. All rights reserved.

1   2   3   4   5   6   7

Library of Congress Cataloging-in-Publication Data

Baró i Cerqueda, Joan.
   [Bíblia. English]
   The Bible : a people listen to God / design by Ignasi Ricart ;
text by Joan Baró i Cerqueda ; illustration by María Rius ;
translation by Carmen Aguinaco.
      p.   cm.
   ISBN 0-8146-2509-6 (alk. paper)
   1. Bible stories, English. [1. Bible stories.] I. Rius, María,
ill. II. Title.
BS551.2.B2813   1998
220.9'505—dc21
                          98-16530
                            CIP
                            AC

Contents

Introduction

Let's talk about this book that you have in your hands, the Bible.

Bible is a Greek word that we've incorporated into our own language. In Greek, *biblion* means book, and *biblia* means collection of books.

You have already noticed that the Bible is a very thick book. That should not be surprising. A combined total of seventy-three books make up the Bible. You may not even have this many books in your home.

The first books were written about three thousand years ago; the last were written about two thousand years ago. So, all seventy-three were written in a span of about one thousand years.

We often use different names in speaking about this combination of books that make the Bible: the Scriptures, the Holy Book. The important thing to know is that we are all referring to the same book.

The history of the covenant between God and people is explained in these books. A covenant is a pact that, in this case, God made with humans. As opposed to other pacts, in which both sides benefit, in this covenant people are always favored. Although people were unfaithful to God, God always returned to protect them and to trust in them.

The Old Covenant is the pact between God and the people of Israel. Jesus, the culminating point of the Bible, represents the New Covenant. Everything before him prepared for his coming.

The Bible is made up of the following:

JESUS

NEW TESTAMENT
27 BOOKS
STORIES ABOUT JESUS

OLD TESTAMENT
46 BOOKS
LONG PREPARATION FOR THE
COMING OF JESUS

Testament is a Latin word that means to establish a covenant, to make a pact before witnesses. In the Bible we find the covenant before Jesus (Old Covenant or Old Testament) and the covenant with Jesus (New Covenant or New Testament). The Bible is the great covenant between God and humans. For this reason, you must know that the Bible is the book of the Word of God.

A People Recount Their Histories

It is believed that the confederation of tribes that later became the nation of Israel was born 1200 years before Christ in Shechem, a city situated in the center of Palestine. Some of these tribes were semi-nomadic; they united with a tribe that left Egypt to avoid the oppression that kept them enslaved.

When they told each other of their histories, they realized that they believed in the same God and had many things in common. Then they created one unique history with the history that each group told.

The particular histories, formed this way into a common history, were transmitted orally, without disappearing. But this story was told a little differently in the northern and southern kingdoms, and these different versions were called the tradition of the north and the tradition of the south.

Starting with the establishment of the royalty, the southern tradition was written around the year 900 B.C.E. The northern tradition was written around 750 B.C.E.

The two traditions were definitively joined together after the Babylonian exile (about 300 B.C.E.), and it gave rise to the current story.

The name of Yahweh, which was the one used by the clan who escaped Egypt, was accepted by all of them and every tribe used it in place of what they used to call God.

The other tribes were also included in the covenant made on Mount Sinai between God and the tribe that came from Egypt. Abraham, Isaac, Jacob, Israel, and their own heroes were considered family.

I
Old Covenant
(Old Testament)

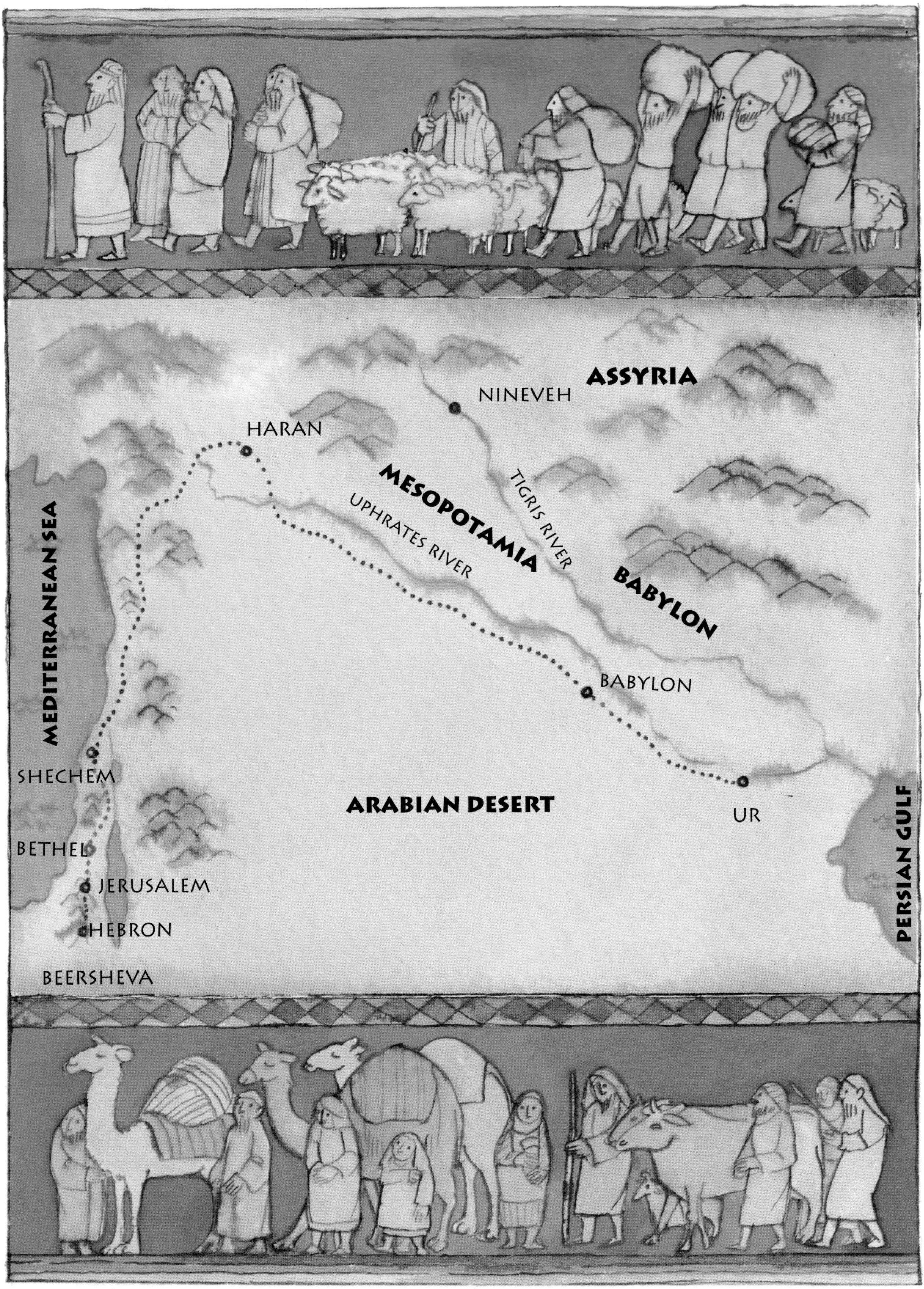

ASSYRIA

NINEVEH

HARAN

MESOPOTAMIA

TIGRIS RIVER

UPHRATES RIVER

BABYLON

BABYLON

MEDITERRANEAN SEA

SHECHEM

ARABIAN DESERT

UR

BETHEL

JERUSALEM

HEBRON

PERSIAN GULF

BEERSHEVA

1.
The Roots of a People

In the beginning, the men and women of the people of Israel could not read or write. At night, each of the tribes or families would sit around and tell the stories of what God had done for them. Everyone kept the memory of the stories about Abraham, Moses, and other important persons. This was the story of the friendship between God and that people.

About one thousand years before Christ, the people of God enjoyed a good life. With King David, the people had conquered the whole territory of Canaan (also called Palestine). This was the land promised by God to their foreparents Abraham, Isaac, and Jacob. They were nomads no longer: they had their own land. God had given it to them.

With King Solomon, the son of David, the people lived at peace. They had the Temple where they could pray and thank God, who had liberated them from the slavery of Egypt. At that time, the learned people of Jerusalem wrote the stories of the tribes of the south.

The northern tribes soon did the same. They did not write like we do now, however: instead of using sheets of paper, they wrote on long rolls of paper.

The prophets wrote what God told them to communicate to the people. Priests, wise men, the teachers of the Law, and poets also wrote. All of them spoke of the great deeds of God. They first wrote in Hebrew and then in Aramaic (the language Jesus spoke). Later, they adopted the language of the Empire: Greek.

The Land Abraham Came From

Long, long ago, Abram lived in Mesopotamia, a country located between two rivers. They provided abundant water and the lands were good pasture for the sheep. Other tribes wished they could have those lands since everything surrounding them, and for miles away, was very dry and desert-like.

These tribes wanted to have Abram's lands, and they attacked constantly so that they could expel the people and stay there themselves. Abram, with the strength of his people and the help of the gods of that land, had been able to defend himself and keep his lands.

Abraham Leaves His Land

At dawn, when the sun rose, a cloud, a luminous sign, pointed in a direction and the voice of the Lord encouraged him to follow:

"Leave your country and go where I will show you. Follow my word and I will make a great people out of you."

And Abram left the country he had earned and kept with so much effort. The influence of gods was so important at that time!

Abram, who was the chief of his family, took his wife Sarai with him, as well as his nephew Lot, all his servants, sheep, and other possessions.

After a tiresome and long journey toward the west, they arrived in the country of Canaan. They saw it was a good place and decided to stay there.

Covenant Between God and Abraham in Cana

Sichem is the country where Abram heard the same voice that made him leave his land. The voice told him, "Abram, I will give this land to you and your people."

Surprised, Abram ran to look for his wife. "Sarai, Sarai, the god I told you about in the land we left behind has spoken to me again. God has promised this land to me and my descendants."

"Lord," Sarai said, "we have walked for so many days that I don't even remember them anymore. It is impossible for the god of our land to be the same that has spoken to you now."

Abram was confused. "It is the same god, the same voice, the same words. Until now, every time we have moved we have honored the new gods we met on our way, but this is something extraordinary. God will be with me wherever I go, if I agree to form God's people. This will be my only God. The Lord, my God!"

"What you say is very strange, and I do not understand it. All the other people of this land do not have that same god. They worship the gods of the land, like everyone else does. Each land has its own god. No one would accept that a god could be united to just one person or a people. They will think you are crazy," Sarai warned.

"I know, but this god is different. This Lord is different. I have built an altar here in Sichem as a sign of fidelity and as a reminder of our pact."

Despite Sarai's mistrust, the pact had already been established.

Hunger Forces Them to Go to Egypt

At that time, they had bad harvests; there was hunger in the land and Abram and his family went to a more prosperous country called Egypt.

"Sarai," said Abram, "if the Egyptians ever learn that you are my wife, they will kill me to keep your beauty for themselves. Say you are my sister, and thus they will want to keep me happy in order to get to you."

Circumstances left no choice for Abram—it was either starvation in Canaan, or the Egyptians killing him to get to his wife. The trick Abram wanted to play would allow him to stay alive. Sarai knew this: "I will do as you say, my lord."

Newly arrived in Egypt, Sarai's beauty was soon known in the royal court. She was so beautiful that Pharaoh—the king of Egypt—gave Abram everything he wanted: animals, slaves, and servants, as long as he could have Sarai as his wife. Abram became wealthy this way.

But, as soon as the Pharaoh took Sarai as his wife, tragedy befell him. He did not know where all his problems were coming from until he discovered they originated with the God of Abram. He should not have married Sarai because she was Abram's wife.

Pharaoh was very angry, and he called Abram and asked him, "Why did you deceive me? Didn't I shower gifts and goods upon you?"

"Forgive me, your majesty. I was afraid that if I said she was my wife, you would have me killed to keep her," Abram defended himself.

"You may be right. But one way or another, I have to stop this spell of bad luck. Leave my country with your wife and your riches. My troubles will then be over."

Separation and Lot's Rescue

They immediately left Egypt and, since Abram's and Lot's herds were very numerous, all along the way the shepherd constantly fought for territory.

"Listen to me, Lot," Abram said to his nephew. "With what you have you can live on your own. We don't need our shepherds to fight over space. Let us separate so that our problems will cease."

"I agree. I will go to the plains of Jordan, to the city of Sodom."

"Very good. I will go back to Canaan where I lived before Egypt."

The two groups parted. But one day messengers came to Abram who told him that Lot had been made a prisoner by an enemy king. Abram wanted to rescue his nephew and ordered, "Have the men ready. We will attack our enemy by night while they sleep. So, even if they outnumber us, we will prevail."

Abram's men stole quietly into the camp of the adversaries who were sleeping. Taken by surprise, the enemy could not defend themselves. They suffered a great defeat, and Lot was liberated. There was great rejoicing in the family and the tribe of Abram.

God Promises Abraham Great Descendants

A few days later, in the middle of the night, when his soul was fully at peace, Abram heard the word of the Lord again: "Abram! I watch over you, and since you have been faithful, I will reward you even more."

"Lord! What do I care about rewards when, if I die, I will not be able to leave an inheritance to anyone? Sarai cannot have children," Abram complained.

"Look at the sky, Abram. What do you see? It is full of stars. There are so many that you would never be able to count them; yet, your descendants will be more numerous than the stars."

"I believe you, my God, and I offer these animals in sacrifice," Abram said, sacrificing two goats as a sign of covenant.

The Lord continued, "Not only will your descendants be many, but I will also give this country of Canaan to them. Before they own it, however, they will have to suffer. They will even be enslaved, but the land will be theirs."

"I am too old for that, but I trust in you," Abram concluded.

Tongues of fire suddenly appeared on the sacrificed animals as a symbol that the Lord was accepting Abram's covenant.

Abraham Has a Son by Hagar

Some time later, Sarai realized that she was getting old and did not have children, so she searched for a solution. She did so in the traditional way at that time. When Abram returned home she said, "My lord, you know well that I have not been able to give you children. Since I am now getting old, I beg you to try to have children with my slave Hagar. In this way, I will have a child through her and our family will have descendants. No one has suffered more with this problem than I, and you are witness that I have tried every possible method. I am an unfortunate woman and I thank you for not having rejected me as many men do in order to look for a woman who can give them children. I feel barren and I don't want to make you unhappy."

"I feel the same," Abram said. "I would have liked to have children by you, but we have to accept divine will. I agree with you, Sarai: a son will consolidate our endowment and from him a great people will come out. I will then try it with the slave."

As a fruit of her relations with Abram, Hagar the slave conceived a child and she felt superior to her mistress, who could not have children. Forgetting that she was just a servant, she was rough with Sarai, who could not endure the situation and talked to Abram.

"Have you seen, my husband, how Hagar treats me since she is pregnant? She despises me, and she acts as if she were the real mistress of the house."

"Sarai, the slave belongs to you, and you can do with her as you please. She should be grateful to you for having allowed her to conceive a baby by your husband. You cannot allow her to pretend she is the mistress, even if she is pregnant."

A little later, Hagar left the house due to Sarai's mistreatment of her. She had not been gone for long when the Lord spoke to her:

"Hagar! Return to your mistress' house and be submissive. Your son will be called Ishmael and great people will come from him."

"Who are you? Are you the god of my lord?" she asked fearfully. "I will do as you say and I will respect my mistress."

Hagar returned to the property and when she saw Sarai she said, "Forgive my behavior. My pregnancy made me arrogant. I did not take into account that you did me a favor by allowing me to have a child for you. If you accept me back I will serve you as faithfully as I can."

"Rise and do your work. I would have regretted losing a servant like you, but I had no choice because of your attitude," Sarai said.

When the time arrived, the slave gave a son to Abram and they called him Ishmael, as the Lord had commanded. According to tradition, the child was considered to be Sarai's and Abram's even though the slave had given birth to him.

Sarah Will Have a Son

A few days after Ishmael's birth the Lord told Abram, "If you are as faithful as you have been up to now, I will give this country to you and your descendants. As a sign of this covenant, your name will no longer be Abram, but Abraham. I will be your God. You will have to circumcise your male children, and Sarai, your wife, will bear a son."

"A son! A son! Sarai's and mine! This is my dream, my lifelong dream. A son! I will do everything as you say," Abraham said full of joy.

When he got home Sarai noticed he looked distracted.

"What's the matter?"

"The Lord has spoken to me. From today on I have been renamed Abraham, as if I had been born again."

"That is a beautiful name. Doesn't it mean 'father of multitudes'?"

"That's right. This name gives new meaning to my life. Now the most important thing is faithfulness to this covenant. You will also change your name; from now on you will be Sarah, because these people will come from the baby who will be born to you," Abraham explained.

"Would that it be as you say! But, at my age, I find that hard to believe."

"You have to believe it because the Lord has already shown his power on many occasions," Abraham encouraged her.

As they spoke, three people arrived, and, being hospitable as their tradition dictated, Sarah and Abraham invited them to sit down and eat. It turned out that the visitors were angels of the Lord, and God spoke through them.

"Abraham, we are grateful for your hospitality. You are a good man. Your wife, Sarah, will be pregnant and bear a son within a year."

Hearing this, Sarah laughed because she was too old to have children.

"Don't laugh, Sarah, because everything is possible for the Lord," the travelers warned.

"I didn't laugh," Sarah lied, realizing she had offended her guests.

Destruction of Sodom and Gomorrah

Once they had rested and regained their strength, the travelers, who were angels of God, wanted to go on to Sodom. Abraham offered to accompany them.

As they were traveling, the three visitors said, "Only evil deeds are done in the cities of Sodom and Gomorrah, and we are going to destroy them."

Knowing that they were speaking on the Lord's behalf, Abraham interceded.

"But certainly there must be good people among the evil ones. It would be unfair for you to destroy everything."

"If there are fifty good persons, the city will be spared. We will not destroy it."

"What if the number fell a little short of fifty?" Abraham insisted.

"It will be forgiven, even if there are only forty-five good people," the strangers accepted.

"What about if there are forty?" Abraham pushed his luck.

"They will also be forgiven."

They continued bargaining for a while. At the end Abraham said, "Forgive my insistence, but, what if there were only ten good people there?"

"Even so, the Lord would forgive the whole city."

As they were speaking, they reached Sodom and settled in Lot's house, Abraham's nephew. When the citizens found out that strangers had arrived, they went to Lot's house demanding that

the strangers come outside so they could do with them what they wished, even if it meant forcing them. Lot tried to reason with them, but meeting their insistence he said, "My brothers, these strangers are in my house and the law of hospitality requires that I protect them."

Instead of calming them down, these words irritated them even more, and they reacted in a threatening way. Then Lot thought of a desperate solution.

"If you are so excited, I will give you my two unmarried daughters."

Lot tried everything before breaking the sacred law of hospitality.

> In those cultures of long ago, the father was the owner of sons and daughters and could do with them as he saw fit. "I offer you my maiden daughters": between the duty to protect his guests and that of protecting his daughters, Lot chose to offer his daughters.

The citizens were not listening, and since they continued to threaten, the angels of the Lord blinded them. Then they gathered Lot's family in order to leave the city, which would be destroyed immediately. They warned him, "Do not worry about what you leave behind. You cannot take everything with you. You just have enough time to flee."

At the beginning they were reluctant to leave so suddenly, but they finally made up their minds and everyone left except Lot's wife, who delayed too long trying to gather more and more of their belongings. She was surprised by a salt shower and the fire that destroyed the cities.

Sarah Protects Her Son

When her time came, Sarah had her child. They named him Isaac, which means "son of laughter" because Sarah had laughed at the divine promises that should not be doubted, even if they sound crazy.

Eight days later, Abraham had his son circumcised as the Lord had commanded.

Circumcision is a small surgical procedure practiced by almost all Semitic peoples. It consists of making a small incision to remove the skin that covers the penis (the foreskin or prepuce). Every Israelite boy was circumcised on the eighth day after his birth.

When the Lord promised Abraham that he would be the father of a great nation, the nation of Israel, God asked him to circumcise all the male descendants. This would be a physical sign of belonging to the people of God.

Abraham and Sarah could not believe their eyes. They wished so much for a son, had imagined the moment for so long, had shed so many tears! And now he was there, in front of their very eyes, and their hearts were filled with joy.

The years went by and Isaac grew up with his brother Ishmael. Sara saw that and she was not pleased. She was afraid that Ishmael, the son of the slave, would acquire as many rights as her own son.

She spoke to Abraham about it. "Lord, the son of the slave shares life with Isaac, and, since he is older, I am afraid he will harm my son or take his inheritance from him. Dismiss the mother and the child so that we can live in peace."

"Don't worry, Sarah. I know what each one is due."

Abraham did not want to send them away because Ishmael was also his son. But Sarah insisted so much that Abraham threw Ishmael and his mother out of the house. They ended up in the desert. When they ran out of water, they thought they were going to die, but Hagar invoked the Lord God. God showed them where there was a spring of water and said to them, "Hagar, your son will also be the origin of a great people who will live in the desert and be master archers."

The Lord God Asks for Isaac's Life

A few years had gone by when one day, while Abraham was praying, the Lord said to him: "Abraham, take your beloved son and offer him up to me in sacrifice upon the mountain I will show you. Do this as a sign of your faithfulness."

Abraham suffered greatly. That was the worst night in his life. He had wished for a son for his whole life! He had resigned himself to not having one, but then Isaac had arrived through the generosity of the Lord God. At that time, Abraham realized how close he was to his son and how much Isaac meant in his life. He cried out of frustration. It was totally unbelievable that the Lord would now be asking for the death of the son God had granted.

But, with his heart wrenched in a knot, he rose early, prepared everything, and, accompanied by his son, went to the place of sacrifice. If Isaac died now, he would not even have the consolation of his other son, Ishmael, the one he had sent away from his house along with his mother.

As they were walking, Isaac had the feeling they had forgotten something.

"Father, this is the first time we are going to offer a sacrifice without an animal. We have wood, we have fire, but we don't have a lamb."

"Don't you worry, my son. God will provide the lamb."

Reaching the place, Abraham arranged the wood on the altar and placed his son Isaac on top. Just at the moment the knife was about to come down on Isaac's neck, the voice of the Lord was heard.

"Abraham! Abraham! Stop, don't kill the child. I have known your faithfulness since you have not refused to sacrifice your only son and have given up your own feelings and desires. Since you have acted this way, I will fill you with blessings. Your children will be as numerous as the stars of the heavens, and the grains of sand on the beach."

Abraham rushed to untie his son, and he broke down in sobs and in uncontrollable weeping. He had been under so much stress! The salt of his tears mixed with the sweetness of the kisses with which he covered Isaac's body.

He had not yet caught his breath when Abraham felt the need to thank God for his generosity. It was as if, by preserving his son's life, he had also saved his own.

A noise from the bush called his attention: it was a goat whose horns had been caught in the thorns. He took the animal and sacrificed it instead of his son. That sacrifice, which was about to be a tragedy, became a feast.

Sarah Dies

The march of time is relentless. Sarah had been slowly losing her strength and she faded gradually until one day she ceased to breathe. In order to be able to bury her, Abraham asked the owners of the land for a piece of land.

"I am looking for some land to bury my wife."

"You are a prince of the Lord. No one will deny you his tomb, since your god is powerful," a wealthy man answered him.

"I thank you, but I would rather buy a piece of land. The other day I saw some I liked. Isn't Ephron in?"

"Here I am!"

"I would be grateful if you could sell me your field since it has a cave that could serve as a tomb," said Abraham.

"You honor me by choosing my field and I ask you to allow me to give it to you as a gift," Ephron offered.

"I thank you, but I would rather buy it. Thus I will own a little of the land promised to my descendants. And this will be the beginning of the fulfillment of the prophecy of the Lord."

When an agreement on the price was reached, and Abraham paid, he buried Sarah in a cave called Machpelah.

Sarah's tomb meant the possession of his first piece of land, and this comforted Abraham in the painful sadness he felt upon the death of his lifelong companion.

It Is Necessary to Find a Wife for Isaac

Sarah's death made Abraham realize that he, too, was getting old and would not live much longer. This thought led him to decide to call the steward who was his most trusted servant and tell him, "Take whatever you need and go to the land of my ancestors where you will find my relatives. You have to find a wife for Isaac to preserve the purity of the lineage. He cannot take a foreign woman from the tribes around us. You will go back by the same way I followed when the Lord asked me to leave the land of the great rivers. We have talked about this many times. You know very well the qualities that my son's wife should have."

"It will be done as you say, lord."

After pledging his loyalty, the steward went on his way, loaded with riches and gifts for the woman he would look for.

The journey was harsher than he had expected, although Abraham had warned him.

Upon arriving, exhausted after the long journey, a young woman appeared offering him water and feeding the camels.

"What's your name, sister?" asked the traveler.

"Rebekah, Nahor's daughter."

"Nahor? Didn't he have a brother named Abraham?"

"Yes. How did you know? Abraham left these lands before I was born. That happened many years ago."

The steward realized that the Lord had placed Rebekah in his way and, upon her invitation, he went to her home to meet her family.

Laban, Rebekah's brother, who had been informed about the arrival, came out to greet him.

"I am the steward of Abraham's house, your relative, who sends me to look for a wife for his son," said Abraham's steward to Laban.

"We are very pleased to get news from Abraham. I have not met him, but I have heard about him from my parents," Laban greeted him. "By the gifts you bring, I see he has really prospered. Come into the house, rest, and stay with us for a few days."

The steward brought him up to date on Abraham's life and was interested in the family so that he could tell his lord. The following day, Abraham's messenger commented, "I would like to ask you for Rebekah's hand for Isaac, my lord's son, so that the purity of lineage can be kept."

"We are delighted that Abraham has remembered us. Rebekah will go with you and will be Isaac's wife," said Laban.

Once the rites and farewell party concluded, Rebekah accompanied Abraham's steward. They wanted to get there soon, but a long, long trip awaited them.

During the trip, based on what Abraham's messenger had told her, Rebekah was trying to picture what the man who was about to become her husband would be like. Just as all the young girls of her time, she had been brought up to accept the man her family chose as her husband, regardless of who he was. Despite everything, she was curious.

After a seemingly endless journey, they finally arrived. They were quenching their thirst at a well when Isaac showed up. When he saw Rebekah, he was glad she was the chosen one. She could only look away. Both of them liked each other immediately.

Isaac took Rebekah as his wife as soon as the necessary preparations for the wedding were completed. She was happy to be Isaac's wife, and they got along well from the very beginning.

Abraham's Grandchildren Will Not Know Their Grandfather

After Isaac and Rebekah's wedding, which ensured the continuation of the lineage, Abraham, who was already very old, died in peace.

As he had wished, he was buried by Sarah in the cave of Machpelah—the first possession in the land of Canaan.

But he might not have died so peacefully had he known that Rebekah could not have children. For several years Isaac was concerned with this. Isaac did not stop asking the Lord for the grace of a son, which was everything he desired.

"Lord, my God! What is the sense of your promises if I don't have any children with whom to form your people?" Isaac prayed.

"Isaac! You have been without children for many years. Now Rebekah will be with child, and she will have twins. Do not forget, however, that although the children are yours, you could not have had them without my help. Therefore, they must carry out my designs according to the covenant with Abraham."

"I thank you, my God. And I guarantee that both my children and I will respect the pact," Isaac rejoiced.

When Rebekah was pregnant, she noticed that the two babies moved inside her and the Lord God said to her, "The two babies who are now quarreling inside you will form two nations and the older will serve the younger."

Isaac and Rebekah were very happy with the two babies coming.

Who Will Be the First of the Children?

At the appointed time, the first baby was born. He was very rosy, and they called him Esau. Grabbing at Esau's heel, out came Jacob.

When they were little it was evident that Esau was adventurous; he always had something to do outside the tent. He looked like his father Isaac.

Jacob was just the opposite. He was more inclined to stay in the tent and spend more time with his mother. Both Rebekah and Isaac showed preference for the son each was closer to.

A few years later, Jacob was in the tent as was his habit, and he had cooked himself a good meal. Esau was exhausted from his work in the fields and said to his brother, "Jacob, I am starving. In these last days I have not caught anything worthwhile. Let me eat of that meal that smells so good."

"I'll let you try it, my brother, with one condition: you must accept, in front of everyone, that from now on I will be the older brother. You will be the second," Jacob said.

"I am very tired and I haven't eaten for such a long time that I don't have any strength. If I don't eat something I will die, and what good will being the older do me? Give me some of what you have cooked and keep the privileges of being the first."

Esau was so hungry that he wolfed the meal Jacob had made. In a minute, he had eaten everything. Once he was satisfied, he left the tent because he could not sit still for a minute.

They Move from Their Land in Order to Eat

There were times of scarcity and the time came when there was hardly anything to eat.

Isaac told himself, "I cannot allow my family and myself to die here. If that were the case, a great people could never come out of me, as goes the promise that our God had made and repeated so many times."

Sensing his concern, the Lord God said to him, "Isaac, do not be afraid. You will establish yourself in the land I will show you. You will go there as an immigrant, but your descendants will possess it. Although now you are going through a bad time, and it is hard to believe, your descendants will be a multitude. All this will be fulfilled as long as you act like Abraham, your father, who respected my laws according to the covenant we made."

The place where Isaac settled was Gerar, the land of the Philistines. His harvests were so abundant that the inhabitants of the land were jealous. After a few years, they had to leave because the Philistines made their lives very hard. With all his family and his possessions, Isaac moved again.

In Beer-sheba, the new land, he continued to prosper. His tribe was so large and powerful that the Philistines went looking for him and said to him, "Let's make a covenant by which we make a commitment to live in peace. You will not attack us and we will not attack you."

Rebekah and Jacob Try to Trick Isaac

Later on, Esau wanted to get married to a woman from the land where they lived, but his parents did not agree. They wanted her to belong to the same tribe. Despite everything, Esau did not pay any attention to them, and, disobeying his parents, married two women who did not belong to his tribe. This greatly worried Rebekah and Isaac.

The years went by and Isaac was getting weaker and weaker, and his eyes were so tired that he could hardly see. He called Esau and said to him, "My son! I am old and death could come any time now. It is necessary for me to bless you before I die so that you can be the heir of the prophecy of the Lord to our people. So go hunting, prepare whatever you catch, and I will eat. Then I will bless you before my strength falters."

> To bless (from bene dicere in Latin) means to "say well." When God says well of someone, he or she becomes whole since the word of God is all powerful and fulfills everything it says. On the contrary, to curse (mal dicere) means to say badly and, therefore, to bring about disgrace.

Obeying Isaac, Esau went hunting for some animal that would please his father.

But Rebekah, who had heard what Isaac had said to his son Esau, ran out looking for Jacob to tell him, "Your father has commanded Esau to cook a hunted animal for him and then he will bless him. If he does so, the rights of inheritance that Esau granted to you will not be worth anything. The prophecy of the Lord will be fulfilled through him and not through you. Go, then, and bring me a couple of goats from the flock. I will cook them the way your father likes them and so he will bless you instead of Esau."

Jacob answered, "Perhaps my father will not recognize me with his sight, but he can do it with his hearing, even if I try to speak like Esau; and if he touches me, he will certainly recognize me. Esau is very hairy, and I am not. If my father realizes the deceit, I will have to bear his curse and that will be worse than not getting his blessing."

"Your father is very old. He doesn't see and he is hard of hearing," Rebekah answered. "I don't think he will recognize your voice. About your skin, I will solve that. Go! Hurry up and listen to me, lest your brother come back before we know it. If something goes wrong, may the Lord bring upon me the curse of Isaac. You will be free from it."

Is Jacob Able to Take Esau's Place?

Jacob did as his mother had told him. Rebekah prepared the best meal she had ever cooked. She told Jacob to bathe in order to lose his odor and made him dress up in his brother's clothes so that he would smell like Esau—since Isaac had a good sense of smell.

In order to deceive Isaac's touch, with the skin of the two goats she had just cooked, she covered the parts of Jacob's body which were not clothed. When she finished, she placed the dish in Jacob's hands and sent him to his father. Jacob went to Isaac and said, "Here I am, father."

"Who are you? Which one of my children are you?"

"I am Esau, your eldest," Jacob lied. "I have hunted the best piece, I have cooked it, and I come to give it to you so that then you can bless me."

"How did you catch it so fast, my son?"

"The Lord, our God, placed it before me. That's why it has taken me such a short time."

"Come, my son. I want to touch you," said Isaac, who was a little suspicious.

Jacob came closer and his father touched him to see who he was. Isaac touched the hairy arms of "Esau" and touched his neck and found it full of hair, too. And he thought, "The voice sounds like Jacob's, but the arms and neck are Esau's."

And he thought his doubts were due to his own old age. That's why he said, "Serve me, my son, that I may eat the meat you brought. Then I can bless you."

After eating, Isaac, who still found his son's behavior strange, said to him, "Come closer and kiss me, my son."

Isaac wanted to see if he smelled like Esau. Jacob kissed him and Isaac could smell Esau's clothes. This convinced him and he blessed Jacob, sure that he was blessing Esau.

"May the Lord give you wheat and wine in abundance. May peoples and nations serve you. May you be lord over your brothers and sisters. May those who bless you be blessed and those who curse you be cursed."

After this, Jacob took his leave from his father and went out.

Esau Asks for the Blessing

A little later, Esau came into Isaac's tent. He brought the meal he had prepared with his catch and said, "Father, here is the animal I have cooked for you. Then you can bless me."

Isaac reacted with surprise: "Who are you?"

"I am Esau, your eldest son."

Confused, Isaac continued, "Who brought me the meal earlier, then? I have eaten and I have blessed him."

When he heard that, Esau let out a cry of anguish stronger than that of a wounded animal. After a while, when he was a little calmer, he demanded, "Bless me too, father. Bless me!"

Hearing his son, Isaac felt the blood freeze in his veins. He would have given his life to be able to bless his favorite son, but he could not do it. Then, dumbfounded, and shaken, he said, "Your brother has deceived me and has stolen your blessing. Now he will be your lord and the lord of the people. You will have to live by your own means, and you will have to serve him. But when you rebel, you will be able to liberate yourself from him."

Isaac had never imagined that he would see Esau—the strong Esau—weeping and whimpering as an abandoned child, helpless and forsaken in the depths of his heart.

That was one of those moments in which, as a father, he would have given anything to be in his son's place. Certainly his old heart would not suffer as much as Esau's, whom he saw writhing in pain.

"This is the second time he has deceived me," cried Esau. "First he made me sell him my rights as the first child and now he has taken my blessing away from me!"

And, full of resentment, he said to himself, "My father cannot live much longer. When he dies, I will kill Jacob."

Jacob Is Sent to Look for a Wife

When Esau left, Isaac thought that, in any case, he was not the older son either, and it was through him that the divine prophecy would be fulfilled. The will of God had decided that Isaac would be the one to inherit the covenant with the Lord, not Ishmael, his older brother.

On the other hand, Rebekah had taken care to remind him of the divine words when the children were still in her womb: the older will serve the younger. Would this be another manifestation of God's plan?

This thought helped Isaac to regain the peace that he should enjoy in his old age.

But Esau's wish to kill Jacob, which had been quieted in front of Isaac, came to Rebekah's ears. She called her younger son and told him, "Jacob, your brother wants to kill you to get revenge. Go to Haran, to my brother Laban's house. Take advantage of the time you are there to choose a wife from among the women of our people.

"In this way, you will let your brother's anger cool off. When he has forgotten what you did to him, I will send someone to fetch you."

Jacob agreed and Rebekah proposed to Isaac, "My husband and my lord, many times we have discussed the tragedy of Esau taking wives from among the women of this land and not from our own as it should be. If Jacob stays here, he will end up doing the same. Send him away to Haran, to my brother's house; he will be able to get married there and then he will return."

Isaac thought Rebekah's proposal to be sensible and called Jacob to let him know. "Jacob, in order to get married you don't have to look at the women in this land of Canaan. Go to Haran, to the house of Laban, your uncle, and look for a wife there. May the Lord bless you, multiply your descendants, and may you inherit the land promised to Abraham."

So Jacob returned to the origins, to his mother's and his grandfather Abraham's homeland.

Esau found out that Jacob was leaving to get married to a woman of his lineage and, in order to make his parents happy, he did the same. He went to his uncle Ishmael's and married Mahalath, who became his third wife.

Jacob's Dream on the Way to Haran

Jacob left Beer-sheba for Haran. After a long day's journey, and when the sun had set, he settled down for the night. He used a rock as his pillow and had a dream:

A ladder joined heaven and earth and a multitude of angels went up and down on it. The Lord God was on top and he spoke, "I am the Lord, the God of Abraham and Isaac. I will give the land where you rest now to you and your descendants. Your descendants will be as numerous as the dust of the earth and will extend from east to west and from north to south.

"All the nations on earth will receive my blessing through you and your descendants. I am with you and will protect you, wherever you may be, and I will return to this land and not abandon you until my promise is fulfilled."

Jacob woke up. He realized that the Lord was with him in this place and he felt fear. Being so close to God could have caused his death. He took the rock that had served as a pillow and set it up as a monument and called that place Bethel. He also made the following promise: "If the Lord God is with me and keeps me, helps me on my way, and returns me safe and sound to my father's house, he will be my God and I will offer up a tenth of everything I own."

He continued on his way. It was a long journey, full of difficulties, heat, thirst, and sweat. Many times during that long trip Jacob felt foolish! He had left his father's house where he had a secured future to go searching for an uncle who lived so far away and who perhaps had already died, or had moved somewhere else. Perhaps all his efforts would be in vain. But his doubts vanished when he remembered the eyes of his brother so full of hatred, the shaking voice of his mother, or the image of his father, so weak.

He must also not forget that he had been blessed. The desires of his grandfather Abraham and his father Isaac met in him.

These thoughts returned his strength to him when he wavered and gave him serenity when he grew discouraged with such a hard journey.

Jacob Finds Rachel

Many days later, Jacob neared Haran. He sat by a well and started to talk to some shepherds who were bringing their flocks to drink.

"Where are you from, brothers?"

In that land it was normal to greet strangers as brothers to show respect.

"We are from Haran," they answered.

"Do you know Laban?" asked Jacob. "I need to find him."

"Of course! You are in luck. There is Rachel, his daughter."

And they pointed to where Rachel was coming.

"I thank you."

Jacob walked toward Rachel. His first impulse was to explain to her who he was. But he was afraid that if he told her she would be nervous and neglect leading her sheep to water.

He knew very well the value of each of these animals for a shepherd, and he could not allow any of them to die because of him. So first he made sure that all the animals had quenched their thirst.

"Sister! Do you want me to help you to give them a drink?" he asked Rachel.

"Yes, of course. Your help will be welcome. The stone that covers the well is too heavy."

When the sheep had finished drinking, he told her who he was. The first reaction for both was to kiss and embrace and cry; that was the same reaction with his uncle Laban. They had not had any news from Rebekah in all the years since Abraham's steward took her away to marry Isaac.

Besides, Jacob was coming from far away. It was as if he had come from the other end of the world.

Laban and Jacob Make a Deal

Laban received Jacob in his house and, after celebrating his arrival, Jacob stayed with them. He worked as hard as he could.

A few weeks later, Laban realized Jacob knew the trade well. He thought it would benefit him if Jacob stayed. So he said to Jacob, "Jacob, during this month that you have worked in my house, you have more than earned your keep. Don't be in a hurry to leave. It is not necessary for you to go back on such a long and tiring journey. If you think we have treated you well, stay and work for me and tell me what wages you want."

Jacob knew that his brother was still very angry with him, and that it would be a few years before his anger subsided.

On the other hand, he was not looking forward to experiencing the crushing heat day after day, or the wind storms that filled his eyes with dust even if he was protected, or the constant dryness in his mouth were he to make the journey home.

Moreover, he saw in his uncle's proposal a possibility to achieve the objective of his visit: his wedding. Thus, he answered: "I will work for you for seven years if you give me your daughter Rachel for my wife."

Laban, who was very shrewd, thought he could kill two birds with one stone and agreed. He was gaining a good worker and solving the problem of getting Rachel married.

Jacob worked for Laban and during that time both were happy. When the time was up, Jacob said, "I have worked for you for the time agreed. Give me Rachel, then, and we will get married."

"Give me a little time to organize the wedding. Then, you can marry her," answered Laban.

Whom Does Jacob Marry?

A little later, when everything was ready, the wedding took place. It was a great day. After the ceremony, there was an extraordinary banquet. Everyone rejoiced and partied.

Laban took care that the wine was abundant for all, especially for Jacob the bridegroom, who, that night, went to the bridal tent. He was walking in darkness and his vision was blurred by the wine. Laban took his daughter there and she was united to Jacob in marriage.

The following morning Jacob woke up late.

It was then, when his head was clear and there was light coming through the window, that he realized that Laban had fulfilled only half of his agreement. By his side in bed was Leah, Laban's eldest daughter, and not Rachel, as he had wished. Furious, Jacob went to Laban's tent and shouted, "Do I look like a fool for you to have deceived me in such a way? Who did you take me for? Didn't I fulfill my part of the agreement? Why did you fool me in this way and make me spend the night with Leah when I loved Rachel?

"You sounded so proud saying I belong to your family, and then you treat me worse than a foreigner. What have I done to you? What kind of love do you have for your sister Rebekah, my mother? Why did you always flatter me only to turn around and do this to me?"

Laban and Jacob's Discussion

Laban needed all his shrewdness to calm Jacob down:

"You are a good worker. You have always known that I hold you in high esteem. Are you mad at me because I have given you the first daughter and not the second? Isn't the first one the most important? Are you scolding me because I have made an exchange by which you benefit?

"If I have kept the second, who is not as important as the first, how have I harmed you? Do you think I have deceived you and given you less than we had agreed? No. I have given you more, so you win.

"Are you complaining that you have been with Leah now that the night is over? Why didn't you bring her back last night, before you slept together? Or should I conclude that a man who is unable to distinguish his wife from another on the wedding night would not make a good husband for any of my daughters?"

"Don't give me any stories now. You knew I loved Rachel and not Leah. Now you are trying to justify your trickery. But don't make me believe that it is my fault on top of everything. Give me Rachel as my wife if you don't want to lose your best worker," shouted Jacob.

"You are too excited and cannot reason. You'll see when you think it over calmly that I have only offered you a benefit.

"On the other hand, you know our traditions: we don't let the younger daughter marry until the older one is married. You should have known that.

"You still love Rachel. So what is the problem? I don't want you to be mad at me. So that you see I trust you, next week I will give Rachel to you as long as you promise to work for me for another seven years."

When Jacob heard he could have Rachel, he calmed down and agreed to do as Laban had said.

In this way, Jacob married Rachel the following week and worked at Laban's house for seven more years.

Thanks to his trickery, Laban managed to get both of his daughters married. This was especially important for Leah, who was not as pretty as Rachel and was not as likely to get many proposals. In addition, he had gotten Jacob to work for him for seven more years.

It was a masterful move. The difficult conditions in those times meant that deceit was, to a large extent, acceptable.

The Children of Jacob

Due to the circumstances in which the weddings took place, it turned out that Jacob lived with, loved, and was much closer to Rachel, while he treated Leah as if she were a second-class wife.

Jacob's behavior toward Leah made her feel despised, so the Lord granted her the grace of fertility. Rachel, however, whom Jacob loved very much, was sterile and had no children.

Leah had four children: Reuben, Simeon, Levi, and Judah. She thought this would make Jacob look at her and pay her some attention.

Rachel, accustomed to being Jacob's favorite, was jealous because Leah had children. Her desire to have children led her to tell her husband, "My lord, give me a son or I will die of jealousy."

"You don't know what you are asking. It is the Lord who gives the grace of children. I cannot do anything," Jacob scolded her.

"Then I will give you my servant as a wife and her children will be mine," added Rachel.

Jacob accepted the deal. Bilhah, Rachel's servant, had two sons from Jacob. Their names were Dan and Nephtali.

Since Leah had not gotten pregnant again she convinced Jacob to have relations with her slave, Zilpah. Through Zilpah she had Gad and Asher.

Some years later, Leah was fertile again and she bore two more children for Jacob, Issachar and Zebulun, and a daughter, Dinah.

These children made Rachel even more miserable since she had not had any of her own. But the Lord remembered her and she had a son named Joseph.

Jacob was happy for Rachel when he saw her happy.

Jacob Prospered

It was too long since Jacob had left his land. So he said to Laban, "My uncle, I have worked for you for all the years we had agreed. Now I would like to go with the women and children."

"Since you have been with me, my wealth has increased greatly. Don't go and I will pay you whatever you ask for," said Laban.

"I will keep the black sheep and the goats with stained skin. In this way, I will be able to build my own farm."

Laban knew that those animals were few compared to the total flock, so he agreed immediately.

When the sheep and goats went to drink, they would mate—sheep with sheep and goats with goats. Jacob tried to get only the stronger ones to mate. Many came out with spots and were very strong, and in this way Jacob's flocks increased.

One day while he was keeping his flock, the Lord commanded, "Go back to your country. I will guide you."

Without any hesitation, he told the women, "The Lord has commanded me to go back to my land. I don't think there is any reason to stay. Your father has deceived me many times. He has changed my wages without asking me, if we had agreed on spotted animals he would change them for striped ones, and if he thought these striped ones were too many, he substituted them for others.

"But the Lord God has helped me, and each time Laban changed a type of animals, the new ones were more numerous than he had intended. So I got richer and richer."

"Let's set on our way as your God has commanded. We don't have anything to do in our father's house. He has mistreated us because he has kept our dowry," Rachel and Leah said.

Return to Canaan

They prepared everything very quietly so that Laban would not realize and prevent them from going.

When they were leaving, Rachel picked up some statues that represented Laban's family idols.

Three days later, Laban learned about it and pursued them. He caught up with them at the mountain of Gilead.

"Why did you leave my house as a fugitive, as if my daughters were prisoners of war, and steal my idols from me?" Laban asked.

"Throughout the years I have served you," Jacob answered, "you have deceived me many times—too many to trust you anymore and tell you about our departure. But your gods are not here. Look for them if you want. If you find them, the offending party will die."

After checking the whole camp without finding them, and when Laban saw that Jacob had power, he proposed a truce. They sealed the pact with the sacrifice of an animal, and Laban returned to his tents.

Because of the animals and the children, the return trip to Canaan was even longer than Jacob's first trip many years earlier. Despite everything, Jacob found it more pleasant. Time went by fast. And Jacob also thought that, although he had gone there with nothing, he was now returning with much wealth.

What Would Esau Do to Jacob?

When they were near the land of Canaan, Jacob knew Esau was coming to meet him. Fearing an attack, he did the following: he prepared five flocks of goats, sheep, camels, cows, and donkeys. Before each of the flocks he put a servant with these instructions: "When you meet Esau and he asks you who you are, you can say, 'We are servants of your brother Jacob, who offers you this gift to ask you for reconciliation. He comes behind as your servant.'"

Jacob knew that everything was pending on the balance of his brother's reaction: his goods, as well as his life and his family members' lives. That's why he asked for the Lord's help.

"Lord, my God, you have promised that my descendants will be as numerous as the sands of the beach. Save me, then, from my brother Esau, because I am afraid he is going to kill everyone."

Jacob was by himself that night and a stranger fought with him all night until dawn. Their strength were so equal that neither could overcome the other. Suddenly, the stranger dislocated Jacob's leg and said to him, "Your name will no longer be Jacob, which means 'intruder,' but Israel, which means 'God is strong.'"

Then Jacob named that place "The face of God" because he had seen the Lord face-to-face and he had not died.

The following day, Jacob saw that Esau was approaching and he stood before his family. He made reverences to Esau, but Esau ran to embrace him and both were very moved by the encounter.

"What's all this camp I have found in front of you?" Esau asked.

"It is an offering to receive a good welcome on your part," explained Jacob. "I beg you to accept it."

Esau already had possessions and did not want to accept anything, but after much insisting on Jacob's part, he took it.

"Gather up your camp and let's go," Esau proposed.

"I thank you, my brother, but I cannot force the children's or the animals' pace. Many could die."

Rachel Dies, Isaac Dies

When Esau left, Jacob took another route just in case his brother relapsed into his old resentment. Thus, he reached Sechem.

In that city, Jacob's family and servants had problems with the people of the town. Then the Lord God showed him the way to Bethel, while God took care to repel the enemies.

But Rachel would never make it because she was pregnant and her time came. Her strength failed her and she died.

Broken-hearted, Jacob buried his beloved wife in Bethlehem, the place where she had died in childbirth.

Jacob took the newborn in his arms and said to him, "Poor innocent. Your name will be Benjamin, and I will love you more than the others, for your absent mother and for myself."

And he rocked him in his arms tenderly. Although he was leaving a piece of his heart at Rachel's tomb, Jacob had to go on his way after marking the tomb with a monument.

At long last, after so many years of absence, he was able to embrace his father when he arrived in Hebron, the place where Isaac lived. Jacob thanked God that he found his father still alive although he was already very old.

Isaac, on his part, had wanted to keep the little energy he had left until his son's return. He knew that Jacob was to assume leadership for the people and defend the covenant with the Lord.

A few days after Jacob arrived, Isaac died, satisfied that he had left the destiny of his people in Jacob's hands.

Isaac was buried by his sons in the cave of Machpelah, where he could rest with his ancestors.

The Brothers Are Jealous of Joseph

Jacob was established, then, in the land of his father. His children were devoted to watching the flocks, but Jacob favored his sons by Rachel. It was very noticeable: Jacob had given Joseph a tunic that provoked his brothers' envy.

One day, Joseph explained a dream to his brothers: "It was harvest time, and we were tying up the packs in the fields. Mine were straight but yours were bending before it. That same instant, the dream vanished and I saw the sun, the moon, and eleven stars prostrated before me."

When the brothers heard these dreams, they said, "He wants to rule over us."

And the envy they felt toward Joseph became hatred.

Jacob also reproached him, "Perhaps I, your mother, and your brothers will have to revere you?"

But, unable to get mad at Joseph, he reflected on the possible meaning of the dreams of his son.

Some time later, Jacob sent his children to a rich pasture field to tend the flocks. As time went by and he did not hear from them, he thought something must have happened. Concerned about them, he sent Joseph there to report back on the situation of his children and the flocks.

When the brothers saw that Joseph was approaching, they said among themselves, "Look, the dreamer is coming! If we kill him right here, we can tell our father that a wild beast devoured him."

But Reuben, the eldest, wanted Joseph to go back to his father unharmed. So he spoke to his brothers saying, "We don't need to dirty our hands with blood. Let's throw him in a dry well and leave him there. It is a solitary place; that will be enough."

Revenge of Joseph's Brothers

The others listened to Reuben and, as soon as he arrived, Joseph's beloved tunic was taken away and he was thrown into the well. Then Reuben went to take care of the flock and his brothers sat down to eat. Meanwhile they saw there was a caravan of traders on their way to Egypt and commented among themselves, "Let us sell the dreamer to the traders and so we will get something. This is safer, because slaves never come back from Egypt."

They dealt with the traders, and Joseph went with the caravan as a slave.

When Reuben returned from tending the flocks, he realized that Joseph was not in the well. His brothers explained to him, "We sold him to a caravan that came by around noontime."

"Yes, that arrogant one who wanted to be served by us will now work as a slave."

"And besides, we have earned a little money. That was a good idea, wasn't it?"

Reuben, who could not reveal his intentions to his brothers so that they would not mistrust him, asked, "What will we tell our father now?"

"Look, we have kept Joseph's tunic. We will stain it with blood and say that a wild animal has devoured him."

They did so. When he got the news and saw the tunic, Jacob exclaimed, "It belongs to my son; some animal has torn him apart. I am so unfortunate! Rachel died and now our son has disappeared. I had placed in him all the love I had for his mother. What will I do now?"

And he wept disconsolately.

Many days after the events, Jacob continued to be as downcast and sad as he was when he first heard the news. None of his other children, who had stayed with him to console him, had any success in comforting him. He kept repeating, "I wish to die to rejoin my beloved son."

Joseph's Fortunes and Misfortunes

Meanwhile, Joseph ended up at Potiphar's house. He was the chief of guard of the Pharaoh, the king of Egypt.

It did not take Potiphar long to realize that anything entrusted to Joseph was a success. For this reason, he finally entrusted him with the stewardship of his goods and house.

One day, Potiphar's wife said to Joseph, "This house is running better than ever now that you are in charge. My husband is very happy, but I am not.

"Your prudence and wisdom have increased our wealth. Don't they advise you to make your mistress happy? Come on! Come to bed with me and my happiness will be complete. You are handsome, educated, and surely you need a woman."

In the face of Joseph's silence, she insisted, "Is it that you don't like me? Many men would give anything to sleep with me. Or is it that you are shy? After the first time, you will lose your shyness. Come on, Joseph, come!"

And she took him by the arm.

"Madam, any man would fall before your beauty. But I cannot betray the trust that your husband has placed in me."

But the woman, who was blinded by her desire for him, did not listen to Joseph.

A while later, Joseph arrived in Potiphar's house to do his work like any other day. The woman, who had made all the men leave the house, came out to meet him and took him by the cloak to take him to her bed.

"Come to bed with me."

But Joseph got away from her and fled the house, leaving his cloak in his mistress' hands.

Upon such rejection, Potiphar's wife flew off the handle.

The desire to have Joseph turned into a thirst for revenge, because he had rejected her. And she started to call the men she had dismissed before:

"Look, look! This is the cloak of the Hebrew man who wanted to force me to go to bed with him; but I shouted to scare him, and he fled. Should I, an Egyptian noblewoman, endure an affront from a man of an inferior race?"

When Potiphar came home, she explained, "Listen to me carefully, my husband. That slave in whom you had placed so much trust—a Hebrew, a lowlife—wanted to go to bed with me. With me, your wife! I defended myself as I could, and made him flee. Look at his cloak which he left here when he ran away."

Fury blurred Potiphar's mind and he ordered Joseph locked up in a royal prison.

What Would Happen with Joseph in Prison?

Despite everything, the Lord protected Joseph. The jail keeper noticed him. Progressively, he gained confidence in Joseph and Joseph ended up running the prison and the prisoners. He made the decisions about what needed to be done there.

After a while, two people—the master cupbearer, responsible for the drinks of the king, and the chief baker—were put in the same prison where Joseph was because they had committed a crime against the king, their lord. One night each of them had a dream that upset them.

Realizing they were upset, Joseph asked them to tell him their dreams so he could interpret them. He said to the master cupbearer, "In three days, Pharaoh will give you back your position as chief and you will serve the wine as you had done up to now. When you get your position back, intercede before Pharaoh so that he will release me from this prison where I have been unfairly placed, because I am innocent."

He also interpreted the baker's dream, saying, "In three days, Pharaoh will take you out of prison and will hang you from a tree; birds will eat your flesh."

Three days later, it was Pharaoh's birthday and he decided that the master cupbearer should go back to his position and that the baker should be hung, just as Joseph had foretold. Despite what had happened, the chief of cupbearers forgot about Joseph and did not intercede before Pharaoh to liberate him.

Joseph in the Presence of Pharaoh

Two years later, Pharaoh had some dreams. Very concerned, he summoned the most prestigious wise men and sages of the kingdom, but none knew how to interpret them.

Then, the master cupbearer remembered the young man who, during his unfortunate stay in prison, had so well interpreted his dream and that of the baker. Thinking he might be useful, he told Pharaoh, who summoned Joseph to his presence immediately.

When he was there, Pharaoh presented the problem: "I cannot find in my whole kingdom anyone capable of interpreting some dreams that bother me. They have told me you know how to interpret dreams."

"In the first place," said Joseph, "I want to thank you for the favor you do me by asking me this. My God, the Lord, will be the one to interpret the dreams through my words, your majesty. Tell me about them, please."

"I was by the river when I saw seven fat and beautiful cows coming up. Behind them came seven skinny and ugly cows, so bone-thin that I had never seen anything so sorry looking in my entire kingdom. These cows ate the fat ones up and, after eating them, they were still as skinny as ever.

"At that time I woke up. When I went back to sleep, I saw seven wonderful and lovely wheat shoots coming out of the same stem. Behind them, however, there were another seven sorry-looking and thin shoots, and they swallowed the good ones up. The dream ended there. Until now, no one has been able to guess the meaning."

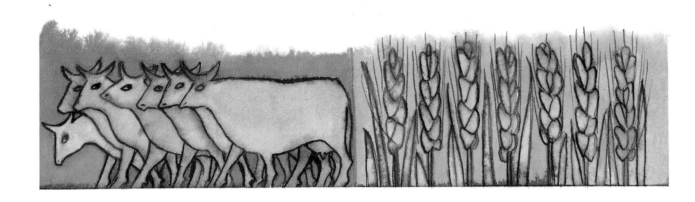

Interpretation of Pharaoh's Dreams

Joseph said to Pharaoh, "The two dreams have the same meaning: the seven fat cows, as well as the seven good shoots, represent seven years of prosperity and abundance. The seven skinny cows, as well as the thin wheat, mean seven years of misfortune and scarcity.

"Due to the responsibility you have for your people, God has wanted to warn you that, after the good and favorable period starting now, there will be another one full of trials and tribulations in which there will be no harvest or benefit; hunger will erase the memory of the good years.

"It is necessary for you to entrust the destiny of your country to a prudent and wise man who, through your servants and under your orders, will be in charge of gathering and storing a fifth of whatever is produced during the years of abundance. Thus, you will have a good reserve which will prevent your subjects from dying of hunger and will help them endure the seven lean years."

Pharaoh was satisfied with what Joseph told him, and proclaimed to the whole court, "I do not know your god. You and your god, however, have prevented the extinction of my people. Not having found anybody in my country who was able to give me this explanation means that there is no man wiser than you. Therefore, I appoint you governor of my kingdom. There won't be any authority above yours except mine, and all will have to obey you."

Pharaoh ordered his decision to be known and Joseph to be carried about in the best cart of the court. He honored him by giving him Asenath, the daughter of a priest, as a wife, and sent him throughout the country to fulfill his mission.

Joseph's Brothers Go to Egypt

During the years of abundance, Joseph gathered the fruits of the fields around each city, keeping them for the time when bad harvests would come. During this time, his two sons were born: Manasseh and Ephraim.

The lean years arrived without warning. Everywhere there was misery and desolation, both inside Egypt and out. Despite this, the people of Egypt did not know hunger because Joseph opened the silos and sold the grain they had kept.

When people from other countries learned that there was wheat in Egypt, they rushed to Egypt to buy it.

The news also got to Canaan and, hearing about it, Jacob sent his sons to Egypt to buy grain.

Benjamin, the youngest, wanted to go also, but Jacob did not allow it.

The rest of the brothers left. When they got to Egypt, they went before Joseph, who controlled the sales of grain.

Joseph recognized them immediately, and remembered the dream of the wheat packs when he saw them there, prostrated before him. They, however, did not realize who he was.

Will the Brothers Be Able to Buy Grain?

Then Joseph thought, "Now I will make them pay for what they did to me." And he talked to them as if they were strangers.

"Where do you come from?"

"From Canaan, to buy food," they answered.

Determined to make them suffer, Joseph alleged, "You are spies. You want to deceive me. You have come to find out our weakness in order to attack us later."

"No, lord, no. We only want to buy grain. We don't have any other intention. If you say that because you see so many of us it is because we are brothers," they excused themselves.

"Have all the brothers come?" asked Joseph.

"No. The youngest has stayed back with our father and we had another brother who died a long time ago," they explained fearfully.

"Do not deceive me. You will be imprisoned because you are spies."

And he put them in prison for three days. On the fourth day, he called them in.

"I don't trust you very much. I am not sure you are honest. In order for me to believe what you have told me, you must bring your youngest brother to confirm your words. One will stay behind as a hostage, and the rest will go back home with the grain for your people."

Then they spoke amongst themselves in their own language, not realizing that Joseph understood them. They commented that what was happening to them was due to what they had done to Joseph.

Joseph was on the brink of making himself known and embracing them, but he did not. He ordered Simeon to be tied up and kept him as a hostage. In the meantime, the others went back with their sacks full of grain. The money they had paid was also inside one of the sacks, as Joseph had ordered.

When they arrived in their father's house, they explained what had happened.

But the grain could not last forever.

When it ran out, Jacob said, "My sons, you will have to go back to Egypt lest we starve."

Judah reminded him of what the governor of Egypt had said. "Our trip will be in vain if we do not take Benjamin. The Egyptian governor said very clearly that without him, he would consider us spies. He could kill us all. You wouldn't want to lose ten of your children at once!"

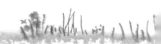

Confused, Jacob mumbled, "You force me to make difficult decisions that break my heart and are not easy to make at my age. Nonetheless, we cannot just sit here waiting to starve. Take gifts from our land to the Egyptian and double the money of the first time, just in case what he returned was a mistake. Let Benjamin go with you, too.

"I hope God will soften the heart of this governor and you will be able to return safe and sound. I place you in God's hands so that you will be successful in what you are about to do."

Hunger Makes Them Return to Egypt

As soon as they got back to Egypt, they were led before Joseph. He immediately realized that Benjamin was with them. Then he ordered that they be taken to his house so they could eat together. But the brothers did not know what was happening, and they were fearful for their lives about going to such an important house. At first they thought that the whole thing might have something to do with the money returned on the first trip, and they said to the governor's steward, "Lord, in our first trip, someone returned the money we had paid for the food, and put it in our sacks, but we didn't know anything. Now we bring it back just in case we should return it."

"Don't worry; the money is yours. I already got paid for the grain you took. Besides, the reason you are here is so you can eat with the governor. He has invited you."

Later Joseph arrived. He said, "Your old father you told me about, is he still alive?"

"Yes, and he gives you honor," they said.

"Is this your youngest brother?"

"That's he," they said.

Joseph excused himself and left the room because he was very moved when he saw his brother. Alone in his room, he cried without being seen.

Making an effort to contain his tears, he went back and ordered the meal to be served. They treated all the brothers very well—especially Benjamin, whose plate was always fuller than his brothers. Everyone had a good time and they laughed, ate, and drank.

Afterwards, Joseph commanded his steward, "Give these strangers all the grain they can take, put the money in each sack, and in Benjamin's, also put my cup."

Without wasting any time, the steward did as his master had ordered.

They Leave Egypt, but Do They Get Home?

The following day, they all said farewell and the brothers returned with the grain, happy with the results of their journey.

They thought they had really scored high when, catching up with them, the steward detained them saying, "I would have never imagined something like this from you. My lord does you the favor of inviting you to his table, and instead of being grateful, what do you do? You steal his cup of silver from which he drinks and sees the future. Why have you done that? You have returned evil for good!"

"How could you think that? We have brought back from Canaan the money from the first trip just in case you claimed it. How do you think we would steal a cup now? We are sure that we don't have it and, if you find it on anyone of us, he will die, and we will be slaves of the governor," the sons of Israel answered.

"I don't ask for that much. Only the one who has hidden it will be the slave of my lord. The rest of you will be free," stated the steward.

They looked through everything: baggage, sacks, and, in the last one, Benjamin's, they found the cup.

When the brothers saw that, they were astonished. And so was Benjamin, who was speechless because he did not know what had happened. The brothers did not want to leave him alone and decided to return to the city as slaves to the governor.

Joseph Identifies Himself to His Brothers

When they arrived, Joseph was still at the palace, and he reproached them. "What have you done to me? Perhaps I haven't treated you well?"

"We don't know what has happened, and we don't know what to say. Take us as slaves to make reparations for the fault," offered the brothers.

"I can't make the just pay for the sinner. Only the person who was found with the cup will be my slave. The rest of you can go."

Then Judah approached him and said, "Lord, if we return without Benjamin, our elderly father would die. Accept me, then, to stay in his place and let Benjamin go that my father can live."

At this point, Joseph was unable to keep the truth from them any longer. "I am Joseph, your brother; I am glad our father is still alive. I am so anxious to see him!"

The brothers went suddenly pale, astonished and speechless. They looked at each other wondering whether it was true or just a dream.

Joseph continued: "I know it is hard for you to believe, but try. I am your brother whom you sold to a caravan of traders traveling to Egypt. Don't be afraid or saddened. The fact that you sold me is no longer your responsibility. You were only instruments of the Lord so that I could come to Egypt.

"In this way now, from my position, I can save all of your lives. The lean years have just started. Go and look for your father and come to Egypt with everything you have; I will support you until the years of abundance come back."

He embraced Benjamin and both cried for joy. Then he hugged all of his brothers, one by one.

Encounter Between Jacob and Joseph

When Pharaoh found out about this he commanded, "Take the chariots you need to move to Egypt. Do not be sad on leaving your land because the best part of Egypt will be yours."

They left laden with gifts, and, when they reached Canaan, Jacob could not believe his ears. He had a hard time believing what his sons were explaining, but he finally had to accept reality.

"My son Joseph is alive! Then it is true. I will go and see him, lest I die before I have the chance."

And his spirits soared with the good news.

They lifted up camp and during the journey they spent the night in Beer-sheba where Jacob offered a sacrifice to God, who said to him, "Jacob, do not be afraid to go to Egypt, for I will make a great people out of you. I will go with you and I will take you out of there."

A short distance from the palace, Joseph came out to meet them. On seeing his father, they hugged, crying and deeply moved.

"My son, you are alive! Now I believe it. You have made me so happy that I don't ask anything else from life. I can die in peace."

"Father, it has been such a long time! I have missed you so much!"

And everyone cried until they had no more tears.

Israel and his clan established themselves in Goshen, one of the best lands of Egypt.

Jacob Dies, Then Joseph Dies

Jacob lived for seventeen years in Egypt and, when he thought his time had come, he called Joseph. He blessed Joseph's sons so that the covenant of the Lord would be fulfilled through him. At the time of the blessing, Joseph realized that Israel, his father, crossed his hands and placed his right on Ephraim's head and his left on Manasseh. Thinking that Jacob was making a mistake due to his tired eyesight, Joseph wanted to change Jacob's hands. "Father, the firstborn is Manasseh."

"I know, my son, I know. He will also be great, but his brother will be greater and of his descendants will come a multitude of peoples."

Then he called all his children together and said to them, "The time has come for me to rejoin my ancestors. Bury me in our sepulcher in the land of Canaan, in the cave that is in the field of Machpelah, the one Abraham bought and is the resting place for Abraham, Sarah, Rebekah, and where I buried Leah."

When he finished speaking, he died, and Joseph covered his face with tears and kisses. He had Jacob embalmed and buried, as he had wanted, in the cave of Machpelah, the origins of the Promised Land.

The burial surprised the people of the country because a multitude of people had come from Egypt: everyone from Joseph's house, those of his father's house, chariots, horse riders, and many animals.

Joseph lived for 110 years. He was able to meet his children, grandchildren, and great-grandchildren. When his time arrived, he said to his children and brothers, "God will be manifested and will lead you out of this land to take you to the Promised Land. Swear to me that, when you go, you will take my remains and bury them in the Promised Land."

They pledged to do so, and he rested in peace, trusting that his bones would reach the Promised Land where they would be together with his people forever.

2.
The Birth of a People: The Exodus

Time went on. The descendants of the patriarchs multiplied, but they experienced the hardships of workers relegated to serving an oppressive pharaoh-king. Israel seemed to be doomed to disappear just like so many other subjected peoples. But then came Moses, a man sent by God, who confronted Pharaoh and succeeded in getting the Hebrews out of Egypt.

The liberation of Egypt took place on a memorable night, the night of the Passover of the Lord. After eating a sacrificed lamb, they started on their journey. They crossed the Red Sea on their way to freedom and arrived at the foot of Mount Sinai. There, Moses solemnly established the covenant between God and the people: God promises the land to those God has chosen. In turn, the people accept the Law—a law which is a true constitution for free persons.

With their exit from Egypt, Israel was born as a people. The memory of such an event has been recorded in the books called the Pentateuch, or the five books constituted by Genesis, Exodus, Leviticus, Numbers, and Deuteronomy. These stories, composed on the oldest traditions, are an interpretation rather than a description of events. It is, however, historically based on the settlement of Semite groups in the Nile Valley and their influence on the Egyptian administration (story of Joseph), as well as on the fact that they were slaves subject to hard labor who left Egypt. These stories agree with what we know of the history of the time.

It is quite possible that these groups of Semites might have abandoned Egypt in different waves and that the story of the group led by Moses was a model for all the other traditions.

It seems that the conquest of the Promised Land was accomplished by three groups. The first settled in the south and formed the tribe of Judah. Joshua's group conquered the center and settled in the mountains of Ephraim. The northern group probably did not go to Egypt, but at that time it had just been freed from the oppression of the Canaanite kings. In time, all these groups gathered together, led by judges, leaders who encouraged the people on in times of trial. So, their traditions fused and they started to share a common faith in Yahweh, the Lord, until in the tenth century before Christ, under the leadership of David, they became the Israelite nation.

The People of God Are Threatened

Joseph had died. The years went by, and the people of Israel grew until they were so many and so influential in the land of Egypt that the Pharaoh at that time thought, "These Hebrew people are too many and very strong in Egypt; if we don't stop them, they'll end up throwing us out of our own country."

And he commanded, "All the members of people of Israel will be forced by foremen to make bricks and tiles. They will also build the buildings and will have the hardest jobs in the land, as if they were servants and not our equals as they have been until now."

Some honest advisors, however, tried to make the king understand in many different ways that Joseph had saved Egypt from extinction and that the Hebrews deserved the gratitude of the country. But Pharaoh did not listen to them.

Despite the harsh treatment they got, the Israelites became more and more numerous. To prevent this, Pharaoh made a radical decision. He ordered the midwives: "You are the ones in charge of births. When an Israelite child is born, see if it is a male. If so, kill him. You can let the girls live."

But the midwives did not fulfill the king's orders, and it was the Egyptian soldiers who carried the command out.

How Is Moses Saved?

Meanwhile, a married couple who were descendants of Levi, one of Jacob's sons, had a son. They hid him for three months, but after that time they could no longer keep him because the Egyptians would discover him. So they placed him in a basket made to float and placed it on the banks of the Nile River. His sister was watching from a short distance.

A few hours later, the sister saw from where she was standing a group of women bathing near her brother: it was Pharaoh's daughter and her servants. When she realized they had discovered the child, she was frightened but she moved closer to hear what they were saying. She heard the princess say, "What a handsome boy! It must be a Hebrew. I don't know how anybody could have the heart to let a child like this die."

The girl who was spying breathed easy and presented herself to the princess. "My lady, would you like me to find a wet nurse for this baby?"

"Good idea. Look for her and I will pay whatever is necessary for her to nurse him," the princess decided.

The girl rushed back home and told her mother the news. The mother could not believe her ears. "And you say they not only have not killed him, but that I can nurse him? You have made me so happy, my daughter!" she exclaimed, hugging her daughter and crying for joy.

The princess had named the child Moses, which means "taken out" (of the water).

Moses Has to Escape

For the Egyptians, Moses was an Egyptian protected by the princess and brought up by a Hebrew woman. But his mother raised him as a Hebrew, and, as he grew up, Moses became more and more aware that his people were being mistreated.

His privileged situation within the people of Israel made him uncomfortable with himself. One day, as had happened many times in the past, he saw an Egyptian foreman mercilessly beating up a Hebrew man. Moses' anger flared. He confronted the Egyptian, and beat him until he killed the man. When he realized what he had done, he buried the Egyptian hoping that no one had witnessed what had happened. He was afraid he would be put to death, even if he was protected by Pharaoh's daughter.

But Pharaoh found out about the death of the Egyptian and ordered Moses to be put to death. The princess, however, warned Moses and he ran from Egypt to the land of Midian.

Upon arriving there, while he was resting by a well, the daughters of Jethro came to give water to their flock. But other shepherds were trying to prevent them from getting near the water. Moses defended them. "These girls have as much right to the water as you do. Why are you refusing? Do you want them and their flocks to die of thirst?"

"Look at the foreigner. You are lucky that we have allowed you to drink. Don't preach to us now. Thank us for the water we have let you drink and get out of here," the shepherds threatened.

Moses, who had been trained for war at the palace, fought them and won.

Moses' Wedding

After the fight, Moses said to the girls, "Come on and let your flocks drink. I will help you." They did so and, arriving in their camp, they told their father about their encounter with Moses. Jethro asked his servants to look for Moses. After they found him Jethro said to Moses, "Few people would have had so much courage. I have to thank you for what you have done. I would like you to stay with us. Here you will have home and a family."

"I thank you for the invitation. It will be an honor to work for you," Moses accepted.

"Then take my daughter Zipporah as your wife. This way we will be a family and you will not feel like a stranger in my house," Jethro proposed.

"You are very generous," Moses said, and, looking at Zipporah, he realized he liked her. "I accept your offer," decided Moses.

At that time, men and women were brought up to accept the spouse their parents chose for them.

Moses married Zipporah a little later and was considered to be a member of the tribe of Jethro.

One day Moses was working as a shepherd when he saw a burning bush in the distance. He did not give it much thought and went on with his work with his flock. Hours later, when he had forgotten about the bush, he looked to the place where he had seen it, and he realized that it was still burning as bright as before.

"How strange!" Moses thought. "That bush is still on fire and has not burned up."

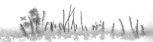

What Was Happening to the Bush?

*The Bible names God in different ways, but the sacred text never tells us how to pronounce the name of God. For the Jewish people, saying the name of a person was almost equal to touching him or her physically. God is different from everything. When God's identity is revealed to Moses from the burning bush, the text shows that only the four letters of the name of God—"Y*HWH*"—express the idea of being and becoming. But, since the Jewish people only wrote the consonants without the vowels, we don't know how this word is pronounced. On the other hand, Jewish people avoided saying this word for fear of using God's name "in vain" (that was forbidden by the Third Commandment of the Law). Since then and still today, Jewish people read "My Lord" (Adonai) every time they come across the letters YHWH.*

The Septuagint, the Greek translation of the Hebrew Bible used by early Christians, purposely used the word Lord (Kryios) when the divine name came up. The New Testament continues this norm and gives Jesus the name of Lord. This Bible you are reading respects the same norm.

Moses approached to see why the bush was not consumed and heard a voice coming from the bush.

"Moses, don't get any closer. Remove your sandals, for the ground you stand on is holy. I am Yahweh, the Lord, the God of your ancestors. I know my people are suffering in Egypt because of the slavery. Go there. I am sending you to lead them out of Egypt into the Promised Land."

Frightened, Moses asked, "Who am I to ask that from Pharaoh? How will my people know I am not lying to them?"

"Gather the elders and tell them that Yahweh-God, the Lord, sends you. Go with them to see the king of Egypt. Ask him to let the Hebrews go. He will not accept willingly, but after the plagues I will send upon the Egyptians, he will let you go," the voice of the Lord said.

"The elders will not believe me. They'll say I am an impostor," Moses replied.

"If they don't believe you, throw your staff in front of them and it will become a serpent; take it by the tail, and it will become a staff again."

Moses did so right there and it happened as the Lord had said. The Lord continued, "If they still don't believe you, take water from the river, and it will be red like blood."

"But Lord, I don't know how to speak; many times I mumble and stutter," Moses objected.

"Your brother Aaron will go with you. He will speak for you," the Lord concluded.

Moses had been living in Midian for two years now and during that time the Pharaoh of Egypt had changed. This made Moses think that perhaps the new Pharaoh would be more understanding.

The Egyptian Plagues Start

After taking his leave from his father-in-law, Moses went to Egypt with his wife and son. There his brother Aaron, who did not stutter, would speak for him.

After listening to Aaron and seeing the wonders worked by Moses, the elders believed in them and went to meet Pharaoh. But instead of granting them an audience, Pharaoh ordered still harder work for the Hebrews. That made life worse for the Israelites.

So Moses and Aaron were heavily criticized by their people, who believed they were to blame for all the problems they had with the Egyptians.

After a time, the two brothers went back to the royal palace and turned Moses' staff into a serpent before Pharaoh, but he was not impressed at all. Then Moses touched with his staff the waters

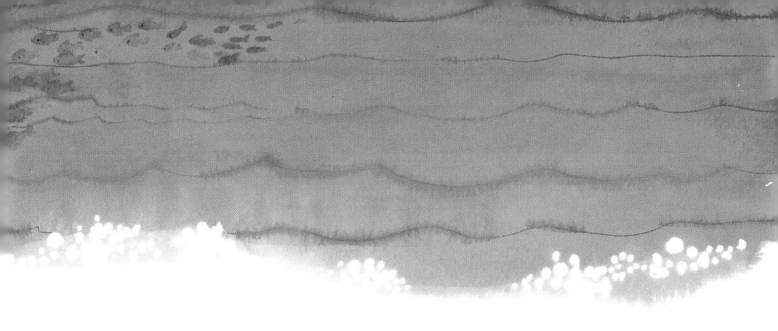

of the Nile River, from which Egyptians drank. All were dumbfounded, for the water was coming down red as blood and the smell was terrible. The fish died and no one could drink from it.

Despite the fact that the Egyptians had to dig wells so they did not die of thirst, Pharaoh did not let the Israelites go. Then, by the order of the Lord, Moses raised his staff over rivers and lakes and all the houses of the Egyptians were filled with frogs. They could not get rid of them because one hundred more would appear for each one they killed. Unable to find a solution, Pharaoh called Moses in.

"Pray to your Lord that the frogs return to the rivers and I will let you leave Egypt."

"We will do it and you will see that not even one frog will be left."

Moses asked the Lord and the country was completely rid of frogs.

Pharaoh Does Not Keep His Word

However, as soon as Pharaoh saw that all the frogs had disappeared, he went back on his word and did not let them go.

Feeling deceived by Pharaoh, Moses raised his staff and everything was covered with mosquitoes. There were so many that no one could be freed of them. The Egyptians themselves begged Pharaoh to send the Hebrews away so that the mosquitoes would disappear. But not even then did Pharaoh pay attention.

Pharaoh was expecting Moses to visit again. Moses told Pharaoh, "If you don't let my people leave Egypt, I will send gnats and they will attack people and all animals. But only Egyptians will be bitten by the insects, for they will leave my people alone. Then you will realize that it is the Lord, my God, who sends you this plague."

All Pharaoh did in response was mock Moses.

Then the gnats came upon the Egyptians. Trying to hide was useless, because the insects were everywhere and they came out of the strangest places.

The Egyptians, seeing their land destroyed by the insects and themselves full of bites, continually complained to Pharaoh; he finally called Moses and his brother and told them, "All right, go if you wish, but make the insects disappear so that my people will stop suffering."

"We will pray to our God for the gnats to leave, but, if you deceive us again, it will be the Lord God who will punish you," Aaron warned.

As they had agreed, all the insects left Egypt. Once again Pharaoh did not make good on his word; he did not allow the Israelites to go.

Consequently, the Lord sent a pestilence on the Egyptian flocks: horses, donkeys, camels, oxen, sheep . . . all died. In contrast, the Hebrews' animals were not affected.

No matter how hard his subjects begged him, Pharaoh did not agree to Moses' petition.

Misfortunes Pile upon the Egyptians

Following the Lord's instructions, Moses then took a handful of dust and threw it up in the air. The wind dispersed it and all the Egyptians were covered with open sores. In contrast, no Hebrew suffered any illness. Despite this, Pharaoh persisted in his stance: the Hebrew people could not leave Egypt.

Moses warned Pharaoh about the following plague: hail would come down so hard that it would kill any person or animal on whom it fell.

And so it happened. All the Egyptians who did not heed the threat and did not take shelter were killed. Never had such a strong hailstorm fallen in Egypt. Everywhere in Egypt, except in Goshen where the Israelites lived, the same thing happened. But in Goshen not even one piece of ice fell.

During this plague, Pharaoh told Moses he would let the Hebrews go as soon as the hailstorm ended. Once again Moses fulfilled his word, and once again Pharaoh broke the agreement. The hailstorm ended, but he did not grant permission to leave.

Then the Lord made locusts appear all over Egypt to destroy what was left of the grain after the hailstorm.

A little later, the land of Egypt was covered by thick fog for three straight days. Everything was so dark that people could not see each other. In contrast, in Goshen, the land of the Israelites, there were not any locusts, nor was there fog.

Tired of the Pharaoh's deceit, Moses complained to the Lord, "Lord, my God, your punishments seem to do no good, since once he sees himself free of them, Pharaoh doesn't make good on his promises. What do we need to do to leave this country?"

"Don't be concerned, Moses, because I have been the one who has allowed Pharaoh to deceive you—so Israel my people has known my power through the plagues I have sent. But everything will change from now on. Warn Pharaoh that tonight, right after midnight, I will go into the houses of all the Egyptians and the firstborn of each family will die. After that, you will be able to leave Egypt."

Moses informed Pharaoh about the new tragedy he would face if he did not allow the people to go, but Pharaoh became so angry that Moses left in a hurry.

At Long Last They Leave Egypt!

For that night, which was to be one of sorrow for Egypt and of joy for Israel, the Lord had given the following instructions to Moses: "Sacrifice a lamb or young goat and eat it as a family. If there are too few people in a house to eat a lamb, share with your neighbors. Before midnight kill the lamb and eat it roasted. With its blood, mark the doorposts of your houses. When I come by at midnight, I will see the blood on your doorposts and will go by without harming anyone in your houses. Warn all your relatives so that no one will be out at that time, because they could die.

"Eat the meat, with your sandals on and the staff in your hand, in a hurry, because this will be the day you leave Egypt. Eat the lamb with bitter herbs and unleavened bread. If there are any leftovers, burn them in the fire, not keeping anything for the following day."

After midnight, the land of Egypt was deep in mourning. Depressed by the death of his firstborn, and without enough energy to be angry, Pharaoh called Moses. With a weak voice, he said, "Despair is prevalent in my country. There is no house where the firstborn is still alive. You cannot harm us any further. Go! Go at once! Go as far away as you can! I don't want to ever hear from you again! Leave my country! Leave us in peace! Let us mourn in peace!"

Moses gave the news to his people. They were not surprised since they were ready to go. But Pharaoh had deceived them so many times that they did not really believe that they would be able to leave Egypt.

They asked the Egyptians for gold, silver, and all kinds of utensils. The Egyptians rushed to give them everything they asked for. They only wanted the Hebrews to leave their land as soon as possible and to go as far away as possible. Hundreds of thousands of people set on their way. The departure was a true party. At long last, after four centuries in Egypt, the intervention of the Lord, their God, would free them from slavery.

In the midst of songs and dancing, Moses reminded them, "We left Egypt thanks to the works of the Lord. So, each year we will have to spend this night in vigil. We will eat unleavened bread for seven days, and we will consecrate our firstborn to the Lord, our God. When we do this, we will explain to our children, and to our children's children, that on a day like today, the Lord freed us from the Egyptians. So this day will be remembered forever."

The Egyptian Army Pursues the Hebrews

Moses took the remains of Joseph with him, as Joseph had requested before his death. The Lord led them through the path in the desert, rather than that of the Philistines, which was the shorter one. That way the Israelites would not have to fight the Philistines. Many of the Hebrews would probably have gone back to Egypt rather than engage in war.

The Lord God walked before them during the day in the shape of a column of clouds, and at night as a column of fire.

As soon as the Egyptians realized that the Hebrews had left, their anger and hatred reemerged. Pharaoh, who had thrown them out of his country, now changed his mind and took his best troops out in pursuit of the Israelites.

The Hebrews were camping by the Red Sea. The cloud of dust of the Egyptian Army was their first warning. They immediately complained to Moses, "The Egyptians are coming and they are armed. They will kill us all to satisfy their anger. Why did you lead us out of Egypt? To end up like this?"

"Do not be afraid. The Lord will protect us. Get ready to cross the sea on foot," Moses informed them.

"Are you crazy? We cannot walk on water."

"Don't you remember that the Lord has saved us from great dangers? Do as I say," Moses scolded them.

The Egyptians Meet Death in the Red Sea

At that moment, Moses raised his staff as the Lord had told him, and a strong wind separated the waters of the sea. A path was opened in the water and the Hebrews could cross the Red Sea. In this way the Egyptians could not keep up with the Hebrews.

Since all the Hebrews had already crossed, the Egyptian Army flung itself after them with horses and chariots. They were very fast, and soon they were in the middle of the sea. At that point, the Lord told Moses, "Outstretch your arms and the waters will go back."

Moses obeyed and Pharaoh's army drowned under the waters of the Red Sea.

Seeing that, the children of Israel recognized the great power of the Lord and broke out in song of thanksgiving. Afterward they rested from the emotions of the day on the other shore of the sea.

The following morning, they continued toward the south desert. They had been walking for three days without water and when they finally saw it, they threw themselves desperately on it. But they were unpleasantly surprised. The water was bitter! Again Moses had to endure the anger of his people, who blamed him for everything. Then, before the unbelieving eyes of the people, Moses threw a piece of wood in the water and the bitterness disappeared. All could quench their thirst.

Thirst, Hunger—Quite a Rough Time in the Desert!

Five weeks later they entered the desert of Zin. Many of them did not even remember their slavery in Egypt. They said, "What are we doing in the middle of the desert, suffocating in the heat, thirsty, and covered with sand? In Egypt we ate bread and all the meat we wanted even if we had to work hard. Why did you lead us out of there?"

On behalf of Moses Aaron answered, "The intervention of the Lord our God will have you enjoy some meat tonight and bread in the morning. At dusk, the camp will be covered with quail. We will be able to eat our fill. Tomorrow, when we rise, we will have as much bread as we want."

And so it was! They could all eat as much quail and bread as they wished.

The Lord had said that each person was to take just a little of the manna (the name of the bread), and to do so before the sun was hot, because the bread would dissolve. Some sneaky ones decided to keep more than they should, thinking, "With this bread we will have enough for a few days." But everything they had to spare went rotten. Only on the sixth day were they able to take more without it spoiling.

Thanks to this bread, which was shaped as a seed and tasted like honey, they could survive the many years they spent in the desert before reaching the Promised Land.

During the long journey, the Hebrews blamed all the difficulties they naturally encountered on Moses or Aaron, forgetting that Moses and Aaron had led the people out of Israel. So, instead of gratitude, the two brothers received harsh criticisms or insults.

The same thing happened on another occasion when the people were without water. Only the deep faith in the Lord God saved Aaron and Moses from discouragement.

This time, in Rephidim, the problem was lack of water. Moses struck a rock with his staff and soon water gushed forth for them to drink. A little later those who had been most critical were praising the Lord and the two brothers that the Lord had sent them.

Renewal of the Covenant Between God and the People of Israel

A few days later, the people of Amalek decided to attack the people of Israel because they considered them a threat. The fight was very even. Moses was watching from the top of a mountain. When he raised his arms, Israel was winning, but if he lowered them, they would lose. The people of Israel were only able to conquer and overcome the Amalekites when Aaron and Hur held up Moses' tired arms.

Three months after leaving Egypt they reached the desert of Sinai. They camped before Mount Sinai. There the Lord came to Moses and indicated to him that in three days the people should be ready to listen to God.

On the third day, Moses and Aaron went up to the mountain. The people were waiting below. The Lord spoke to them amidst smoke, thunder, and lightning.

"I am the Lord, your God, who has freed you from Egypt. Fulfill my commandments and I will be with you: I will be your only God. You will not carve images to worship. You will not use my name without a good cause. You will dedicate to me the seventh day of the week. Love and respect your parents. Do not kill. Do not desire your neighbors' spouse. Do not steal. Do not lie. Do not desire what belongs to others."

The Israelites, seeing the dazzling spectacle of fire and light, were afraid and exclaimed, "Moses! Make the Lord speak to you and we will listen to you. Ask God not to speak to us because we are very scared."

"Don't be afraid. The Lord God has wanted to be shown before you so that you will know God's power. Fulfill God's commands and you will have nothing to fear," Moses explained.

"We will do as you say and will obey all the commandments."

Moses poured the blood of animals sacrificed to the Lord on the people. This symbolized the acceptance of the Commandments on the part of people and divine protection. This was the covenant: God would help them in everything and they would keep God's rules.

The People Turn to the Worship of Idols

A few days later, the Lord called Moses to the top of Mount Sinai to give him the Commandments carved in stone.

Many days had passed since Moses had gone to Sinai and no one had heard from him. The rumor spread that he had died, and the trust of the people in the Lord collapsed.

But Moses came down from the mountain with the Law engraved by the Lord on stone tablets. As he was getting near, he saw that the people were worshiping a golden calf. He was red with fury and threw the tablets down against a rock.

"What on earth are you doing?" asked Moses.

"Forgive us. It had been so long since we had heard from you that we thought you had died. The people felt the need to give shape to the God who had taken us out of Egypt. We collected all the gold we could and melted it to create this calf."

"Don't you remember what the Lord has done for us? Wasn't that more important than growing discouraged because you didn't know where I was? The Lord has known your unfaithfulness and has allowed you to fall. You can't imagine how hard it has been to calm God down."

Despite Moses' warnings, a group of Israelites had grown fond of the golden calf and did not listen to him. Then Moses called forth the men of the house of Levi who had stayed faithful to the Lord. He said to them, "Destroy those who have sinned against God and don't want to change their attitudes."

So, those who did not change their behavior given the chance were punished.

Not much later, the Lord God ordered Moses to go back to Mount Sinai to receive the new tablets of the Law. When Moses came down the mountain, his face was shining because he had been speaking to God. Seeing this, people felt a great respect for him.

Moses explained to them what the Lord had said to him and showed them the new tablets of the Law as a testimony of his words.

They placed the tablets in the ark of the covenant (a box made of gold and fine wood with two angels, one on each side) and placed the ark in a tabernacle, which was a richly decorated tent made with good, strong canvas. It was also called "tent of the sacred encounter" and served as a sanctuary. It represented the presence of God among the people. It was there that Moses met the Lord.

Miriam Is Jealous of Moses

It had been more than two years since they left Egypt; they lifted the camp and continued on their way. When they were in Hazeroth, Miriam, Moses' sister, was badmouthing him. She was critical of the fact that Moses had taken a non-Hebrew woman as his wife. But the truth was that she was jealous. Miriam complained, saying, "If the Lord speaks through Aaron and me, how come only Moses is considered a prophet of God?"

The Lord, who knew what was going on, made the three—Moses, Aaron, and Miriam—meet in the tent of the sacred encounter and spoke to Miriam.

"Miriam, and you too, Aaron, why do you want to be like Moses? If you had been chosen, I would speak to you in dreams or visions. If I speak to Moses face-to-face it is because he has earned it through his faithfulness. Do not make me angry, for you should be setting a good example for the people."

When she left the tent, Miriam contracted leprosy as a punishment from God. Moses took pity on his sister and begged the Lord to heal her. The Lord ordered, "Send her away from the camp for seven days. Afterwards you can welcome her back in your midst."

The word of the Lord was fulfilled. After the appointed time, Miriam was back to her old self. After what had happened, she understood that the Lord decides through whom God will be manifested.

They continued on their journey and arrived in the desert of Paran, near Canaan, the land that had been promised to them.

One Step Away from the Promised Land

God commanded the chiefs of all the tribes to explore the lands.

They spent many days scouting the land in order to know it well. Upon their return, they reported on their findings.

"This land is very rich and fertile. Its fruits are plentiful and water is abundant. We could live as kings, but it is populated and very well protected. The people who live there—Hittites, Amorites, and Hivites—own weapons and are used to fighting. Besides, these men are tall and strong, like giants. Compared to them, we look like beetles."

With these words, they were exaggerating the difficulties of establishing themselves in Canaan, and the Hebrews were frightened. Only Joshua and Caleb encouraged them, saying, "Do not be afraid, we will overcome them. Or perhaps you don't remember the wonders the Lord has done for us? Now we will be able to overcome the enemy. The Lord will help us conquer the land we have worked so hard to reach, and then we will enjoy it."

No one paid attention to what they were saying because the chiefs of the tribes kept insisting that it was impossible to occupy the land. Moses and Aaron could not change their minds either. All were grumbling against them, saying, "They have been playing games with us all these years. How many times they have repeated the promise of a fertile land! And now that we are near, we cannot stay here. We don't want those tribes of warriors to kill us."

God Punishes the People's Lack of Trust

Moses went to the tent of the sacred encounter to ask God what he should do. To begin with, he had to bear the anger of the Lord.

"Haven't I worked enough wonders in Egypt and in the desert? If you had come this far enduring difficulties and overcoming enemies, how can they think I have abandoned them now? I am tired of this people who forget me as soon as the slightest problem comes up. I will destroy them and will bring out of you another people who will be faithful to me. How can I have any consideration toward them when they don't have any for their God?"

"Lord, you are absolutely right, but I must ask you to forgive them and not destroy them. It is not that they don't deserve it, but you are our God, generous and compassionate. Grant them your forgiveness. Besides, the Egyptians and all our enemies were amazed to see what we were able to do with your divine protection, and now they would think you are evil by first protecting us only to kill us later."

The Lord answered, "I will listen to your plea, not because of the merits of your people, but because you are asking me, you who have been faithful and never doubted my word. I will not kill them, but they will have to pay for their mistrust: not one of the adults who has doubted me will enter the Promised Land. They will go back to the desert and wander around for forty years before they come back to these lands. Only their children will enter. Likewise, those who have explored this land and then discouraged the people with their bad faith will also die."

When the people of Israel saw that their chiefs were dying, they renewed their trust in God and wanted to go to war with the inhabitants of Canaan.

Moses warned them, "Don't go, because the Lord does not want you to. God will not protect you and you could be defeated."

And so it was. Israel was defeated. After this they had no choice but to listen to the word of God and return to the desert.

Rebellion Against Moses and Aaron

After a time, three Levites—Korah, Dathan, and Abiram—led an insurrection against Moses and Aaron. They accused the brothers, saying, "You have managed to take us far away from the Promised Land and have brought us back to swallow the dust of the desert. If the Lord speaks through your lips, he can also do it through any of ours, because the whole people is sacred."

Moses answered them, "We are only instruments in the hands of the Lord. May God prove right whoever is right. Stand before your tent and the Lord will show whether you are mistaken or not."

At that instant there was a deafening noise; the earth opened at the foot of those who had rebelled and swallowed them up. But the people, instead of believing in the Lord, threatened the prophet brothers, saying, "You are guilty of all the deaths that happen among our people. You are guilty!"

Then the Lord sent a plague, a strange illness that brought them to the brink of death. The illness subsided only when Aaron came out among the people with incense as an expiation rite. Despite this, the grumblings against Moses and Aaron did not cease.

"What right do Moses and Aaron have to boss us around?" they asked.

"Bring a staff for each tribe of Israel, each one labeled with the tribe's name. The one that blooms in the night will indicate the chosen one," the Lord said.

The staff with Aaron's name was the one representing the tribe of Levi.

The following morning everyone could see that the only staff that had bloomed was Aaron's.

From then on, Aaron and the Levites remained the priest servants of the tabernacle of the Lord God.

Miriam and Aaron Die

They continued on their journey, and arrived in the desert of Zin. Miriam, Moses' sister, died and was buried there.

In Meribah they had no water and they again grumbled against the brothers.

"Speak to the rock and there will spring water from it," the Lord told Moses.

But Moses thought that he would be ridiculed by the whole people if no water came out of the rock when he spoke to it. So, instead of doing what the Lord had said, he struck the rock with his staff and water came forth instantly.

This mistrust of Moses, even if it seemed insignificant, was severely punished by the Lord. "Neither you nor Aaron will enter the Promised Land, since you doubted that I was capable of making water come out of the rock with just a word."

When they were in Kadesh, on the border of the kingdom of Edom, they asked the king's permission to cross his territory. He did not grant permission, so they were forced to go around his territory. Following that path, they came to Mount Hor. It was there that, by divine decision, Aaron gave his children the garments that identified him as the high priest of the Lord. Then Aaron died. Everyone mourned him for many days and many nights.

The harsh conditions they were enduring during the journey made the people complain again. "In Egypt we lacked for nothing. But here we only see trial and hardships."

Angered by those comments, the Lord sent serpents that killed all who were bitten.

Moses interceded again before the Lord, and his plea was answered. He molded a bronze serpent and placed it on the end of a staff, and all who looked at it were cured of the serpents' bites. It was because of this that the people survived.

King Balak Cannot Summon a Curse for Israel

After a time, they had to cross the land of the Amorites and Bashan. They sent messages to the kings seeking permission to cross, but in response armies were sent to fight them. The help of the Lord was crucial and the Israelites were victorious.

Some time later, they camped in the plains of Moab. Balak, the king of that region, was afraid of them and sent messengers to look for Balaam. He wanted Balaam to curse Israel so that they could be defeated.

To curse (male dicere in Latin) means to "say evil" so that misfortune ensues.

Balaam set on his way to serve Balak. But every now and then, the donkey went astray or stopped and refused to go on. In anger Balaam beat the donkey, but the donkey spoke up and said, "Why are you beating me, when I am really saving your life? Cursing Israel does not please God; if you did it, God could punish you with death. Do not abuse me any more because I am helping, not hindering you."

At that time, Balaam saw an angel of the Lord in their way, and he apologized. "I am sorry. I did not know why my donkey did not continue walking. Tell me what I should do."

"Go and see Balak, but you will only tell him what the Lord inspires you to say," the angel said.

When Balaam was in the presence of the king, Balak tried three times to have him curse Israel, but Balaam blessed Israel instead, by the will of the Lord. No matter how many riches the king promised to him, Balaam did not curse Israel. Finally Balak gave up and withdrew his army, at the same time that Balaam went back home.

Relationships with Non-Hebrew Women Are Forbidden

The people of Israel went on their way and settled in Shittim, in the territory of Moab. But a little later, seduced by the beauty of the women of the land, they joined them and started worshiping their gods.

This infuriated the Lord, and he ordered that all those who had sinned by worshiping Baal, the god of that region, be put to death. Even after some died, the plague that the Lord had sent on them did not stop. Aaron's grandson discovered that an Israelite had continued his relationship with a Midian woman, a worshiper of Baal, which was prohibited. He then killed them both and the plague disappeared.

Despite all this, the Lord asked for revenge against the Midianites because they had caused Israel to sin. The Israelites formed an army and defeated the Midianites with the Lord's help. From the riches they seized from the war, they kept a part for the Lord and gave the other part to the Levites, who were servants of the tabernacle.

When they neared the Jordan River, the tribes of Reuben, Gad, and half of the Menassah tribe requested of Moses: "Allow us to stay here, in Transjordan. These are good lands for the animals. We will build houses for the women and children. The men will go with you to help you conquer the land, until all Israel is well settled."

Moses said, "I think that's a good idea. Do it. But remember that you will have to continue helping Israel and fighting for our cause until everyone is settled."

So those tribes established themselves on the right bank of the Jordan.

Moses Passes the Power to Joshua

When the hour of death had arrived for Moses, he followed the Lord's command and went up to Mount Nebo after naming Joshua his successor.

"You, Joshua, will be in charge of bringing Israel into the Promised Land. Respect the covenant present in the tables of the Law, and make the people respect it. Be faithful to Yahweh, the Lord, in everything. You know I will not be able to go into the Promised Land because I doubted. Go and establish yourselves in that land that we have reached after so much trouble. May the Lord bless you!"

Moses did not come down from Mount Moeb where he died at the age of 120. All the people of Israel mourned him for many, many days. Once Moses was dead, Joshua received the divine inspiration. He said to the people, "Prepare to cross the Jordan in three days."

Joshua did not have to do much convincing to get the cooperation of the tribes that had settled in Transjordan. The armed men enthusiastically agreed to cross the Jordan, keeping the promise they had made to Moses.

On the other side of the river was the city of Jericho. This was the first one they would have to conquer. Since the Lord was helping them in their fight, they placed a ban on the city. They killed all the inhabitants and destroyed everything so they would not keep any of the spoils for themselves. In this way, all the benefits would be for the Lord, so that no one would forget that the victory was the Lord's, rather than the work of human hands.

Jericho Is Conquered

Joshua sent two spies into Jericho. The king of the city found out and ordered that they be followed. The Israelites went to the prostitute Rahab's house. Instead of betraying them she protected them. The spies promised, "As soon as we destroy the city, we will save you and your family. Gather all your relatives here and place this red ribbon on your window. No one will harm those in this house."

When the spies returned, everyone prepared to cross the Jordan. On the appointed day, the priests were carrying the ark of the covenant. When their feet touched the river, the waters separated forming a passage for them to cross without getting wet.

In this way, with the ark held by the priests in the middle of the Jordan, all the Israelites could cross the river. When the ark was placed on the other bank, the waters returned to their course. The Lord had told them so, and so it had happened.

Israel's enemies heard the news of the Jordan crossing, and they were filled with fear.

The Israelites camped in Gilgal and, before attacking the city, they prepared themselves before the Lord. All the male adults and children who had not been circumcised before the Israelites left Egypt, were now circumcised.

They celebrated the Passover. It was the first time they enjoyed the fruits of the land instead of the manna that had fed them during the long years in the desert. From then on manna did not fall from heaven, because they no longer needed it. The products of the land were more than enough to nourish them.

When they were ready for war they followed the Lord's rules: during seven days, they circled the walls of the city of Jericho, carrying the ark of the covenant and playing the trumpets. On the seventh day, they circled the walls seven times, and at the end of the last round the people shouted the cry of war. Suddenly, the walls collapsed and so they could enter the city and raze it. The entire population perished. Only Rahab and her family were saved.

Victory Is Real Only If the Covenant Is Respected

Since it had been so easy to conquer the city of Jericho, the Israelites became complacent and sent only three thousand armed men to the small city of Ai.

The Israelites were unexpectedly defeated, and the people grew discouraged.

Joshua consulted with the Lord and the Lord said, "Why are you surprised? You have broken the covenant. You were supposed to save the spoils for me, but you left only half. That's why I did not protect you. Eliminate those among you who have broken the pact."

Joshua started investigating immediately and found those who had kept a part of the spoils for themselves. Those who broke the pact were immediately stoned. Then the Lord watched over the people again.

It was necessary to overcome the defeat at Ai. Joshua devised a plan inspired by God: with just a few men, he went to fight the enemy. Soon after the battle had started, the Israelites pretended to flee. All of the people of Ai came out to pursue them, leaving the city walls open. When they were quite far away, five thousand Israelites who had been hiding nearby went into the city. They did not meet with any resistance and set Ai on fire. The flames were the signal for Joshua and his men to turn and confront their pursuers. At the same time, the Israelites who had gone into the city attacked the population of Ai from behind. The citizens of Ai were caught in the middle and could not save themselves.

The Hivites lived in four different cities near the site of these events. The most important city was Gibeon.

Does Joshua Control the Moon and the Sun?

The people of those towns, who had heard of everything that Israel had done, were frightened. To avoid being killed, they decided to pose as travelers from other lands and went to see Joshua.

"We are pilgrims and come from afar. We want to make a pact with you to keep our lives. Take us, if you wish, as your servants, but let us make a peace pact."

Joshua accepted the foods they offered. He did not realize the deception until days later. Although he was enraged, he could not attack them because he had given his word. To punish them for having lied to him he decided, "They will not die, but they will work as woodchoppers and carry water for the whole people of Israel."

The Gibeonites were lucky. Although they were slaves, they still had their lives; they were better off than the neighboring tribes that had been killed.

The rest of the kings of the area learned of the pact between the Gibeonites and the Israelites. This seemed treason to them, so they united against the Gibeonites. The Gibeonites asked Joshua for help.

The people of Israel helped defend Gibeon. When they were near the city, they attacked the besieging Amorites. In addition to their courage, they counted on God's help. A powerful hail fell on the Amorites. More were killed by the hail than by the sword. While they were fighting, night fell. The darkness would have allowed the Amorites to flee. Then the Lord granted Joshua's plea.

"Sun! Stop!"

And the sun stopped without setting.

"Moon! Do not move forward!"

And the moon did not continue on its journey. The night was delayed until the Amorites were completely defeated.

The five enemy kings, who had not died in battle, were captured in a cave. They were hung from a high tree for having defied Israel. All the surrounding tribes found out about these events.

The Conquest Ends

People and cities fell to the power of the children of Israel. They did not leave anyone alive, nor did they take the treasure, because everything was for the Lord. In this way, they soon had conquered all their enemies and returned to their camp in Gilgal.

Then the kings of the land north of Canaan joined forces and created a large army in an attempt to defeat the Israelites. The army camped in Merom, a place near Israel, and waited for a good opportunity to attack.

But Joshua was faster than they were. The Israelites fell on their enemies and caught them by surprise. Soon the scales of the battle tipped in favor of the Israelites, who pursued their enemies and put them all to death.

Once the coalition of kings had been defeated, Israel conquered the cities north of Canaan. This was a process that took many years, since there were many towns and cities there.

Once the conquest was ended, they divided the lands that they had obtained according to the needs of each group and tribe.

As soon as everyone was established in their own land, the warriors of the tribes of Transjordan, who had only joined the others to help them in war, received Joshua's permission to return to their lands.

"You have fought courageously as if you were conquering lands for yourselves. You haven't abandoned your brothers. The Lord is happy with you. Return to your families and rest. Always remember that you, too, are Israel. Keep the precepts of the Lord. Do not be unfaithful to God."

He then blessed them and bid them farewell.

Joshua's Death

Many years after the wars were over, Joshua, who was feeling old, convened an assembly in Shechem. All the chiefs of the tribes of Israel attended. He said to them, "From the time of Abraham, our father, until today, the Lord has not ceased to work wonders for Israel. Realize that all we have we owe to God. We have defeated peoples who were more numerous than us and who would have defeated us had the Lord not helped us. Never think that we owe what we have to our own strength. If the Lord ever abandoned us, we would be nothing. Remember that. Don't ever deny the Lord or adore any other gods. You know well God would not allow it. Be faithful as God has been faithful to us despite the constant lack of trust of our people."

"We want to serve the Lord our God, and will never separate ourselves from God's Law," the people responded.

"Very well then. Let us build this monolith as a testimony of your words for centuries to come. Now, return to your places and fulfill the covenant with the Lord."

A little later Joshua died having fulfilled the mission entrusted to him. He was buried on his property and the people mourned him for many days. They also buried Joseph in Shechem on the land that Jacob had purchased many years before. So, Joseph's wish that his remains would find a resting place in the Promised Land was fulfilled.

Deborah Saves the People

When the people of Israel found themselves without a chief through whom the Lord may speak to them, they forgot the promises they had made in Shechem and worshiped the gods of other lands.

The Lord, who had favored the Israelites up until then, turned his back on them. The Israelites were defeated by their enemies, robbed by bandits, and very few things went well for them.

Jabin, the Canaanite king of Hazor, had been oppressing the children of Israel for over twenty years. Deborah the prophet emerged as leader of the Israelites and sought a way to overcome Jabin's oppression. After consulting with the Lord, she called for Barak and said, "Take ten thousand men with you and go up to Mount Tabor because the Lord will deliver Sisera, chief of the Canaanite army, into your arms."

"I will go if you come with me," Barak answered.

"Let's go! But you will lose the opportunity to be the victor, because people will say a woman conquered."

Sisera gathered together all the chariots and the troops he had before Mount Tabor. Seeing the number of enemy troops present, the Israelites hesitated. But Deborah encouraged them on.

"Let's go. The Lord is with us."

The attack confused Sisera's soldiers, who did not know how to defend themselves. The battle turned into persecution. The whole camp of Sisera was annihilated, but the chief escaped.

He escaped and ended up in the tent of Jael, a Kenite woman. After giving him something to drink Jael hid him, covering him with a blanket. At the moment when Sisera was most unsuspecting, Jael killed him. Just then Barak arrived looking for Sisera. The courageous Jael showed him Sisera, dead in the tent.

The victory gave strength to the Israelites. They organized themselves and, a little later, conquered and killed Jabin, the enemy king.

And Deborah, as a prophet, sang a song to the Lord to celebrate the victory.

Gideon, Chief Chosen by God

After the victory over Jabin, the Israelites lived in peace for forty years.

After this period, Israel once again started worshiping false gods and lost the Lord's help. For the next seven years they were under the rule of the Midianites. Their lives became very difficult, for they hardly had anything to eat. When the time came to harvest the fruits of the earth, the Midianites appeared and razed everything.

Gideon, son of Joash, was harvesting the wheat and putting it in a pail so that the Midianites would not see it and take it away. At that point, the angel of the Lord appeared to him and said, "The Lord is with you, courageous warrior!"

"What are you saying? If that were the case, we wouldn't be in this situation, furtively seeking a little grain. We are abandoned."

"The Lord God is sending you to free Israel from the Midianites."

"I don't understand. I am the youngest of the family and my tribe is not important. What can I do?" Gideon resisted.

"You will defeat the Midianites because the Lord will be with you."

"Give me a sign to demonstrate the truth of your words," asked the young man, "because I can't believe it."

Gideon took food for the stranger and put it on the rock. At that moment fire came out of it and consumed the meat and the bread. This fact served to convince Gideon that an angel of the Lord was before him.

Gideon Gathers an Army

That night, the Lord God ordered, "Take ten men and destroy the altar to Baal. Build one for me and sacrifice an animal."

Gideon did so. The following morning everyone saw that Baal's altar had been destroyed and they looked for the culprit. They suspected Gideon and went to Joash's house. They demanded, "Make your son come out. He has to die because he has destroyed a holy altar."

"Don't worry," said Joash. "If Baal is god, he will avenge it. It won't be hard for him."

In the meantime Gideon had sent messengers to different regions of Israel to recruit an army.

Gideon continued to wonder why he had been chosen. He asked the Lord for another clear sign. That night he stretched his coat out on the grass, and the following morning he found it covered with dew, while everything around it was dry. The following day the opposite happened: the coat was dry and everything around it was wet.

Gideon's call was a success: there were already over thirty thousand men for the army. Then the Lord said, "You have too many men. I will deliver Midian into your hands. If there are so many of you, you will think it is all your doing and not my power. Tell the more fearful to go home. Ask the rest to come down to drink from the stream. Pay attention and keep only those who drink with their hand. The rest can go home."

After the fearful ones withdrew, ten thousand stayed; of these, only three hundred drank with their hand.

Three Hundred Israelites Defeat Thirty Thousand Enemies

Gideon divided the three hundred into three groups. He gave each a horn and a torch in a jar. Then he warned them, "When you hear my signal, do as I do."

His group entered the Midianites' camp and the other two surrounded them. It was well into the night when Gideon broke the jar and, holding the torch with his left hand, he played the horn with his right. The three hundred did the same, and there was great confusion in the camp of Midian; the Midianites ran from side to side trying to flee. They suffered a terrible defeat.

Gideon, however, wanted to take advantage of the opportunity to exterminate the enemy. Although they were exhausted and hungry, he sent the men to the other bank of the river Jordan in pursuit of the fugitives. When he passed through the cities of Succoth and Penuel, he asked for some food for his army. Neither city wanted to help.

The enemy armies still had 15,000 men, but they had lost 120,000.

There was widespread discouragement among the troops, which was enough for Gideon to launch a surprise attack from which they could not recover. His army captured the two enemy kings and decided to take them to his camp.

Now that he was a victorious hero, Gideon did not forget to go through Succoth and Penuel. In Succoth, he collected thorns and thistles from the desert to use to whip the leaders of the city as punishment; in Penuel those who had despised him were put to death.

When they were in the camp, several witnesses accused the two kings of having killed many warriors in Israel; the two kings were decapitated.

After this, the Israelites said to Gideon, "Govern our people, you who have saved us from Midian."

"It won't be I, but the Lord."

From then on, and for many years, Israel lived at peace with Gideon at the helm.

Jephthah Is Named Chief of Israel

Once Gideon was dead, the children of Israel turned back to the worship of Baal. With this behavior, they lost the favor of the Lord.

Tired of the oppression of the Ammonites and Philistines, they turned to the Lord God and received an answer: "I have saved you many times, and you are always unfaithful. Haven't you adored other gods? Ask them to help you."

Hearing that, the Israelites rejected the false gods and returned to the Lord, their God. In this way, the Lord calmed down and returned to Israel's side.

The Israelites had been organized to fight, but they could not find anyone to lead them.

Considering this, the elders of Gilead thought that Jephthah, a young warrior accustomed to fighting, could serve them. But Jephthah had been outcast from the city by the noblemen and his own brothers. So he said, "And now you come to look for me? A long time ago you expelled me from my father's house in Gilead because I was the son of a prostitute," Jephthah recriminated.

"If you come with us, you will be our chief. You will have the command and we will obey you in everything."

This helped him make his decision. He went from utter rejection to the full respect of the city.

Jephthah Has to Sacrifice His Daughter

As a judge of Israel, Jephthah sent messengers to negotiate with the Ammonites. After a few unsuccessful attempts at peace, the only solution was war.

Then Jephthah invoked the Lord saying: "Lord-God, if you grant me victory over the Ammonites, I will offer you in sacrifice the first person who comes to welcome me when I return."

The Ammonites suffered a terrible defeat. More than twenty cities were destroyed with the help of the Lord.

As soon as Jephthah returned home, his only daughter came out to welcome him. Jephthah remembered the promise he had made to the Lord and was deeply saddened. But he could not go back on his word, and, heartbroken, he fulfilled the vow he had made to the Lord.

After six years governing over Israel Jephthah died and was buried in Gilead.

A little time later Israel, forsaken by the Lord because people were again worshiping other gods, was under the power of the Philistines. They abused the Israelites, making them the victims of their pleasures and whims.

Samson Chosen by God

Manah, of the tribe of Dan, lived in those times. His wife was sterile, and they wanted a son more than anything.

An angel of the Lord spoke to the wife of Manah and said, "You will have a son who will be consecrated to God. Don't ever cut his hair, as a sign of his dedication to God. From now on don't eat or drink anything that could jeopardize your pregnancy."

"You can't imagine how happy you make me. That was my only desire. I will do as you say."

The woman explained everything to her husband. Manah asked, "And he hasn't said what we must do when he is born?"

"No, he has only told me this," confirmed his wife.

Manah asked the Lord to tell him how he should raise his child.

The angel of the Lord came back and explained, "The child must never take wine or try any impure food."

"Don't leave so soon. I want to invite you to eat with us," offered Manah.

"Thank you. I will not eat anything, but if you want to offer a sacrifice to the Lord, it will be welcome."

When they offered the sacrifice, the flame of fire rose to the sky and the angel disappeared in it. With this wonder they knew that he truly was an angel.

The child came at the appointed time and they named him Samson.

Samson Kills a Lion with His Bare Hands

When Samson was a grown man, he met a Philistine woman whom he liked. He told his parents, "I want you to ask for her hand."

"My son, there are enough women to choose from in our own people. Why do you have to look for a Philistine?"

When they were on their way to ask for her hand, a lion came out and tried to kill them. Due to the extraordinary strength that God had granted Samson, he killed the lion with his bare hands. The following day, walking by the same place, he saw a beehive inside the dead lion and he gathered some honey.

While they were celebrating the wedding banquet, Samson proposed a riddle to the Philistines gathered there. He bet thirty tunics. "I give you a week's time to guess this riddle: 'Food comes out of those who eat, and sweetness from the strong."

The Philistines did not want to pay for the thirty tunics, but the days went on and they could not find the answer. They threatened Samson's wife to get the answer from her husband. She was so insistent that Samson finally told her the answer. On the seventh day, the Philistines came before him.

"We already know the answer: 'What is sweeter than honey? Who is stronger than the lion?'" Samson had no choice but to pay the bet. More angered by the betrayal of his wife than by having been forced to pay the debt, he went to a Philistine town and killed thirty men. Their clothes were the payment for the riddle. This betrayal helped him realize that he could not trust his wife, and he returned home with his parents.

Samson Conquers a Thousand Philistines

Some time later, when the wheat of the Philistines was ripe, Samson went to see his wife. His father-in-law told him, "Don't come in. I was so convinced you wouldn't come back that I gave her to another man. If you want to, you can have the younger sister."

Samson felt abused. To take revenge on the Philistines, he captured three hundred foxes, tied burning torches to their tails, and set them loose in the Philistine's fields, which caught fire and were burned to the ground. Afterwards, so as not to be found, he hid in a cave. Then the Philistines went out searching for him and attacked the Israelites. The children of Israel took up arms to find Samson, since they did not want to die for him. They tied him down, and he allowed himself to be led to the Philistines. They rejoiced when they saw him arrive like that, thinking that they had him in their hands.

Samson effortlessly untied his cords, and, using a jawbone he found on the ground as his only weapon, he confronted them. More than one thousand Philistines died that day.

The struggle left him exhausted and he cried out to the Lord for help, "Thanks to you, Lord, my God, I have defeated the Philistines, but if I don't have some water to drink immediately, I will not be able to move and I will fall into your hands."

And the Lord made water spring forth from a nearby rock so that Samson could recuperate.

On another occasion, Samson went to Gaza to visit a friend. When his enemies found out, they waited for daybreak to kill him, since they could not escape from the city at night because the gates were closed.

At midnight, however, Samson wanted to leave. He took the doors off their hinges, and took them to the top of a nearby mountain. In this way he escaped death.

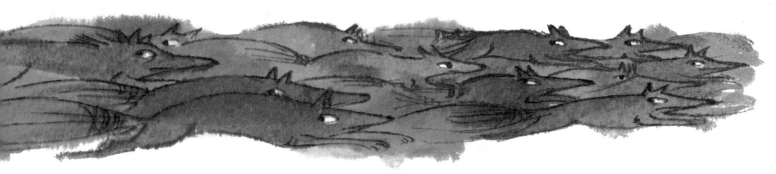

Samson Is Betrayed by Delilah

A little later, Samson fell desperately in love with Delilah, a beautiful young woman.

When the Philistines found out, they went to see her and told her, "If you succeed in finding out what is the secret of his strength, we will pay you with many coins."

"I agree. I will tell you," Delilah replied, aware of the power she held over Samson.

One day, amidst kisses and caresses, Delilah said to him, "Listen to me, Samson. If you truly love me, explain to me the secret of your strength."

"If they tied me down with seven brand new ropes, I would lose all strength," Samson answered.

And, while he was sleeping, Delilah did exactly that. When she had finished, she said, "Samson! The Philistines!"

Samson woke up and broke the ropes easily. Delilah realized he had deceived her, and she asked him the same question. Samson answered, "If you tie me with new and unused ropes, I will lose my strength."

Delilah tried it, and Samson again broke the ropes effortlessly.

Every time Samson was with Delilah, they had the same conversation.

"You have tricked me many times. What is the secret of your strength?"

"If you tie the braids of my hair to the weaving rods I will lose strength," Samson commented.

Delilah tried it again, and when she warned him of danger, Samson woke up and broke the bar of the weaving loom almost without realizing it.

Delilah pretended she was mad and would not let Samson touch her. She repeated the same question day and night until, finally, Samson revealed his secret. "I am consecrated to the Lord. If they cut my hair, I will lose my strength and I will be like any other man."

Delilah felt that this time he had said the truth and she warned the Philistines. While Samson was sleeping, she cut his hair. When she finished, she cried out, "Samson! The Philistines are attacking!"

This time, Samson could not defend himself because Delilah had sold him to the Philistines. They captured him, blinded him, threw him in prison, and forced him to turn the stone of a mill in the city.

Samson Brings the Temple Down

Time went on. On one occasion, the Philistines went to offer a sacrifice to Dagon, their god, and prepared a great feast. They wanted to have fun, and they called Samson in to mock him.

Samson asked the young boy who guided him to place him between the columns of the temple. Everyone was laughing at him, but Samson, whose hair had grown, invoked the Lord, "Lord, my God, give me strength for the last time to avenge the Philistines, my enemies and the enemies of my people."

He concentrated, and, with all his might, he moved the columns that supported the temple as he cried out, "Let me die with the Philistines!"

Suddenly the temple collapsed and all who were there were crushed.

Despite what had happened, the Philistines continued to oppress Israel.

Samuel Is Consecrated to God

In the tribe of Ephraim there was a man named Elkanah who had two wives. Penninah had given him children, but Hannah could not bear any children. So Penninah was always mocking her. Hannah was very sad because she could not be a mother, and the words of the other woman really hurt her. Concerned, she prayed to the Lord, saying, "Lord God almighty, so far I have not been able to have children. If you grant me a son, I will consecrate him to your service. I will not cut his hair, as a sign of his consecration."

The Lord listened to her. Hannah got pregnant and gave birth to a son, whom she named Samuel.

When the child grew up and did not need his mother's milk any longer, Hannah took him to the Temple and presented him to the priest Eli.

"I am bringing you my son, who is consecrated to the Lord, so that he can live with you and serve the Lord in your Temple."

And Eli kept Samuel.

Eli's sons, who were also priests of the Temple, kept part of the offerings presented to the Lord for themselves. In turn, they despised the offerings that the Israelites made to the Lord God. Eli tried to correct them, but they paid no heed.

Each year Hannah visited her son and brought him whatever he needed. Samuel grew up in body and in spirit before the Lord.

Samuel's Prophecy Is Fulfilled

One day, while Samuel was sleeping in his room, he heard someone calling him. He rose and presented himself before Eli. "Here I am; you called me."

"I didn't call you; go back to bed," Eli answered.

The same thing happened three times, and the third time Eli understood that it was the Lord who was calling Samuel. He said to the boy, "If you hear the voice again, answer, 'Speak, Lord, your servant is listening.'"

And Samuel did so.

"Samuel! Samuel!"

"Speak, Lord, your servant is listening," Samuel answered.

"The house of Eli will be punished because his sons curse the Lord and he hasn't been able to bring them up as he should. There is no sacrifice capable of erasing their sin."

The following morning, Eli called Samuel in to ask him what the Lord had said to him.

Samuel was saddened because this was bad news for Eli, but he had to explain in detail what the Lord had manifested. From then on, the news that the Lord spoke through Samuel traveled fast throughout Israel.

At that time, the Israelites and the Philistines were preparing for war. In the first battle Israel was defeated.

The sons of Eli went to look for the ark of the covenant in the Temple to ask for God's help. But they had offended the Lord too much for God to grant them favor now. The Philistines attacked again, and, again, they were victorious. The Israelites dispersed and the sons of Eli died.

One of the survivors who escaped went to tell Eli. When he heard the news, he fell on his back and broke his neck.

Samuel Conquers His Enemies

The ark was in the hands of the Philistines, but they did not know where to place it. In the temple, it would destroy the image of their god; when it was in a town, the inhabitants would get ill. In this way, they took it from one place to another, but wherever they placed it, there would always be some tragedy. Finally they decided to return it to the people of Israel to prevent it from destroying everything.

They placed it on a cart pulled by oxen and brought it back to Israelite territory. The whole people of Israel rejoiced at having been able to retrieve the ark of the covenant.

Samuel governed over Israel at the time. After a few years, the Israelites felt deeply sorry for having sinned by worshiping other gods. Samuel told them, "Remove the alien gods from your houses. Return to the Lord, our God, and you will be freed from the Philistines. Fast and be purified."

They did so. Later they gathered in Mizpah to confront the Philistines. During the battle, Samuel offered a sacrifice to God. The sacrifice pleased God, who made the Philistines flee from there. Thanks to that victory, Israel was considered by the other nations to be a terrible enemy. No one transgressed their borders or attacked them while Samuel was governing Israel.

3.
The People Want a King:
David and His Descendants

Around the year 1000 B.C.E., Israel was consolidated as a monarchy. Israel wanted to be like other nations, with a king to govern it. Samuel and King Saul took the first steps, but the one who really brought change was King David. His kingdom was glorious: from Jerusalem, the capital of the kingdom, he organized the administration, and his court flourished. His son Solomon caused culture to flourish and fostered a great influence on neighboring peoples.

This was a country, a king, and a Temple where God became present to the people. Literature started. The memories of the past started being written down: the Exodus—or liberation from Egypt—became the basic experience in which the people discovered God as savior and liberator. The story of the Patriarchs (Abraham, Isaac, Jacob) was written emphasizing how the promise God made to Abraham was fulfilled in David. The writers also went back to the origins of the world: God not only wants to save Israel, but also the whole humanity.

Solomon dedicated special attention to buildings and increased the splendor of the court and army. All this brought about great consequences: the people were taxed on practically everything they earned in order to pay for the construction of the Temple, palace, and other buildings; this implied a progressive impoverishment of the people, with a subsequent political crisis which broke out at the time of Solomon's succession.

After Solomon's death, the kingdom was divided into two: Israel in the north, with the central and northern tribes, and Judah in the south, with the tribes of Judah and Benjamin. The two kingdoms had a tragic end: Israel was destroyed by the Assyrians in 722 B.C.E. and Judah was deported to Babylon in 587 B.C.E. All this placed the people of Israel in a desperate situation. If we stop to think, all that happened could have meant the end of this people: they were without land, without a king, without a Temple, and forbidden to practice their Law. Normally this people, like so many others, would have been banished from history.

The Israelites Want a King

Samuel, who was already old, was visited by the elders of Israel, who told him, "All the other nations have a king, which gives them security and protects them from enemies. We, too, want one. This way we won't have to be worried about what to do if we are attacked by the surrounding peoples."

Samuel answered, "You know perfectly well that our king is the Lord. God gives us protection, provided we are faithful. No king, no matter how powerful, can do what the Lord has done for us. Don't provoke the Lord with your petition."

But, since the people insisted, Samuel set them at ease. "If you are so concerned, I will transmit your request to the Lord. But don't get your hopes up because, until now, God has refused to accept a king for this people."

After Samuel presented the request of the Israelites, the Lord said to him, "Perhaps my protection is not enough for them. You know by now, Samuel, how it feels when they don't take you into account. You have led them wisely as a judge. They, however, want a king. They don't appreciate the effort of so many years. They also don't realize that the king and the whole court will make them work more in order to collect taxes to maintain the kingdom. They want a king? Very well then, we will give them one. But they should be very much aware of all the burdens they are taking on. I will show you how to choose him."

Samuel told the elders what the Lord had said.

The First King

Some days later, Samuel entered the city to offer a sacrifice. A handsome man asked him, "Do you know where the man of God is?"

"I am. What is going on?"

"My name is Saul, son of Kish. Our donkeys are lost and we cannot find them. We came to ask you to tell us where they could be."

"Don't worry about them. Come with me to offer a sacrifice."

Samuel realized, by all the details that the Lord had given him, that Saul was the one chosen to reign over Israel. When they finished offering the sacrifice, Samuel asked him to stay until the following morning. At dawn, he poured oil from a vessel on Saul's head and said, "The Lord has chosen you as a king for the people of God. You will be just and save it from its enemies. On leaving

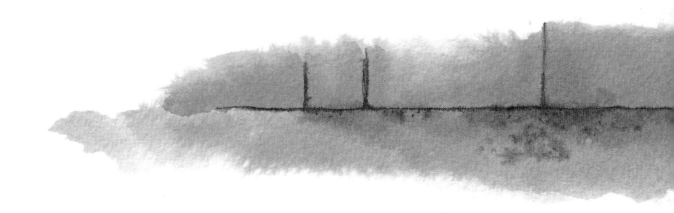

here, you will find two people who will tell you where your animals are. The spirit of the Lord will turn you into a new man. Afterwards go to Gilgal and wait there for me for a few days. When I arrive, I will tell you what to do."

The Ammonites, enemies of Israel, attacked the city of Jabesh. The Israelites who lived there were about to surrender because they were weaker. But they had sent messengers asking for help. As soon as Saul learned about it, he gathered an army and went in search of the aggressors.

At dawn, he divided the troops into three groups and they fell upon the enemy camp. The Ammonites who could save themselves escaped hurriedly. Saul had achieved a magnificent victory. This served so that all the Israelites, even those who had doubted him, would accept him as king.

After the battle, Samuel spoke to the people: "Now you have a king as you wished. My task as the leader of your people has finished. From now on I will only act as prophet of the Lord, to teach you what is right and what is not. Remember that both you and your king have to respect the Lord's Commandments because we all depend on the Lord."

Saul Is the King, but God Is God

The Philistines wanted to stop the Israelites before they could attack them. They called together a multitude of warriors, with chariots and all kinds of metal weapons. In contrast, since the Philistines had not allowed them to have blacksmiths, such weapons were not available to the Israelites. For this reason, the Philistines were convinced they could easily defeat the people of Israel.

The Israelites were afraid and fled Gilgal. Meanwhile, Saul waited for the arrival of Samuel. But, since the prophet was taking longer than expected, Saul decided to offer the sacrifice to the Lord himself. In this way, he would ensure the Lord's help if the Philistines should attack.

On arriving, Samuel scolded Saul. Even if he was a king, he could not offer a sacrifice; only a priest of the Lord could do that. Despite this, the Lord helped them. God created such confusion among the Philistines that they were forced to flee. This victory reaffirmed Saul's authority.

On another occasion, the Lord ordered Saul, "I want to punish the Amalekites. Attack them and kill all living things there. Furthermore, you will offer me the spoils."

But Saul did not do it, and a little later he had to listen to the Lord speak through Samuel: "I regret having chosen Saul as the king of Israel. He is not faithful. He thinks that because he is king he can decide for himself. He doesn't obey me. What is that bleating of sheep and that bellowing of oxen I hear? Hadn't I ordered that everything be exterminated?"

"The people wanted to keep the best animals to sacrifice to the Lord," Saul objected.

"The Lord appreciates the faithfulness of the people and obedience to God's word more than all the sacrifices they can offer. You have kept them out of self interest. Don't try to convince me otherwise," Samuel reproached.

"I have allowed myself to be influenced by the people. Forgive me and ask the Lord to be favorable to me once again," the king pleaded.

"You have rejected the Lord's word and now he rejects you as king of Israel. God will find someone better than you who knows how to be faithful. Have you perhaps forgotten you are king not out of your own right but because the Lord wished it so? You cannot act without him," Samuel reminded Saul.

Who Will Be the New King?

A few days later Samuel, at the Lord's suggestion, went to Jesse's house in Bethlehem to choose the future king from among his sons. The sons came before Samuel expecting the Lord to identify who would be the elected one, but no one was chosen. Surprised, Samuel asked Jesse, "Don't you have any other sons?"

"Yes, the youngest, who is tending the flocks of sheep."

"Go fetch him, so we can find out whether he is the chosen one of the Lord, our God," requested Samuel.

When the boy arrived—with his lovely eyes, fair hair, and strong build—the Lord told Samuel he should anoint him the king of Israel. As soon as he did so, the Spirit of the Lord came upon David (that was the name of the Lord's chosen one).

Messiah is a Hebrew word that means "anointed with oil." It designates a special person who is consecrated and whom God has entrusted with a particular mission for the salvation of the people. King David is a kind of messianic king. The hope for a messiah was forged after the Babylonian exile. It centered in particular around the figure of a SON OF DAVID/SON OF GOD, in a liberator who would come at the end of time. Jesus answered those hopes: he was the awaited Messiah.

After a time, David's older brothers were waging war, like all the available men of Israel. They were part of Saul's army. The Philistines attacked again and it was necessary for them to defend themselves.

Jesse told his son David, "Go to the camp where your brothers are and take to them the food I will give you. When you see they are all right, come straight back here to report to me."

David hurried to do what his father had ordered. When he was in the camp, he heard a loud voice coming from the other side: "Israelites, you cowards! For days I have been proposing a one-on-one fight with any one of your warriors. Haven't you found anybody who wants to fight me, you chickens?"

That man was laughing loudly at the fear of the Israelites. It was a justified fear, because by his stature and strength he looked like a giant rather than a man.

What Will David Do?

David was enraged to hear that arrogant bully ridiculing the army of the Lord. So he presented himself before Saul and said, "I will fight the Philistine who is laughing at us."

"You, my boy? Don't you see that he will kill you with the first blow? Are you crazy? We can't allow you to do that," Saul forbade him.

"The Lord, our God, has protected me when I have defended my flock against bears and lions. Why wouldn't God favor me today?"

This answer impressed Saul, who withdrew his prohibition. "Go. May the Lord go with you."

The suit of armor was too heavy for David, so he faced the Philistine with only a staff and a sling. When the Philistine saw this he was angry. "Listen, little boy. What do you think, that you are coming to shoo a dog away with a staff? If you get close, I will feed your flesh to the beasts. Who has prepared you for war?"

"You are only a dumb bully. You may be big and strong, but you don't have God's protection; his power will help me defeat you," David answered decidedly.

When Goliath, the enormous Philistine, was ready to attack, David loaded his sling with a stone that he carried in his backpack. He aimed carefully, and the stone hit his adversary right in the middle of his forehead. Goliath fell to the ground. David came up running, and, with the sword of the haughty Philistine, he cut off Goliath's head and took it back to the Israelite encampment.

So Much for a Thank You from Saul!

The Philistines were really surprised to witness the tragic end of their champion. They were frightened and escaped in disarray. The Israelites pursued them and killed many of them.

Sauk kept David in the army and gave him more responsibilities as time went on. David and Jonathan, Saul's son, had much in common and became fast friends.

Anything Saul entrusted to David, he did well and swiftly. There was no battle from which he did not emerge victorious. Among the Israelite people, David's fame surpassed that of Saul, and Saul was jealous. His jealousy got so out of hand that, one day while David was playing the harp for the king, Saul saw that David was distracted, so he attacked David with his spear. Thanks to his good reflexes, David was able to dodge the spear that almost pierced him.

Saul could not bear the fact that David was more popular than he was. From then on, he spent most of his time plotting to kill David.

King Saul proposed that David marry his daughter Michal. In exchange, he asked David to bring back proof of having killed one hundred Philistines. In truth, Saul hoped that David would be killed fighting the Philistines, but David survived the feat.

On another occasion, Saul took advantage of the darkness of night and ordered some assassins to kill David. Thanks to his wife, David was able to save himself.

Because of all this, David went into hiding to stay alive.

Helping David Could Cost You Your Life

Jonathan did not understand why his father treated David like that.

"Father, please explain to me why you want to kill David, because I can't for the life of me understand. He has risked his life for you in many battles and has always been faithful. What do you have against him?"

When Saul saw that his own son spoke up in defense of David, he was enraged. "What has he given to you to make you take his side in this way? I am your father, not him. You have to defend me. My power, which you will inherit, is in jeopardy as long as he is alive. What you need to do, since you probably know where he hides, is to bring him to me so that I can kill him."

"I can't believe David wants to do us any harm. He would never try to take your power. I don't see any reason for him to die."

Saul was beside himself and, without letting Jonathan finish, he took out the spear to attack his son. Luckily, he did not wound him.

Jonathan realized that his father would never let David live in peace no matter how much he begged. He immediately explained to David what had happened.

David had to keep running. He came upon Nob, a priestly city, and they helped him. But Doeg, Saul's main shepherd, saw David in the city and went to inform the king.

"Ahimelech, the priest, has given David provisions, and, in addition, he has given him Goliath's sword."

"Make him come together with his whole family."

Ahimelech presented himself before the king, "Here I am, my lord."

"Why have you helped David when he was fleeing from me?"

"I didn't know he was fleeing from you. On many occasions I have helped him because I thought he was your best servant."

But the king did not want to listen to reason. When he spoke about David, he ranted and raved, "You and your whole family will die because of your treason."

He also told the soldiers, "Go to Nob and kill all of the priests of the Lord who have been disloyal to me."

The soldiers, however, did not want to obey the king, since they feared the Lord's punishment. Then the king ordered Doeg to do it. He went to the priestly city and killed all the priests.

Now David Can Take Revenge

In the meantime David was taking refuge in a cave in the mountains. Many men, who were also fugitives for different reasons, joined him. David was the leader and slowly they formed an army.

With this army David freed the city of Keilah from the Philistines, through the intercession of the Lord. David longed to stay there, but he did not because he knew Saul wanted to capture him. For a time, David wandered through mountains and deserts, fleeing Saul.

In their flight, the fugitives settled in the mountains of Engedi. King Saul was informed of their whereabouts and took his soldiers to capture David. When they arrived, Saul went into a cave to relieve himself. It turned out to be the cave where David and his men were hiding.

"The Lord has placed him in your hands. Kill him now while he is defenseless so our lives as fugitives will end," the soldiers encouraged him.

"I cannot do such a thing, because he is the anointed one of the Lord. I must not harm him," David argued.

It was only when Saul had left the cave that David came before him saying, "My lord, why do you think I want to harm you? I will never have a better opportunity than today. When you were vulnerable in the cave, my men and I were watching you. See what I have in my hand: it is a piece of your cloak that I cut while you were relieving yourself. Had I wanted to, I could have killed you. However, I neither killed you nor allowed my men to do it."

Saul was impressed by David's behavior and said, "Is that you, David? Yes, that's you. I can't believe you would allow me to go free after what I have done to persecute you. You have shown me your kindness. Now I know you will reign over Israel and that the people will be safe in your hands. Swear to me that, when I die, you will not kill off my family."

"I swear, I will respect your descendants," David assured him.

When they finished speaking, Saul returned home and David went up to the shelter with his men.

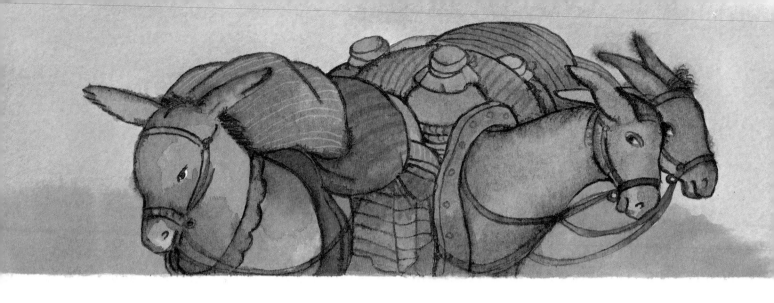

Samuel Dies, Abigail Escapes Death

In those days people from all over Israel gathered together. It was a meeting of cries and lamentation. Sadness spread throughout the cities and towns of Israel: Samuel, judge and prophet, had died. They buried him at his home in Ramah.

In the desert of Maon, where David and his men were stationed, Nabal, a rude and uneducated man, owned many properties. David sent messengers to tell him, "Peace to you and your family! We come from David to ask you to give us whatever you can to feed us. Your shepherds can tell you we have never taken anything from them even when we were hungry. We have let them watch their flocks, and we have never bothered them."

"What are you asking? If you decided to leave your homes in order to have a nomadic life that's not my fault. Why should I help you now? Besides, all is reserved for my family and my workers. Don't count on anything," said Nabal, dismissing them rudely.

They explained to David what he had said. A moment later four hundred armed men were on their way to Nabal's house. In the meantime, a servant went to tell Abigail, Nabal's wife, what had happened.

"My lady, David's men have come peacefully to ask your husband for help. Not only has he refused, but he has also insulted them. They have never bothered us or taken anything from us when we were watching our sheep. They are good people. Now I am afraid your husband's reaction may make them angry and return with their weapons. And if they get here, you know what will happen: they are warriors and we are shepherds."

Abigail acted swiftly. She ordered all kinds of foods and went to meet David. He was coming down from the mountain and had decided to kill Nabal and his whole people when he saw Abigail. She prostrated herself before him and apologized. "Lord, I am Abigail, Nabal's wife. Let the blame be mine. He is a bad and ignorant man. I did not see the messengers you sent. As soon as they warned me, I ordered food, and I come to offer it to you. Here it is," she said, pointing to the packets. "Consider us your servants: we are at your disposal in case you should need anything else. Out of kindness, I hope you do not attack my people."

"Blessed be the Lord who has given you wisdom and has placed you on my way. In this way, you have prevented me from falling upon your camp before dawn and killing everyone. I accept your food. Go back home in peace and warn your husband of what almost happened," David answered.

A Second Opportunity for David

Nabal died the following day. When David found out, he asked Abigail to be his wife; she immediately accepted. Since David had already taken Ahincam as his wife, Abigail would be his second wife. This was a common practice in those times. Michal, however, did not live with David because her father had married her off to another man.

On another occasion, Saul went with his soldiers to the hill of Hachilah in search of David. The king was sleeping in the center of the camp. David and his nephew managed to sneak by the guard unnoticed and came upon the place where Saul was resting. The nephew said to David, "Allow me to pierce him with his own spear."

"He has been chosen by the Lord and therefore we cannot do any harm to him. We will take the spear and the jug of water he has by his side, and they will serve us as proof. When he realizes we could have killed him, he will be astonished."

And they left the enemy camp unnoticed. When they were halfway up the mountain, and far from Saul's men, David shouted, "Awake! Rise! We could have killed the king. What were you doing while we were by his side? Look!" he cried, showing them what they had taken. "Aren't these the king's spear and jug? Is this the way you protect the anointed of the Lord?"

"David! Is that your voice?" asked Saul, who had recognized him.

"Yes, it's me. You have been shown once again that your life has been in my hands. Will you stop pursuing me? You have seen for yourself that I don't want to harm you in any way. If that were so, I would have killed you with your own spear."

"David, come back to me. I regret having chased you. You have respected my life and I wanted to take yours. I have erred," the king realized.

David knew only too well that the king could change his mind and kill him as soon as he was within reach. That's why he did not accept the offer, and at dawn he went back to his people while Saul withdrew.

David, at the Service of the Philistines?

It did not take long for David to get the news that Saul continued looking for him in order to kill him. David and his men went to serve the Philistines so the king would not be able to find him.

They settled in the city of Ziklag. They often left the city to attack the enemies of Israel, making Achish, king of the Philistines, believe that they had attacked the Israelites. David became popular among the people of Israel for helping them in this peculiar way.

Once, the Philistines decided to attack the Israelites. Achish called David in to ask him to help in the battle, and David could not refuse. But the other Philistine princes recognized him and did not like the idea of having him among them: they feared he could betray them halfway through the battle and go to the Israelites' side. Then Achish ordered him, "Go back to the city. I have always been very happy with you, but the Philistine princes believe that you could rebel against them, and I haven't been able to convince them otherwise. Go in peace and reserve your strength for other battles."

"I had wanted to fight for you, my king," David said, hiding the joy he felt at Achish's order, "but if that is your wish, I will return to the city, much to my dismay."

When they arrived in Ziklag, David and his men met with an unfortunate surprise: the city had been attacked and the inhabitants had been imprisoned by the Amalekites. After consulting with the Lord God, David and all his followers pursued the assailants. On the way there, they met an Egyptian slave of the Amalekites who led David and his men to them.

The enemies, spread throughout the camp, were eating and drinking contentedly, celebrating their victory. Taking advantage of the moment, David attacked. Except a few who managed to escape, all died. David recovered all the people and things taken from Ziklag, as well as a splendid spoil from the Amalekites. David divided the spoils among the camps and cities where he had lived while he was wandering. All were very grateful.

David Succeeds Saul

While all that was happening, the Philistines and the Israelites were furiously fighting. A short while later, the Philistines won the battle. Then Saul realized he was lost: his sons had been killed and the army had dispersed. In order not to fall into the Philistine's hands, he committed suicide by throwing himself on top of the sword. All the people of Israel who lived in neighboring cities fled inland to avoid the Philistines' revenge.

David was informed of Saul's death. He mourned him. Later he went to Judah where he was proclaimed king. But only the tribe of Judah recognized him as such; the rest of the tribes of Israel crowned Ishbaal, son of Saul, as king. So, Ishbaal and David fought to reign over the whole people of Israel.

The chief of Ishbaal's army was Abner. One day Ishbaal and Abner had a heated discussion and got angry with one another. Then Abner took David's side to dethrone Ishbaal. But one of David's lieutenants tricked Abner by posing as his friend. When Abner was near, David's lieutenant killed him: Abner's betrayal of his king was paid back with another betrayal.

Once Abner died, all the chiefs of Ishbaal's army were sure that they would never be able to defeat David. They killed Ishbaal while he was sleeping so that David would be indebted to them. But they were in for a big surprise: instead of being grateful, David ordered them executed for having needlessly assassinated their king, the son of Saul.

At the time of these events, David had already been reigning over Judah for seven years. At that point, the elders of all the tribes of Israel gathered together in Hebron to accept David as the king of all Israel: David had achieved his goal.

The Ark Enters Jerusalem, the Capital

As king of Israel, David conquered Jerusalem, which was occupied by the Jebusites.

Other enemies, the Philistines, were alarmed when they heard that David had unified the whole Israel. They were afraid he would conquer them, so they attacked him twice. Both times the Lord granted favor to David, helping him to win.

So Jerusalem became the capital of the kingdom; it was also the religious capital when the ark of the covenant was transported there. To celebrate the occasion, David danced in front of the ark. Michal, Saul's daughter who had returned to David as his wife, scolded him.

"Do you think it is appropriate for everyone to see you, a king, dancing like a fool?"

"I have danced, and I will dance always before the ark of the Lord, because I am nothing without God. I don't mind humbling myself or being ridiculed," David answered without hesitation.

Michal's attitude made David separate himself from her. She had not given him any children, so she did not have the honor of being the mother of a possible heir to the king.

While he was at home, David realized that he had many luxuries, while the Lord had a simple tent as a home. So, he went to talk to the prophet Nathan.

"Because I am a king, I live in a wonderful house. Doesn't the Lord perhaps deserve a better house than I have?"

"The Lord is glad to see the interest you have in God's house; but this is not the time to build it. Whoever reigns after you can do that; it is not your task. However, since you were concerned, you will be rewarded: your family and your house will endure. If any one of your descendants does not fulfill the pact that the Lord has made with Israel, he will be punished, but the Lord will never abandon him," the prophet answered.

Then David prayed in thanksgiving to the Lord.

David Loses His Senses over Bathsheba

Having solved that, David continued to focus on the tasks he had ahead as a king. He learned that the king of the Ammonites had died, so he sent messengers to give his condolences.

But the Ammonites thought it was a trap by David, so they sent the messengers back after taking away their clothes and shaving their beards, the worst thing they could do to a man of those times. As a result of this, war broke out between the Israelites and the Ammonites.

While the army was at war, David stayed in Jerusalem. One day he spotted an attractive woman bathing. David ordered her to be brought before him and they had sexual relations.

A while later Bathsheba, as the woman was named, told David that she was pregnant. Bathsheba's husband was Uriah, one of the men who was at war. King David ordered him to come and said to him, "I have learned that you are a good fighter. Your courage deserves a rest. Go to your home and rest so that when you go back to battle all your strength will be restored."

"I thank you for the honor, but I can't go home. If I did, I would die of shame thinking of my companions. They are on the battlefield sleeping in the open air. I cannot be the only one to enjoy the pleasure of resting at home," Uriah refused.

David wanted him to spend the night with his wife so that the baby she was expecting could be attributed to Uriah and not to him. He tried everything, even getting him drunk, but Uriah did not go home. Then king David sent Uriah to war again with a letter for the commander saying, "Place Uriah in the most dangerous position so that the enemy can kill him because it would be to my advantage."

Not two days had gone by when Uriah was dead. Once the period of mourning for Uriah's death was over, David took Bathsheba as a wife.

David Gets Angry at Himself

After what had happened, the prophet Nathan came before David and said, "Listen to what happened between two men. One was very rich and had many flocks of sheep and cows. The other man was poor and only had one sheep, which he had bought with great sacrifice. That sheep was like one of his children, and he fed it and loved it as one of the family. One day the rich man received a visit and, instead of taking one of his animals to welcome the stranger, he took the sheep of the poor man, cooked it, and served it to his guest."

David became angry with that man, and exclaimed, "Whoever has acted that way deserves death. He should pay dearly for that sheep to see the pain he had caused."

"You have behaved like that rich man and therefore the Lord has gotten angry. After saving you from Saul, he made you king of Israel. You have inherited Saul's women. Why, then, have you disobeyed the Lord? You have caused Uriah's death and kept his wife. Tragedy will visit your house since you haven't limited yourself to what you had," Nathan said menacingly.

"Pray to the Lord to forgive the sin I have committed against God," David asked.

"The Lord forgives you. You will not die, but the son you two have conceived will die," the prophet ended.

David's son got very ill. David fasted and slept on the hard floor as his penance to see if the Lord would spare the child. But on the seventh day of his sickness, the son died. When David found out, he went to comfort Bathsheba.

A while later the Lord gave them another son, Solomon, who was favored in the eyes of God.

Amnon Cannot Control His Lust

A while later Amnon, a son of David, fell in love with Tamar, who was his sister, although not of the same mother. He became obsessed with her: he could not stop thinking about her day and night; he could not eat, could not sleep, could not live without her.

One day he feigned sickness and Tamar went to prepare his food. When she got near to serve him his meal, Amnon grabbed her and said, "Sleep with me. I cannot live without you, my sister."

"No, Amnon, that cannot be. You know that our people don't do things like that. Speak to the king, perhaps he will allow us to marry," Tamar objected.

But passion was blinding Amnon, whose only thought was that Tamar was there, close to him, and that he could hold her. So he forced her to behave as if she were his wife. A few minutes later the love that Amnon thought he felt for Tamar turned to hatred.

"Go away from me! Get out of here! I don't want to see you here," Amnon yelled at her.

"It wasn't enough that you forced yourself on me, but now you want to throw me out like a dog? You aren't satisfied with the harm you have caused me, so now you want to offend me by kicking me out of your house? I don't have anywhere to go; if you do this to me no one will want me," Tamar protested.

Amnon was beside himself and was unable to listen to anyone. He threw her out of his house without a second thought.

Amnon's Evil Brings Him Misfortune

Once Tamar was thrown out of Amnon's house, she dressed in mourning for what had happened to her. Tamar covered her head with ashes and tore her tunic, the symbol of her virginity. With her hands on her head, she went away crying.

She ended up at her brother Absalom's house. He started plotting revenge on Amnon for the offense committed against his sister. But first, he calmed Tamar down. He knew the appropriate moment to avenge her honor would come.

"Don't cry or complain about it anymore, or everyone will know what happened. Calm down and don't suffer."

Inconsolable, Tamar stayed in Absalom's house. King David was very angry when he found out, but he did not reprimand Amnon, because he was his first born. David did not want Amnon to be upset. Absalom did not say anything to Amnon either, but for a very different reason: he did not want Amnon to suspect he was plotting revenge so he could take him by surprise.

Two years later, Absalom invited all the king's sons to a banquet. At Absalom's orders, the servants waited for Amnon to get drunk. Then they killed him. His sister's honor had been avenged.

To escape the king's ire, Absalom fled to another land and stayed there for three years. After that time, David called Absalom and he returned to Jerusalem. But the king did not allow him to come to the palace. Another two years passed. The passage of time cooled David's fury against Absalom, and he allowed his son to come before him.

"I am your servant. If you consider me guilty, kill me, but don't force me to live in the city without being able to come to see you," Absalom said to the king.

The king made Absalom, kneeling before him, rise and kiss him, for he was his son. Father and son were thus reconciled.

114

Absalom Is Too Eager to Be King

Absalom, who wanted to dethrone his father so that he could become king, dedicated himself to winning over the people of Israel. He would stand on the road into Jerusalem and talk to those who went to the city seeking justice.

"If I were the judge, I would impart justice and defend your interests," he would tell them.

And he did not allow people to prostrate themselves before him, but he embraced them.

After four years, Absalom went to Hebron to offer sacrifices to the Lord God. From there he would start his rebellion against David. He managed to get all the tribes of Israel, with the exception of Judah, to consider him their king and lend him their support.

David was informed of all that happened. When he knew that Absalom had the recognition of the majority, he fled from Israel with his followers, those of the tribe of Judah. The priests Zadek and Abiathar wanted to take the ark of the covenant with them, but they returned to Jerusalem with the ark and the mission to spy for David so he would be informed of everything Absalom was plotting.

Ahithophel, David's main adviser, had also joined Absalom. In order to compensate for the influence of the treacherous advisor over Absalom, David sent his faithful Hushai to Absalom. Hushai would pretend he was on Absalom's side and in this way he would try to upset the plans of the rebels to destroy king David.

Absalom had entered Jerusalem as king. He accepted Hushai as his servant and continued with the custom of royal successors of keeping his father's wives so that everyone would accept him as king.

What Strategy Will They Choose?

Absalom soon started to plot to destroy David and his followers. Ahithophel advised him, "Let's take twelve thousand men and go against David. We will trap him by night, when he is resting. The surprise of our attack will make his people run in different directions. As soon as his followers have abandoned him, we can kill him easily."

Everyone agreed with Ahithophel's plan, both Absalom and the elders. However, Absalom wanted to find out Hushai's opinion before deciding what plan they would carry out. Once he was consulted, Hushai said, "Ahithophel's strategy would work on common enemies. But consider that we face awesome warriors with a courageous and experienced king leading them. If they are attacked, they will fight as wild beasts pushed on by the anger of having been dispossessed of what was theirs. Be certain that David will not allow his men to rest quietly. They will always be ready for battle.

"If we had many casualties in the first battle, all Israel would know and that would discourage many of the men who want to fight. To ensure victory it is better for Absalom himself to lead the largest army possible. In this way, their anger and fury will be for naught. They will be eliminated to the last man."

Absalom and all those gathered there thought that Hushai's advice was wiser than Ahithophel's and agreed to follow it. Hushai explained to the priests the decision they had arrived at so that they could inform David. Knowing this, they could cross the Jordan river and free themselves from Absalom's attack.

Who Shall Overcome: David or Absalom?

The sons of the priests were in charge of taking the news to David. On the way they were almost taken prisoner. Someone had betrayed them and they were being followed. They were lucky enough to find a hiding place in the house of some friends. The lady of the house led them into a dry well in the garden. A wheat cover hid the well from view.

After looking everywhere, Absalom's soldiers could not find them. They returned empty-handed. So David was informed of what was going on and, before the following dawn, his men had crossed the Jordan. They settled in the city of Mahanaim where people treated them very well and they could recuperate from the exhausting journey through the desert. Absalom, with his army, also crossed the Jordan, pursuing them.

David had reviewed the troops and had reorganized the army perfectly in groups of one hundred and one thousand. He told them, "I will go before you to confront the rebels who want to dethrone me. We will fight courageously. Let us pray to the Lord for help so that we can be victorious in battle."

But his men told him, "You don't have to go to combat. If one of us falls, that is not very important, but if you die the army would be discouraged and that would be the end of us. Stay in the city. If necessary, you can come out later to help us."

"All right; I will do as you say. Go carefully and don't kill my son Absalom. Out of the faithfulness and appreciation you have for me, treat him well," ordered David.

David's army went to face the rebels. The battle, which was fierce, was going in David's favor. Absalom was defeated after twenty thousand of his men were killed and the rest fled.

Did David Cry for His Victory?

Absalom also tried to escape, but his long hair got tangled in the branches of an oak tree and he could not free himself. Seeing it, one of David's soldiers ran to tell Joab, the chief of the army. Joab reproached him.

"You had the chance to kill him. Why didn't you?"

"I couldn't because the king gave orders to respect his son's life and I would have been punished."

But Joab did not heed David's order. He went where Absalom was still trying to free his hair and shot some arrows at him; Joab's assistants finished the job. Then Joab ordered the horn to be played. That was the signal to stop pursuing the conquered.

Joab sent a messenger to David to tell him of the victory. Immediately David asked, "Is Absalom all right?"

"He was killed in action," the messenger answered.

From that moment on, David looked like the defeated rather than the victor of that battle. A bitter and profound sadness overcame his heart. Sobbing, he could not stop lamenting, "Absalom! My son! I wish that I had died instead of you!"

When they found out that the king was mourning his son's death, the victors returned quietly to the city, without any inclination to celebrate their victory. Seeing the attitude of his men, Joab told the king, "The one who was seeking your misfortune and your death is dead. He wanted to kill his own father and rob him of everything that was his. My men and I have been faithful to you, have risked our lives for you, for your family and your throne. You can feel sadness as a father, but as a king, you have to show respect to your army, lest now that you have defeated your enemies, you lose the loyalty of your men."

David realized that Joab was right and he sat by the door so that the army could pay their respects to him.

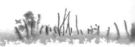

Even More Treason

In order to gain the trust of the elders, David placed Amasa at the head of the army and returned to Jerusalem. When he was there, they faced the rebellion of Sheba. Amasa went out to pursue Sheba. On the way, Amasa met Joab, the former head of the troops. Joab bent as if to kiss Amasa, but instead he pierced Amasa with the sword, killing him instantly. At the head of the army, Joab continued to pursue Sheba, who had taken refuge in a city which was later besieged by Joab and his men. When they were getting ready to bring the walls of the city down, a woman spoke to Joab from inside the city.

"What do you have against this city? We have not trespassed in any way. Why are you trying to destroy a city of Israel that keeps all the traditions?"

"I don't want anything from your city. I only want Sheba, who has rebelled against the king," Joab clarified.

"Don't worry. We will kill that traitor from above the city walls," the woman promised.

And she did so. As soon as Joab had Sheba's head in his hands, he withdrew his troops.

David had to fight the Philistines, and once again he defeated them. When there was peace again, he broke out in a song of thanksgiving to the Lord.

"Praised be the Lord. Blessed be the one who helps me! May the God of my salvation be exalted, the God who gives me gladness, the one who subjects nations to my power."

Both Adonijah and Solomon Want to Succeed David

King David was getting old. His body tired easily. David's son Adonijah believed he would be heir to his father, and he behaved as though he was. He organized a party and he invited other sons of the king and some important people who acclaimed him as monarch.

David had promised Bathsheba, the mother of Solomon, that Solomon would be heir to the throne. Bathsheba spoke to David because she was afraid that Adonijah would end up being king.

"Lord, you swore to me that Solomon would reign after you. Adonijah has invited people to a party and they are shouting, 'Long live Adonijah, the king.' You should have said clearly who will sit on the throne after you."

Then Nathan, the prophet, came in and said, "Do you realize that Adonijah is gathering people in celebration because he intends to take the throne? There are others crying out, 'Long live Adonijah, the king.'"

"Today I will crown Solomon king, as I promised," David decided.

And so it happened. Once the anointing of Solomon as king was over, he was paraded through the whole city, among music and clanging. Adonija's supporters , who were eating, heard the noise, but did not know the cause of so much clamor.

"What is going on, that there are so many shouts and noise?" Adonijah asked.

"By order of King David, Solomon has been proclaimed king and has sat on the royal throne. King David and the new King Solomon are constantly receiving congratulations," Jonathan, son of the priest Abiathar, told him.

Adonijah and his followers were afraid and hid so that no harm would come to them. When Solomon found out, he forgave Adonijah and set him free.

Solomon, King, Rich, and Wise

A little while later David, who was already very old, died. Before dying, he gave Solomon a last bit of advice: "Fulfill the Lord, your God's commands, so that you will be successful in everything you propose. Never go astray from God's ways, and he will continue to help you as he has helped me."

For many days the Israelites, young and old, mourned David, the best king they ever had.

Not much later, Adonijah started complaining. He claimed the throne was his by right and started thinking of the ways to get it. When Solomon heard about this, he was very angry. Solomon had forgiven Adonijah and set him free—even after his disloyalty. Instead of being grateful, Adonijah wanted to destroy Solomon. Solomon had Adonijah killed as punishment for his unfaithfulness to Solomon. In this way, Israel could live in peace for a long time without any struggles for the royal throne.

Solomon wanted to offer a sacrifice to the Lord and went to Gibeon where the most important shrine was located. When he was resting there, the Lord spoke to him in his dreams.

"Solomon, what would you like to ask of me?"

"Give me a wise heart so that I can be a good judge among your children of Israel. The people are very numerous and many problems arise. I won't be able to move ahead without your help," Solomon asked.

"It pleases me that you are not asking for material wealth. So I grant you wisdom to solve the difficulties that you will face, as well as material wealth. Both one and the other you will receive in abundance, so that no one will compare to you," the Lord granted him.

All the world found out that Solomon was very wealthy and also very wise. The news reached Egypt. So Solomon, who had such admirable qualities, married Pharaoh's daughter.

Whose Newborn Son Is This?

One day two prostitutes presented themselves before the king and one, sobbing inconsolably, said, "Lord, do me justice!"

"Don't cry, I can't understand what you are saying. Explain to me what has happened," Solomon asked.

"This woman here and I each had a son at the same time. One night she fell asleep while she was nursing her baby. When she woke up in the middle of the night she realized that she had fallen asleep on top of the baby and had suffocated him. Without making any noise, she came to where I was sleeping and exchanged the baby. I woke up at my usual hour. When I realized the baby was not breathing, I wanted to die. When I calmed down a little, I realized that he wasn't my baby; this one has thicker lips and doesn't have two spots on his neck; mine has a navel that sticks out and his eyes are lighter," said the first woman, crying, while she showed him the dead baby.

"That's not true! It's a lie! It's a lie! Everything she has said is false. She wants to take my baby. She was the one who fell asleep on top of the baby. She suffocated him and now she wants to steal mine. Since she took care of my baby for two days, now she knows all the details of his body. She has made up this story so that she won't be without a baby. Do justice and punish her, lord king," said the second woman.

There was a long pause in the royal palace. King Solomon was not saying anything, just thinking. At last, his words resounded in the court.

"Let the executioner come with a well-sharpened sword. He will split the live baby in two and we will give half to each woman."

At that moment the executioner came in and was about to grab the baby, when the first woman implored, "No, good king! Give him to her. Give him to her! I'd rather have her keep him alive than have him dead," said the first woman, fighting back the tears.

"All right, all right! Cut him in half! That way neither of us will have him!" said the second woman.

"Stop!" said the king to the executioner. "Give the baby to this woman, who is his true mother," he said, pointing to the first woman. "And you, get out of my sight, since you have already been punished with the death of your son," the king concluded, addressing the second woman.

Everyone heard about the result of this trial. And all, awed by the royal verdict, agreed that they had a wise and just king.

What a Temple, What a Palace!

Solomon did not neglect one of the functions assigned to him: building the Temple. He sent thousands of workers to neighboring countries to extract first class materials. He also called the best experts in each one of the construction areas so that the Temple would be unique. The Lord God deserved that and much more. It took several years to complete. Once finished, the Temple dazzled both Israelites and foreigners because of its beauty and splendor.

Solomon also built a royal palace. Temple and palace won the admiration of all.

In order to transport the ark of the covenant from the tent where it was to the new Temple, an impressive feast was organized. The elders came from all over Israel for the great event. The transfer of the ark happened among cries for joy, dancing, and music. Thousands of songs and sacrifices confirmed the importance of the event.

When everything was over, the Lord appeared to Solomon in his dreams and said to him, "I accept the Temple you have built to me. I will stay there and assure the permanence of you and your sons on the throne, provided you fulfill my commands. Imitate David, your father. He kept my support by his behavior. Never divert your attention toward other gods, because that would only bring disgrace upon you and this magnificent Temple would be brought down to its ruin. Never provoke my anger."

Solomon's renowned wisdom prompted the queen of Sheba to visit him. That way she would be able to deal with him and see for herself whether the wealth and wisdom were as great as people said.

As she approached first the royal palace and then the Temple, the queen's eyes widened is disbelief at what she saw. Inside the palace, the queen rubbed her eyes in amazement to make sure she was seeing right. The queen's surprise at what she saw paled in comparison to what she felt when the king answered her questions.

It had been a long time since Jerusalem had seen as many gifts of perfumed wood and gold as the queen of Sheba offered Solomon.

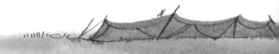

Solomon Falls out of Grace and Dies

Things were going very well for Solomon, but little by little he had forgotten the promise he had made to the Lord his God. He got together with many foreign women and they diverted his heart from the Lord. Solomon started worshiping strange gods. So the Lord withdrew his trust from Solomon and told him so.

"What good are my warnings if you don't pay attention? Since you have not respected your part of the pact, I will not keep mine either. Your kingdom will not continue with your descendants. Despite everything, I will allow your successor to have a tribe, as a remembrance of the faithfulness of David, your father."

After this warning to Solomon, Jeroboam, one of the king's stewards, was leaving Jerusalem and he ran into the prophet Ahijah. Ahijah was carrying a cloak that he divided into twelve parts. He said to Jeroboam, "Take ten parts, because the Lord has manifested that he will take the kingdom away from Solomon and will give you ten tribes. If you keep his laws and are faithful, he will keep your kingdom and house."

Solomon found out about that encounter and ordered the death of Jeroboam. But Jeroboam escaped into Egypt to be out of Solomon's reach. At this time Solomon was very old and, after a long life, he died. He was buried with all honor. People came from all corners with messages of condolence. King Solomon, the great one, the wise one, had died.

Israel Is Divided Between Jeroboam and Rehoboam

The whole of Israel got together in Shechem to proclaim Rehoboam, son of Solomon, king. The elders of Israel told him, "Solomon, your father, burdened us with taxes and duties. Make our load lighter and we will serve you as your people."

"I will keep in mind what you ask me. You will have an answer in three days," Rehoboam promised.

The young king asked for advice. He first asked the elder councilors, who said, "Do as Israel asks of you. Address them with gentle words and you will reign with peace and happiness."

He then received the counsel of his young friends.

"What do you care if they have one less sheep? You need money to have as much fun as possible. You have to ask for more taxes, and impose more obligations on them."

Rehoboam heeded the advice of his young friends instead of following the recommendations of the elders. He communicated his decision to the elders of Israel. Seeing his attitude, they decided not to accept him as king. Furthermore, they found out that Jeroboam had returned from Egypt after learning of Solomon's death. They sent for him and crowned him king of ten of the tribes. Only the tribes of Judah and Benjamin continued to be faithful to Rehoboam.

In any case, Jeroboam was concerned about his subjects going back to Jerusalem to offer sacrifices. He was afraid that in the long run, they would want to rejoin Rehoboam's kingdom because the holy Temple was in Jerusalem. To prevent that, he ordered two golden calves to be built as representations of God. He placed one in Bethel and one in Dan. He also built temples on different holy mountains. In addition, he appointed priests who were not of the tribe of Levi, to whom the priestly functions belonged, to care for the temples and the calves.

Jeroboam Is Unable to Protect His Son, the Temple, or the Palace

Jeroboam was in Bethel, ready to burn some incense, when a man of God spoke to him saying, "The Lord God wants you to know that there will be a day when you and the priests will be burned upon the altar. This very altar will open up to demonstrate that the Lord speaks through my lips."

Jeroboam reacted by pointing to the intruder so that someone would arrest him. But his hand was paralyzed while the altar opened up. Only when the prophet interceded before the Lord did Jeroboam return to normal.

A little later, Jeroboam's son fell ill. The mother went to see the prophet Ahijah to ask him about her son's future. Ahijah told her, "The Lord God of Israel speaks thus: I took the reign away from Rehoboam to give it to you. How did you thank me? You have built golden calves, have built them temples, and forced your subjects to worship them. Listen to your punishment now: no one in Jeroboam's house will survive. Moreover, no one will be buried. You can only bury the son who is now ill and who will die as soon as he enters the house."

Everything happened as the prophet had said.

But Rehoboam, king of Judah, was not faithful to the Lord either. He copied the gods of neighboring lands and the ways to worship them. So the Lord left him at the mercy of his enemies. Rehoboam had not even been reigning for five years when Shishak, the king of Egypt, attacked Jerusalem. They could not prevent him from taking all the treasures from the Temple and the royal palace. On the other hand, he was constantly at war with Jeroboam, and neither of them ever achieved a total victory. After reigning for seventeen years, it was time for Rehoboam to die.

The Prophet Elijah and the Widow

A few years later Ahab was proclaimed king of Israel. This king strayed even farther from the Lord than previous kings. One day the prophet Elijah came before Ahab and said, "Because you strayed from the Lord's commands there will not be rain or dew for years."

Elijah had to hide under a waterfall so that Ahab's men would not kill him. As the Lord had told him, some crows brought him bread and meat regularly. With that and the water from the waterfall, he survived. After a time, the waterfall dried out. According to the word of God, Elijah went to Zarephath where a widow would feed him.

When he was about to enter the city, he met a widow who was gathering wood. He approached her and said, "Please bring me a glass of water, because I am thirsty. And a piece of bread, even if it is small. I will be grateful."

"I only have a handful of flour and a little oil, just enough to make you a small loaf. Afterwards my son and I will await death because we won't have anything else to eat," she answered.

"Don't be afraid. Go in and do as you have said. But first, bake a loaf of bread and bring it to me. After that you will be able to bake as many loaves as you want. The Lord tells you that neither the flour nor the bread will end," Elijah told her.

The woman did as Elijah had asked her to do. Amazed, she saw that the flour did not run out and the jug of oil was never empty.

A short time after Elijah's arrival, the widow's son got sick to the point that he stopped breathing. The woman complained to Elijah, "Did you come here to bring me misfortune? My son has been sick since the day you arrived."

"Bring me to your son," Elijah replied.

The woman accompanied him to where the child was lying. The prophet invoked the Lord to return the child to life, and he lay on top of the child three times. After a while, Elijah returned carrying her son alive in his arms. Choking with tears of joy, she exclaimed, "Now I realize you are a man of God and only the truth comes from your mouth."

Elijah Faces Baal's Priests

After three years the Lord ordered Elijah, "Go to meet King Ahab and tell him I want to send rain."

Elijah met Obadiah, Ahab's steward, and told him, "Inform Ahab that you have seen me."

"I would do anything for you, but you don't know what you are asking. If I say that to Ahab, he'll send for you, and if he finds you, he'll kill you."

"Go and tell him that I'll come before him today," Elijah asked him after thinking it over.

Obadiah informed the king. A little later, Ahab himself was talking to Elijah and reproached him, "Are you the one who brings misfortune upon Israel?"

"It isn't I but you, because you abandoned the Lord and started to worship other gods. If you want to see how false they are, call that group of prophets and priests of Baal that you are feeding so lavishly. Ask them to come to Mount Carmel and we will see who the true God is," Elijah proposed.

Then the people of Israel, the prophets of Baal, and Elijah met on Mount Carmel. Elijah spoke to them.

"Bring two calves. Have the priests of Baal choose one and place it on their altar. I will do the same with the other one. Neither of us will set the calves on fire. The god who makes fire come from heaven to consume the offering is the true god."

Everyone thought it was a reasonable proposal. The prophets of Baal sang and danced around the altar and shouted loudly, "Baal, listen to us! Make fire come down to burn down the calf we are offering."

They carried on until noon. They even wounded themselves to see if their god would heed their plea. Elijah mocked them saying, "Shout louder; perhaps your god is sleeping or is busy with his own affairs, or perhaps he is a little absent-minded."

Then Elijah got ready to fulfill his sacrifice. He rebuilt the altar of the Lord which had been destroyed. He placed the wood on twelve stones, one for each tribe of Israel, and on top of that he placed the calf cut up in pieces. Three times he ordered the assistants to pour water on the calf so that it would be harder to set on fire. Then he prayed, "Lord, God of Abraham, Isaac, and Jacob, listen to my prayer. Send me fire so that they will know that you are the God of Israel, the true God. Then they will acknowledge that I have done all this in your name."

Then the fire of the Lord God came down from heaven and consumed everything: wood, calf, and stones. There was not a trace of the water they had poured. So the people prostrated themselves saying, "The Lord is God! The Lord is God!"

None of the false prophets survived. The Israelites took them before Elijah, who killed them. A little later, Elijah told Ahab that the rains were coming. And so it was: a tiny, insignificant cloud at the beginning turned into a huge rainstorm.

Elisha, the New Prophet

Ahab's wife did not like the fact that Elijah had killed the prophets of Baal, so she ordered that he be sought and killed. Elijah had no choice but to flee. After forty days of walking and being fed with the help of the Lord, he came to Horeb, the mountain of the Lord. It was there that the Lord passed before Elijah: he had to bear a great blizzard, an earthquake, and fire, but the Lord was not in the fire, the earthquake, or the hurricane. He then noticed a gentle breeze and the Lord spoke to him from it.

"Go back the way you came. Look for Elisha, the son of Shaphat, and anoint him as prophet and your successor."

Elijah went looking for Elisha. He found him toiling in the fields. He threw his cloak on Elisha, a sign that he was investing him as a prophet. Elisha understood the meaning of it and said, "Let me go say goodbye to my family and then I'll come and follow you."

"Go," Elijah granted.

A little later, Elisha was back and ready to serve Elijah.

In the meantime, Ben-hadad, king of the Arameans, who had many more men, chariots, and horses than Israel, went out to attack. However, the Lord gave victory to Israel both in the first combat on the mountain and in the second on the plain.

Defeated, Ben-hadad went before Ahab, king of Israel. The two kings established a pact. Ahab agreed to free him. He wanted Aram to be a defensive wall against the powerful Assyrian army, who represented a threat to the Israelites. But, by doing this, Ahab showed very little trust in the Lord, and the prophet called him on this. When he was walking back to the city, the prophet said to the king, "Thus says the Lord, 'Since you freed the man whom you had defeated with my help, you will have to be responsible for him and your people for his. In this way you will learn to trust in my power.'"

These bad omens had Ahab sad and worried by the time he arrived in Samaria.

Naboth Is Assassinated Due to His Vineyard

But other affairs required the king's attention. Near the palace there was a vineyard, the property of Naboth. King Ahab said to Naboth, "Give me your vineyard so that I can make a garden. I will pay you whatever you ask, or I will give you another vineyard in exchange."

"I cannot do that because it was my parents'. If I got rid of it, I would offend their memory," Naboth explained.

126

Naboth's refusal displeased the king, who was so upset that he went to bed without eating anything. His wife Jezebel came to him and said, "What's the matter? Why are you in such a bad mood that you even lost your appetite?"

"I was unable to convince Naboth to sell me his vineyard," Ahab complained.

"Don't you worry. A king like you is going to act like this over an insignificant thing? I will get that vineyard for you. Come on! Get up and eat something," his wife said to calm him down.

Then the woman gave instructions to have Naboth framed for a crime he did not commit and then stoned to death. Her instructions were followed to the letter. A few days later, Naboth was stoned. As soon as Jezebel found out, she told Ahab, who went immediately to take possession of the vineyard.

While Ahab was taking a walk in the vineyard he had acquired, he received a visit from Elijah, who reproached him.

"You have committed a murder and now you take the vineyard. You must know that in the same place where the dogs are licking Naboth's blood, they will also lick yours. Jezebel will be maimed by the dogs and no one in your family will be buried; those who die in the city will be devoured by dogs; those who die in the fields will be eaten up by crows."

When Ahab heard those words, he was so regretful that the Lord decided to carry out the threat on his son, but not on him.

Micaiah Confesses the Truth Despite the Danger

A few days later, Ahab received a visit from Jehoshaphat, king of Judah, who proposed to him, "I think it is high time that we reclaim the city of Ramoth of Gilead, which is in Aram's hands. Would you come with us to attack it?"

"Yes, I will. We will join forces. That way it will be easier for us to be victorious," Ahab agreed.

In order to know whether the action would be successful, they consulted the prophets. Jehoshaphat also insisted on hearing the opinion of a prophet of God, so they called Micaiah. All the other prophets had made favorable predictions, but Micaiah said, "I see the people of Israel scattered through the mountains without any leader. The king has died. Those prophets tell you what you want to hear. Don't go because you will not return."

Ahab got angry at Micaiah, who failed to predict what Ahab wanted to hear. He threw Micaiah in jail and went to battle. The Arameans fought fiercely against the king of Israel, wounded him, and, a few hours later, he bled to death.

Elisha Has to Do Without His Teacher

After that, Elijah knew that his hour to pass from this world had come. He wanted Elisha to stay where he was, but Elisha did not allow Elijah to go by himself. They went through Bethel and Jericho. In each city, the prophets warned Elisha that the Lord wanted to take Elijah that very same day. So Elijah said, "Stay here, since I need to go down to the River Jordan."

"For the Lord's sake, I swear I will not leave you," Elisha answered firmly.

They then went to the River Jordan. Elijah made the waters of the river part. The two crossed on dry land. When they had crossed, Elijah asked Elisha, "What can I do for you before leaving this world?"

"More than a teacher, you have been a father to me. So don't be upset if I ask you for what would be the inheritance of any heir: two-thirds of your spirit."

"You ask for much, but if you are present when I leave this world, it will be given to you."

At that point, a chariot of fire came and took Elijah and his cloak fell on Elisha. With this cloak, the spirit of Elijah came to rest on Elisha.

Later, every time Elisha went to Shunem, a good woman gave him hospitality and food. As a reward to her generosity, Elisha called her in to tell her, "Next year you will have the son you so long for."

The woman had not gotten pregnant although she had been married many years, and now her husband was getting old. So she said to Elisha, "Don't deceive your servant. How am I going to have a child?"

The child arrived just as Elisha had promised. The child grew up healthy, then died suddenly of an illness. The Shunemite went to see Elisha.

"Did I ever ask you for a son? Why did you grant it and now take him away?"

And Elisha went to the house of the Shunemite woman. He infused his spirit on the dead child and he came back to life. The mother was so happy that her heart was filled with joy.

Jezebel and the Priests Meet Their Maker

On another occasion, Naaman, the army commander of the king of Aram, found out that Elisha could cure his leprosy. With this in mind, he went to Elisha's house. The prophet, who was familiar with the situation, sent him a messenger with this instruction, "Go and bathe in the River Jordan seven times."

After some hesitation, Naaman did as he had been told and his sickness disappeared completely. Impressed, he went to see Elisha and admitted, "Now I know that there is no other god in the entire world than the God of Israel. As a token of my gratitude, please accept the gifts I bring you."

But Elisha did not want to accept anything. His servant, however, took advantage of the opportunity and took Naaman's money. When he found out, Elisha cursed the servant, who was then stricken by leprosy.

On the other hand, Joram, king of Israel, displeased the Lord as much as his father Ahab had. For this reason, Elisha anointed Jehu as king. Joram tried to defeat Jehu, but did not succeed because the Lord was on Jehu's side. He was in charge of fulfilling Elijah's prophecy to Ahab: Joram and the other descendants of Ahab were exterminated and Jezebel, Ahab's wife, was thrown down from the city walls and eaten by dogs.

In order to finish with the priests of Baal, Jehu had an idea.

"Let all the priests of Baal who live in Israel come to make a great offering since I, Jehu, want to honor Baal more than Ahab ever did."

All the priests of Baal wanted to take advantage of the opportunity to flatter the new king. When they were all in the temple, Jehu made sure that none of the Lord's faithful were in the temple and ordered his soldiers, "Come in and kill them all! Let no one escape! If anyone runs away, you will answer with your life."

They went in and, after killing all of Baal's worshipers, set the temple on fire. In this way, Jehu made Baal disappear from Israel. He, however, continued to worship golden calves as images of God, which greatly displeased the Lord.

Death of Elisha and Disappearance of Israel

After some time, Joash was reigning over Israel. This king went to visit Elisha, who was sick in bed. The prophet put his hands on the king's head and said, "The Lord God will give you victory over Aram. You will defeat him easily."

Elisha's hour had come and he surrendered to his illness.

After Elisha's death many kings succeeded one another in the kingdom of Israel until the time of King Hosheah. The lifelong threat of the Assyrians was finally carried out.

Hosheah could not confront them because the Assyrian army was very numerous, so he submitted and paid taxes to them. In order to get rid of them, Hosheah attempted to make a covenant with other nations, but when the Assyrian king found out, he invaded the whole Israelite territory and took all his population to Assyria by force. The kingdom of Israel had vanished because of its many sins against the Lord.

Isaiah Is Called by God

At the same time, in the kingdom of Judah, Isaiah was discovering his vocation as a prophet. He saw God, the Lord, sitting on a throne with a tunic that covered everything. God had many angels around him who proclaimed, "Holy is the Lord! The glory of the Lord God fills the earth!"

Dazzled by the surprise, Isaiah exclaimed, "What will happen to me now? I am a man of impure lips and I have seen the Lord, whom no one can see and not die."

An angel touched Isaiah's lips with an ember and said, "Your impurity has disappeared. You are a clean man."

And the voice of the Lord was heard asking, "Whom shall I send to this people? Who will go?"

"Send me," Isaiah answered.

That is how, as a messenger of God, Isaiah went to speak to Ahaz, king of Judah.

"The Lord will give you a sign of hope: a young girl will be pregnant and will bear a son, whom she will call Emmanuel. Hard times will be upon us as never before; captivity and destruction await you. This child will free you. Expect the king of Assyria to destroy you, because people have not wanted to heed the warnings that I have been making for a long time so that you could return to the faithfulness you owe me."

Judah Disappears

A few years later, Hezekiah reigned over Judah. That's when Sennacherib, king of Assyria, attacked Judah. He took over all the walled cities and then went against Jerusalem. King Hezekiah of Judah sent messengers to Isaiah. He told them to tell the king, "Do not be afraid. You have been faithful to the Lord. Jerusalem will not be conquered, nor will Judah be vanquished while you are alive. The Lord grants you help. Remember that no army can be victorious without God's consent."

And so it was. The enemies withdrew. The angel of the Lord had attacked the camp during the night and when they woke up they only saw corpses everywhere.

Sennacherib was also killed, assassinated by his own sons while he was making an offering to his god.

But years after Hezekiah's death, when Jehoiakim was reigning, Nebuchadnezzar, the king of Babylon, attacked Jerusalem. The king and noblemen were imprisoned, and Nebuchadnezzar crowned Jehoiakim's uncle Zedekiah king instead of Jehoiakim. All the treasures and valuable objects of Jerusalem were taken to Babylon.

A few years later, because of a rebellion led by Zedekiah, the Babylonian king destroyed Jerusalem; the houses were burned to the ground and the temple was destroyed. All the sons of Zedekiah were murdered and, after gouging his eyes out, the Babylonians took Zedekiah as a prisoner to Babylon. The walls of Jerusalem came down and the majority of the people were forced to move to Babylon. The invaders named Gedaliah as governor of Judah, which became a province of Babylon.

The kingdom of Judah had disappeared. What would become of the divine promises if Israel and Judah did not exist anymore?

4.
The People of Israel in Exile

The fall of Jerusalem (587 B.C.E.) and the deportation to Babylon mark the end of the Israelite monarchy. Some people believed that the deportation to Babylon would mean the end of this people; the people exiled to Babylon, seduced by the splendor of the conquerors, could be tempted to forget their humble roots. The promises made to Abraham, Isaac, and Jacob were in danger of disappearing and being forever forgotten.

The Jewish people lived in Babylon for half a century. They had no temple, worship, king, or opportunities to offer the fruits of the earth as a sacrifice to God, since such fruits were not theirs to offer now that they lived in a foreign land. The only thing remaining, thanks to the prophets, was their faith in God and in their traditions. They would start to meditate on them, reflect, and review their past history in order to find meaning.

The exiled were far away from Jerusalem and the Temple. But even if they had broken the covenant (the friendship) with God, God was faithful to his love and did not abandon them. God always accompanied his people, even while they were deported and exiled in Babylon. So, around the year 538 B.C.E., God helped the people escape from slavery to freedom. God used the Persian King Cyrus to give the people their freedom back.

The Lord is the "Saving God" because he helped them go from being nothing, scattered throughout Babylon and Judah, to become once again the people gathered and reborn until the trial of their deportation. After God saved them (liberated them), they also discovered that God had created the world.

Jeremiah Is Called as a Prophet

Hilkiah the priest lived in Anathot with his son Jeremiah. This was the time when Josiah, the grandson of Hezekiah, reigned over Judah.

One day the voice of the Lord came to the young Jeremiah and said, "I have made you a prophet. When you were in your mother's womb, I had already chosen you."

"How can you want me, Lord, to go before the people, since I am still a boy?" Jeremiah protested.

"I will always be with you to help you. I will put my words in your mouth, and I will tell you the gestures you have to make," the Lord assured him while he touched his hand to Jeremiah's mouth.

"And who will listen? No one will pay any attention to me."

"I am placing you over peoples and nations to build and to destroy. It is not your family or your age that will make you say what you must, but the fact that I have chosen you," the Lord affirmed.

From that time on, Jeremiah proclaimed the words the Lord put on his lips. That's why he started to preach, "The Lord remembers when the relationship between you, people of Israel, and God was so close that it seemed like a relationship between lovers.

"Why did you have to break the commitment established between you and the Lord? God had always kept the commitment. He took your ancestors out of Egypt where they were slaves. What has God done to you to make you behave this way now? Instead of being grateful, you have denied him and worship false gods. And you still have the nerve to go to God when you need something.

"Look to the north: the punishment you deserve is coming from there. Everything will be destroyed because you have despised the Lord."

Israel and Judah, Unfaithful Wives

But King Josiah had rejected the veneration that Manasseh, his grandfather, had felt for alien gods. He had always been faithful to the Lord.

It so happened that a priest found a book in the Temple where the covenant with the Lord had been inscribed. The king listened attentively to the reading of this book. Consequently, he rejected all the alien gods and ordered that everything that did not belong to the worship of God be cleaned from the Temple of the Lord. He also destroyed many images that represented false gods.

Judah had not seen celebrations and feasts as big as these in honor of the Lord in a long, long time. Unfortunately, Josiah was killed in a battle against the Egyptians. Josiah's successors did not want to follow his example and went back to worshiping alien gods.

On the other hand, Judah had become a people subject to the Egyptians, to whom they had to pay taxes.

Many times Jeremiah would explain simple stories to the people to help them understand his words. For example:

"Once upon a time there were two young sisters who had a good and affectionate husband. One of them was Israel and the other Judah. Israel soon started deceiving her husband, and going with other men. Judah, instead of reproaching her sister for her behavior, started to imitate her. Neither of them respected the commitment they had made to their husband. Both one and the other only remembered him when they needed something.

"Israel was banished from the face of the earth as punishment; all memory of her was erased. Judah did not repent and continued with her lies. So Judah deserves an even greater punishment."

So the people understood that the first woman represented the kingdom of Israel, which had been devastated, and that those of the kingdom of Judah—that is, themselves—would have to endure an even greater misfortune than Israel's punishment.

Jeremiah Wants to Prevent Divine Punishment

Jeremiah, who did not want the people to be destroyed, interceded before the Lord.

"Lord, my God, have compassion on this people and don't destroy them. They offer you sacrifices occasionally; that means that they haven't completely forgotten you."

"What good do their sacrifices do? My Law does not tell them they have to offer sacrifices to me. In contrast, it does say that they should worship no other gods but me. If they don't do this, their sacrifices are meaningless."

"If you don't do it for them, do it for me. Spare them from being destroyed."

"Don't intervene on their behalf because they don't deserve it. I have sent them people and signs to show them, clearly, that they have to change their ways. And how have they reacted? They don't pay attention. You yourself are tired of warning them. What more do they need? The fate of Israel, hasn't one warning been enough?"

Jeremiah tried to think of more arguments to convince the Lord.

"They are circumcised men. Circumcision meant your protection was upon them. You cannot abandon them now."

"Circumcision was an external sign of a two-sided covenant. I will keep my commitment as long as they keep theirs. If they don't go back to being faithful to our pact, circumcision means nothing," the Lord answered coldly.

"But on other occasions they have also broken the pact by worshiping false gods, and you have never sent such a harsh punishment. The destruction of the ancient Promised Land is too great a blow. Remember how much they suffered during the long time in which they couldn't reach it," Jeremiah said, exhausting his arguments.

"It is because I have been patient with them so many other times that I feel patience is not the solution. Only if they turn to me with all their hearts, which they have now turned toward false gods, could they avoid the punishment that awaits them," the Lord concluded.

Jeremiah was greatly worried because he had not succeeded in convincing the Lord to forgive the people. He made every effort to tell them what would happen if they did not turn their hearts to the Lord. But he achieved nothing; the more he insisted, the less they listened to him.

The People Have Decayed Like the Material of a Belt

Another time the Lord ordered Jeremiah to buy a belt of cloth. Carrying out the word of the Lord, he wore it for a while until he received another divine word to keep the belt in the opening of a rock by the bank of a river. After a time he went to look for it. He found it all rotten and useless.

Then the Lord spoke to him, "The cloth of the belt has rotted because there was moisture around it. Moisture has saturated the belt and ruined it. Now, what would you do with it?"

"I will have to throw it away. It isn't good even as a cleaning rag," answered Jeremiah.

"You said it. It is good for nothing. So this people will end up in the same way, after receiving all the harm I am sending their way. I have united myself to the whole house of Israel and Judah just like that belt that you had worn on your waist. Time went on and they allowed themselves to become rotten by being influenced by the ideas and gods around them, until they were totally saturated. Now neither your belt nor mine has a remedy," the Lord said in anger.

"But why do I have to remind the people of the fate that awaits them if they don't change their attitude? You chose me as your prophet, and I behave as such, but I have earned enemies everywhere. All curse me and many scoff at me. I am not sure I will be able to endure it," Jeremiah complained.

"You will bear it because I will always be with you, as I have up until now. You will be stronger than iron. They might fight you, but they will never win. I will be your support," the Lord assured him.

136

Will Judah Be Able to Stop Babylon?

The official priests of the Temple of the Lord were angry at Jeremiah because he went about proclaiming doom and gloom for the people. Hearing him, Pashur, one of the priests, put him in prison for one day. When he was about to set him free, he had to listen to the prophet, who said, "Thus says the Lord, 'You are making false prophecies by saying there will not be destruction in Judah, placing obstacles and imprisoning the true prophet. That's why you will be deported to Babylon, together with the rest of the priests, and you will die there, far from this land.'"

It happened just as Jeremiah had said. Nebuchadnezzar, the Babylonian king, conquered Judah after forcing the Egyptians to withdraw. All the important people from the land were deported to Babylon. Among them was Ezekiel, priest of God, who would work as a prophet among the exiles. The year was 598 B.C.E.

In Babylon, the deported felt discouraged and defeated, but they maintained the hope that Jerusalem would remain intact. One of their kings reigned there and the Temple had not yet been destroyed. Nebuchadnezzar had imposed Zedekiah as king of Jerusalem, although he was still a subject of the Babylonians.

After all these events, Jeremiah found two baskets with figs in front of the Temple. The Lord asked him, "What do you see, Jeremiah?"

"Two baskets with figs. From their appearance, the ones in the first basket are very good, but those in the other basket are so dry that they look pitiful."

"As with these good figs, I will deal with those who have been deported, so that when they return, they will do so with all their heart. But Zedekiah and the other ones will be treated like those in the second basket," the Lord said.

New Attack on Jerusalem

Time would prove Jeremiah right. Zedekiah, the king, trusted the priests instead of listening to Jeremiah. This conviction made him rebel against those living in the city.

When he found out, Nebuchadnezzar set on his way with a large army in order to conquer Israel once and for all.

In order to make the citizens realize that they had better yield to the Babylonian king, Jeremiah put a yoke around his neck and walked around saying, "It is to your advantage to subject yourselves to the Babylonian king. If you do, you won't be forced to leave your land or suffer any harm. Resign yourselves to the Chaldean yoke. You can work and live normally."

"Why do we have to trust you and not the priests? They say we are well protected and not in jeopardy," they said.

With the same passion with which he had preached disaster, Jeremiah now wanted to inspire confidence. That is why he bought a field in Anathoth and kept the deed for the land in a secure place. In this way, he wanted to express that he had no doubts that the people would go back to that land after the exile.

Nebuchadnezzar's army arrived at the city's gates and surrounded the city, besieging it. But the news arrived that the Egyptian army was on its way to wage battle against them. This forced the Chaldeans to leave the city for the time being and go to confront the Egyptians. At the same time the Egyptians withdrew and Nebuchadnezzar returned to besiege Jerusalem.

Prison: A Good Payment for Defending the Truth

To those who would listen, Jeremiah preached that it was necessary to surrender to the invading army. There was no possibility of victory because this was a punishment from the Lord. Therefore, they should submit to their enemies. This was the will of God. Thus they would save both their own lives and the city.

Despite all this, Jeremiah's message fell on deaf ears throughout the whole city; people thought that it was impossible for Jerusalem, the holy city, to be destroyed and the Temple razed. On other occasions throughout their history they had wandered far from the Lord and nothing of this kind had ever happened to them; so they were certain it would not happen now, either. Although it was very recent, they refused to remember that the Northern Kingdom, called Israel, had been erased from the map about one hundred years before.

Sick and tired of hearing Jeremiah announce gloom and doom, the noblemen of the city imprisoned him without any food, hoping he would starve so they would be rid of him.

King Zedekiah did not defend Jeremiah for fear that he would be taken for a traitor, but he wanted to know of the messages of God told by Jeremiah. So he called for Jeremiah and asked him, "Does the Lord still want to destroy the city?"

"The city and the people. The only way to be saved is to surrender to the enemies. I can't deceive you. The Lord speaks through my mouth," Jeremiah repeated.

"I see nothing is changed. They say they will keep you without food or drink. You will be a prisoner in my house; there you will be able to eat. Come on, go!"

In this way, Jeremiah could save his life and, later, regain his freedom.

Death and Destruction in Jerusalem

When he was free, he immediately went back to proclaiming, "Those who stay in this city will be killed by the sword, or will die of hunger or pestilence; however, those who surrender to the Chaldeans will be rewarded with life and not die."

It was evident that the priests and noblemen were enraged to see him free, so, to end his life, they caught him and placed him in a cistern full of mud.

Jeremiah saw his end approaching, but a foreigner informed the king about Jeremiah's situation.

King Zedekiah gave the foreigner permission to secretly take Jeremiah out of the cistern. The time for the prophet had not yet arrived.

Jerusalem was a city in disgrace. It had been a long time since provisions had arrived. No one could go in or out because of the blockade the Chaldeans had on it. There was no bread, very little water, and people were getting sick. It was not long before it succumbed to the attacks of the Babylonians.

The noblemen, priests, and princes were murdered. King Zedekiah was chained and brought to Babylon after his eyeballs had been gouged out. The city was burned to the ground in the summer of 587 B.C.E.

Nebuchadnezzar then appointed Gedaliah as governor of the country and the survivors.

Jeremiah was not among the thousands of captives they had taken prisoner to Babylon, but was jailed in the country. Ten days later, the captain of the guard freed him, saying, "Your god had announced that this misfortune occurred because the people had sinned against him. It has happened just as God said. I am setting you free. You can go wherever you want: you can come to Babylon with me, go anywhere in the country, or live with Gedaliah who is the governor now."

"I appreciate it. I will go to Gedaliah's palace," Jeremiah answered.

Jeremiah Has to Die Away from His Homeland

At that time, since all he had said had been fulfilled, everyone respected him greatly, and they even offered him the opportunity to live with the governor.

Gedaliah had joined all the survivors in Mizpah. The king of the Ammonites, who were enemies of Judah, found out and sent men there to murder him. That way the few Jewish people who had been left with Gedaliah would disperse and the people of Judah would no longer be an obstacle for the Ammonites.

Gedaliah was murdered. Ishmael, the assassin, took the captives to the lands of the Ammonites, but about half-way there they were saved by the Jewish people who had regrouped outside the cities.

They consulted with Jeremiah on whether they should go to Egypt or stay in the country. The Lord answered through the mouth of the prophet, "If you stay here, you will have peace and prosperity. Do not fear the Chaldeans or any other enemies, because the anger of the Lord has abated. If you return to him with all your heart, God will be favorable, and you will have nothing to fear. But only death and doom await you in Egypt."

This was not the answer the rebel leaders of the Jewish people wanted to hear. So, turning a deaf ear to the words of the prophet, they forced everyone—including Jeremiah—to start on the way to Egypt.

Jeremiah was elderly and his strength had diminished. The people of Judah had failed to listen to him, as did those who took him to Egypt. Despite all the difficulties, he was happy that he had fulfilled God's will.

The hour of his death had arrived. He was only sorry that he could not die in his homeland. He did not know then that the lifetime he had devoted to warning people about the forthcoming destruction would later be instrumental in helping the Jewish people regain confidence in the Lord and unite them as a people.

Ezekiel, Prophet in Babylon

While Jeremiah was carrying out his mission in Judah, Ezekiel, who had gone with those deported after the first conquest of Jerusalem, was a prophet in Babylon.

One day, when Ezekiel was by the river with his people, he saw the heavens open and a chariot with a dazzling light coming out. He could see that up in the middle, there was someone sitting on a majestic throne: four figures, half-human, half-animal, surrounded this person. After a while, he understood it was the Lord appearing to him. He clearly heard a voice that said, "Ezekiel, I am charging you with an uncomfortable mission. I will send you to those who did not pay any attention to me when they were in their land. Perhaps now that they are far away they will listen. Keep in mind that they are very stubborn. Don't think it will be easy to make them listen. You will have many difficulties, but I will be with you, and I'll give you as much help as you need."

This sudden apparition made Ezekiel fall to the ground; then he rose, speechless. Turning his head, he saw a hand stretching out to him and offering him a book, while the voice of the Lord continued saying, "Eat this book. Be not afraid to do so; all that is written in it will become a part of you. So you will know what you have to say."

Ezekiel could not believe he would be able to swallow such a book. He was amazed and dumbfounded when he realized that, in his mouth, the book became edible and tasted like honey.

"Go and tell the people my words," said the Lord. "Warn them that they are not acting right. Tell them to go back to my Commandments and to keep them. Do that with all those I will indicate. If you tell them and they don't pay attention, it will be their fault; but if they don't keep the Commandments because you haven't warned them, it will be your fault."

Immediately, in the midst of a clanging noise, the chariot rose to heaven until it completely disappeared.

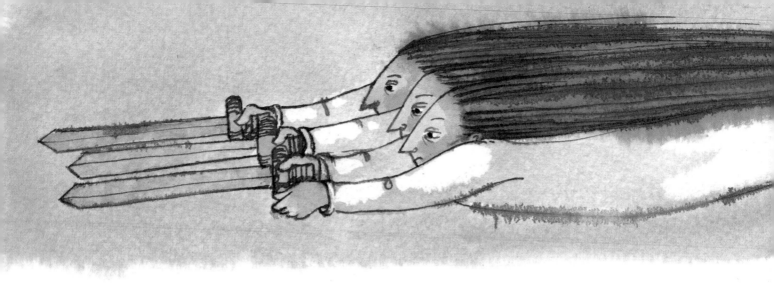

Why Isn't Ezekiel Speaking?

Ezekiel set out to preach as the Lord had commanded him. He made every effort to make his fellow citizens understand that they had to give up their false gods and return to the Lord with all their hearts and behave according to the Commandments. Attending worship services was not enough to be reconciled with the Lord.

It could not exactly be said that he was successful; people did not listen to him. Ezekiel could explain a thousand different ways that the misfortune of the Jewish people was a consequence of having wandered far from God, but he accomplished nothing.

Seeing the situation, the Lord spoke to Ezekiel and said, "I told you so. Getting them to listen to you is not easy. But they are more careless than I thought. If they don't want to listen, it's up to them. From now on you will be struck dumb. You will only be able to speak when I instruct you to tell them something."

In this way, Ezekiel could only speak when he had to transmit a statement from the Lord. Then, on a clay tablet, Ezekiel drew the city of Jerusalem surrounded by people who represented an attacking army. Whoever wanted to, without need for words, would understand that Jerusalem would be destroyed.

After a time, the Lord showed Ezekiel the city of Jerusalem. Although he was in Chaldea (or Babylon), the Lord transported him so he could behold what the Jewish people were doing in Jerusalem. He was panic struck. They were worshiping false gods in the sacred Temple. They believed the Lord had forsaken them and were trying other gods. Almost everyone was doing the same. It was so difficult to find a group of people who maintained trust in the Lord!

New Covenant with the Lord

Afterward he saw how the angels walked through Jerusalem marking the people who were faithful to the Lord. Once they had done so, they killed everyone who was not marked. They carried out a huge massacre; it was a terrible scene. Ezekiel interceded before the Lord saying, "Do you want to end up exterminating the whole people of Judah? They don't deserve your forgiveness, but have mercy on them. Death is too harsh a punishment."

"I have had patience and forgiven them many times. Has it been good for anything? No. They have gone back to their bad conduct when they knew they wouldn't be punished. Now is not the time for mercy. I will be inflexible. Unfortunately, they don't understand any other language," the Lord answered.

There was no way the Lord would change his mind and stop the massacre that Ezekiel was witnessing. Even then, the Lord did not want to leave the people without hope; so he indicated to Ezekiel he should tell the people, "The Lord will gather you up from all the corners where you are dispersed, and he will gather you again in the land of Israel. He will change your heart; he will take out this heart of stone and will give you one of flesh capable of loving God. You will give up any other gods. You will be God's people, and he will be your God.

"You will make a new covenant with him. You have violated the covenant made to the Lord. Despite everything, he will forgive us. He will put you back on the right path if you repent from all the evil you have committed until now."

Ezekiel's Account

In the same way that he had been transported to Jerusalem, Ezekiel was returned to Chaldea where he explained to people his vision and the divine message.

Since Ezekiel was announcing such an unpleasant reality, he had to endure his people's mistrust. Furthermore, he had to confront the false prophets, whom the people preferred to listen to over him. He pointed out these prophets' falsehoods so that they would not deceive the people, and in the process he gained enemies by upsetting people.

Ezekiel, like other prophets, was in the habit of telling parables inspired by God. These were brief stories which, once their meaning was explained, helped people to better understand what the prophet wanted to say. Let's read such a parable:

"There was once a great eagle, of long feathers and enormous wings," Ezekiel had started the story and the whispers were dying down until there was absolute silence. "This eagle flew to the land of Judah. Once there it used its beak to bite off the highest shoots of the tallest cedar, the most important and tender part of the tree, and took the shoots to a city of merchants, where the eagle's house was located.

"When it finished, it took seeds from the same country of Judah. It sowed them in an appropriate place, with water and salt. Soon there was a beautiful vine, but it was not very tall. It had deep roots in the earth and branches that reached up to the eagle. Nothing was missing. It could have a long and quiet life.

"The vine knew that there was another great and powerful eagle. Then it decided to stretch its branches to this other eagle.

"What do you think the first eagle will do with the vine?" There was noise of people whispering and answering the question of the prophet, but Ezekiel continued. "The eagle had left the vine well placed so that it could live without any problems; but the vine despised this situation and wanted to look for one it considered even better. What will the eagle do? It will pull out the vine and let it dry on fertile land, by the waters of life."

When he got to this point, Ezekiel kept quiet. Now the whispering had turned to clear words and discussion on what the prophet had just told.

What Does Ezekiel's Parable Mean?

Then the prophet explained the parable:

"The first eagle represents the power of Babylon. The cedar is Jerusalem. The highest shoots of the tree are the most important people of the city. The transfer of the shoots refers to the exile of the leaders of Jerusalem. The city of merchants represents the land of Babylon, where the noblemen of Jerusalem were taken by force. The seeds of Judah symbolize the princes of the same house of Judah, who were authorized to stay there to reign.

"The vine symbolizes the small, insignificant, and powerless reign they have formed. The branches oriented to the eagle mean the submission of this reign to Babylon. The deeply planted roots represent keeping the union of Judah with its ancestors. This means special treatment since, as you know, the Babylonians are used to deporting all the conquered out of their homelands.

"How has the king of Jerusalem shown appreciation for this favor to the Babylonians? It has directed its branches to the second eagle. This eagle is the image of Egypt, the other powerful country. The branches directed to Egypt are the ambassadors sent to that country to ask for help against the Babylonians. What will Judah get out of all this? Only total destruction. Egypt will not help them, and Babylon will raze the country until nothing is left in the land of Israel or that of Judah.

"This will be the punishment that Judah will receive for not listening to the warnings that the prophets of the Lord made and constantly repeated. The prophet Jeremiah and I have been preaching in Babylon the need to surrender to the Babylonians. How many times have you heard us say this is the will of the Lord?"

There was a long pause in response to Ezekiel's words, and then he continued, "So it will be done since you wanted to be apart from the Lord and not heed so many of the warnings you have received through the prophets."

However, when people do not want to understand, it is better not to tire oneself out. Nothing that is said will be absorbed by them, and it will seem as if they did not hear a thing. This was what happened to Ezekiel. He had tried to explain to them in a descriptive story (the parable) so as not to bore them with what he had to say. He had explained it in detail, step-by-step, so that they would understand and reflect on it. Their only answer was, "Why do you always speak in parables? We can't understand what you are trying to tell us."

So, no matter how loud you shout, people do not hear what they do not want to hear.

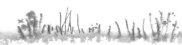

It is not necessary to explain how Ezekiel felt when he saw that his efforts to convince his fellow citizens were so unsuccessful. Sometimes he grew discouraged and sometimes he despaired. He realized it was like shouting in the desert. Had it not been for the trust he had in God, he could not have endured it.

Will Ezekiel Endure What the Lord Demands of Him?

On the other hand, the Lord was not making matters easier for him; in addition to being mute, he had to bear the misunderstanding of his people. But the Lord wanted even more: God wanted to take away the person Ezekiel loved most. What would he do if the only person who supported him in the most bitter moments was no longer by his side? Who would comfort him?

The Lord informed Ezekiel, "Ezekiel, your wife will die today, but I don't want you to cry or mourn for her, or do anything that might express sorrow. You must be calm and be an example for your people. Only wear your turban and your sandals, as if you were about to go on a trip."

The Lord took away the woman he was in love with, the only one who supported him. And not only that: he forbade him to express his feelings, God asked Ezekiel to behave as if nothing had happened. Is it reasonable to ask this from a person?

Ezekiel had no choice but to convince himself that God's will comes first. The motivations of the Lord should be important. God comes before his wife. He was forced to repeat this to himself hundreds and thousands of times in the most absolute loneliness, in order to soothe the pain piercing his heart.

The Lord had taken away the woman who comforted him at his most difficult times. In addition, he was not allowed to take comfort in mourning her death—he was about to go crazy. Only faith in the Lord helped him overcome that hard trial.

When people realized that Ezekiel did not follow any of the Jewish traditions, dress in mourning, or shed one single tear after his wife's death, they asked, "What does it all mean? Why don't you cry, dress in mourning, cover your beard?"

"See what the Lord wants to tell you with all this, 'I will not allow my sanctuary in Jerusalem, my Temple, on which you have placed your hopes, to be profaned or destroyed. Your sons and daughters, who have stayed behind in Jerusalem, will die by the sword, and Jerusalem will disappear.

"'You must behave as Ezekiel has. You will not allow a single tear to swell up in your eyes, nor will you dress in mourning. You will wear your turbans and sandals to mean that the count down for the return to your land has started.

"'On the other hand, when this has happened, nothing will remain from Israel or Judah. Do not expect, then, for me to cry for the disappearance of your people, even if in other times your people were like my wife. Ezekiel has done exactly as I will do when destruction comes.'"

Jerusalem Is Destroyed; Ezekiel Speaks

In the meantime, Nebuchadnezzar, king of Babylon, had learned of the betrayal of Zedekiah, the king whom he had tolerated in Jerusalem. Enraged, Nebuchadnezzar decided to send a large army there. In this way he would completely destroy that insignificant kingdom that was bothering

him. Now he regretted not having razed it in the previous battle. He knew Zedekiah had asked for support from Egypt, and he would not allow that.

In order to prevent the Egyptians from helping Jerusalem, Nebuchadnezzar fought against them. It was not hard to defeat them. Immediately after, he devoted his time and efforts to the conquest of Jerusalem.

One day, twelve years after Ezekiel had been deported to Babylon, a fugitive from Jerusalem came and informed him, "The city has fallen, people have been massacred and the Temple is destroyed. Everything is fire and devastation."

From that moment on, Ezekiel could speak freely, as the Lord willed. God had made Ezekiel mute so that he would not constantly insist on the fall of Jerusalem. Now that the city had been conquered, it made no sense for Ezekiel to be unable to speak.

A new group of Jewish people arrived in Babylon. This time they were not only the nobility, but all those who had been taken captive.

The deported Jewish people in Babylon were going through bitter times; discouragement was rampant. They no longer had a king in Jerusalem or the city of Jerusalem as a symbol. The Temple and ark of the covenant had been destroyed. The people were scattered everywhere. Nothing that had made them a people remained; none of what had identified them as the people chosen by God endured.

Bad Priests; Reviving Corpses

At that time many priests were taking advantage of the people, rather than guiding them and helping them. Through Ezekiel's lips, the Lord scolded them.

"Your mission is to be shepherds of the people, but you are the ones benefiting. You take their food and money, but you don't watch over them or guide them. Where are my sheep? They are scattered all over the place. But that is not the worst; the worst is that foreigners own them. Your mission is to guide them so that they do not leave the fold and join another. How are you going to do that if you are only concerned about your own profit?

"You should make them understand that the cause of their misfortunes is my anger at their behavior. You ought to tell them that their bad luck will last until they accept me in their hearts as their only God. But you have neglected your ministry. You tell them pleasant lies so that they will reward you. Therefore, you will not be the shepherds of my sheep any longer. I will take away the sheep from you so that you don't take advantage of them any more."

A few days later, Ezekiel was transported by the Lord to the middle of the desert where there was a pile of bones. It was a cemetery for the remains of the many Jewish people who had not endured the hard journey from Jerusalem to Babylon and had died on the way. Before those bones, the Lord asked Ezekiel, "Do you think these bones can come back to life?"

"You know it, Lord, my God, I don't," Ezekiel replied.

"Prophetize that these bones will be filled with flesh. Then infuse the spirit in my name," the Lord commanded.

And Ezekiel did as the Lord had ordered.

"Dry bones, get flesh and nerves in the name of the Lord God. May skin cover you that you may live."

The bones joined together to make a body. Then they were covered with nerves, flesh, and skin, amid a great clamor; but they could not move, were not alive. Then Ezekiel proclaimed, "May the four winds bring spirit to infuse life to these bodies."

Immediately, the spirit came into the bodies. All rose and started moving about as normal people. They were so many, they seemed like an entire army.

After this, the Lord said, "In the same way that only a little while ago those people were only bones, I will open the tombs of the house of Israel and make the dead alive again so that they may enter again the land of Israel."

Jerusalem Prepares for Return

Fourteen years after Jerusalem was destroyed, the Lord took Ezekiel to the land of Israel. God placed Ezekiel on top of the mountain where there was a city similar to Jerusalem. Ezekiel met a man who was making measurements to rebuild the Temple. He was measuring everything very carefully for the building of a new Temple.

When he was done measuring, the Lord appeared and ordered, "Describe to the people of Israel all the characteristics of the Temple: the entrances, exits, structures, and arrangement of everything. Let them know its order, rites, and laws. Put it in writing for them so that they won't forget and they will practice it."

The Lord took Ezekiel again to the gates of the Temple. God showed him how there was a fountain springing from it that became a wide and deep river, while the Lord said, "This river will be a source of life. Everyone who touches this water will live. If there are any sick people, they will be healed by touching it."

Immediately God gave instructions for dividing up the land among the various tribes, as if this were a new entrance into the Promised Land. Ezekiel was listening very attentively so he would be able to convey everything to the people without leaving anything out.

Where Do We Come From? Has God Abandoned Us?

During the Exile, people often had the feeling that the history of their people was coming to an end. And since they could not resign themselves to that, they felt the need to ask themselves about their origins as a people, and also about the origins of the world and of human beings. They could not believe the Lord would abandon them, nor that their Lord had been defeated by Babylonian gods. They were very clear that if that had happened it was because the Lord had willed it thus. The true prophets did not cease saying it.

The constant warnings of the prophets had been basic. Had they not existed, many Jewish people would have turned to worship Babylonian gods, convinced that they were much more powerful than the God of Israel.

These priests wanted people to understand that—in God's plans—the sad situation they were going through at the time was not the last chapter in the history of Israel. So that they would understand it better, the priests would tell stories such as these:

How Did the World Begin?

Before us, before our parents and grandparents, and the grandparents of our grandparents, before all things we see—houses, trees, rivers—before all this existed, the world was very different. Everything was mixed together: the sea, the sky, and the earth. The darkest darkness covered everything. You could not tell one thing from the next.

And God thought, "I should put some order in all this mess."

Everything was so dark that God thought nothing could really exist without light. Then God said, "Let there be light."

And there was a small ray of light which gave enough clarity to make darkness withdraw until everything was lit up. God saw it and liked it. God called the light day and the darkness night. That is why we see days separated from nights. And that was the first day.

The water still covered everything, and there was nothing dry, not even a little earth. On the second day, God wanted to separate the waters—he placed some up and some down. The sky

appeared in the middle. That is how we can refresh ourselves with rain water, or, if we prefer, we can bathe in the ocean.

So the world seemed to be a little neater, but everything was sky and water. So God said, "Let earth appear under the water and stay higher than the waters."

So, the land that was not covered with water dried up and hardened when it came in contact with the air.

But the earth was a dust color, without any shade, and it was not very pleasing to God. God solved this by making the grass, flowers, and woods grow. Many different colors appeared. The world now appeared more joyful. The third day had ended.

The following day, God created the heavenly bodies: the sun to give us light during the day, and the moon so the nights would not be so dark. He also created other planets, to give name to the days of the week or to celebrate feasts. And those starry nights? Why do you think we have them? Because on that fourth day God also placed stars in the heavens.

On the fifth day God realized that everything was too calm and quiet. There were not any beings to give joy and variety to things. So God said, "May the birds populate the heaven and fly from

one place to another; may fish of all kinds live in the rivers and oceans and swim in the waters, and may all grow and multiply to fill the places where they live."

That is why you can now hunt for birds or go fishing to feed yourselves.

The heavens and the waters already had their dwellers, but the earth did not, so the Lord said, "May the earth produce animals of all sorts: reptiles, pets, and wild beasts."

And each kind of animal appeared in the area that was most suited for its characteristics. The fifth day had ended.

God was pleased with all these works, but could not communicate with any of them. That is why God made a being with whom to communicate. From the dust of the earth God created man

and woman. And God spoke to them, saying, "I am giving you these plants and animals for you to be fed. You will rule over all the animals. You will use them according to your need.

"I am giving you my breath of life to help you in this task that I am entrusting to you. Have children; may they in turn have children when they grow up, and so on for every generation until the earth is full of human beings."

It was the sixth day when God made man and woman. Then God looked around and reviewed everything that had been made. God was pleased with everything and felt happy.

Creating the world and putting everything in its place had been hard work. God needed six whole days for the task. It was time to rest. So God dedicated the seventh day to rest. That is why we have to stop working on the Sabbath, just as God did. (The Sabbath was the day of celebration at that time.) We dedicate this day to praying and recuperating from the week's work.

Woman and Man, God's Favorites

Since the Lord God loved the human beings he had created, God placed them in a garden where they lacked for nothing. The grass was like a soft carpet caressing their feet. The trees gave many kinds of tasty fruits. The song of birds made a soft music. There were many animals and they lived together peacefully. Since it was never cold, they had no need for clothes. It was truly paradise.

The man liked all the things in paradise, but the company of the woman was the best of all. Of all the creatures, only she had feelings similar to his own, reacted like he did, laughed with him, and understood him. Only the woman provided the satisfaction he needed. He loved her so much that without her he was uncomfortable, he felt as if something were missing, he felt incomplete. (That is why men and women leave their parents and join together to be a single and complete being.)

The Lord God chose humans as his favorite beings. God would communicate only with them—only human beings would rule over all the other beings. The difference was clear. God had placed them in a wonderful place where all their needs were met, in the same way that the Lord had granted the Promised Land to our ancestors. The fact that they had power over all other things and were the only beings in contact with God may have made them proud. And they were merely creatures made of dust.

To prevent them from being tempted to want to be like God, they had one prohibition, a prohibition that served to remind them that they were simply human, mere creatures. The Lord God would care for humans, and human beings must follow God's commands, as God had demanded that the people of Israel keep the Commandments.

So the Lord God ordered, "In the middle of paradise there is a tree: it is the tree of the knowledge of good and evil. Do not eat the fruits of this tree. If you do, you will die. Everything else is at your disposal, except the fruits of this tree."

Was Not Knowing Good and Evil Better Than Knowing?

Life in paradise, what a pleasure! Good food, great weather, and the possibility of doing whatever they pleased all day long. That was complete happiness. But, each time they went by the forbidden tree, they were tempted to try its fruits. The fact that they could rule over everything except that tree bothered them.

In the beginning there were simple observations. The man, Adam, would say to the woman, "I don't understand why we cannot eat the fruit from that tree. It isn't anything special."

"I am sure that if we just try a bite, God wouldn't be angry at us," she would answer.

This scene was repeated day after day. On another occasion, when Eve, the woman, was playing hide-and-seek with a serpent, it climbed the tree of good and evil. Once there, it said to her, "Look, what a fresh fruit. Is this the one God has forbidden you to eat? Why don't you try one? Nothing will happen. Aren't you God's favorites?"

The serpent told Eve what she wanted to hear, so she could not resist the temptation of trying one piece of fruit. Adam, not wanting to miss the opportunity, also picked a piece when he arrived.

Then they realized why that tree was called the tree of the knowledge of good and evil. The fruit tasted just like that of any other tree, and they felt sad and displeased with themselves for having betrayed God's trust for nothing.

But, why are all people marked by this sin? Man and woman represent the king and queen of creation—they are models for the people. When the chief of a country declares war, he takes the whole people with him, because all of them are in solidarity with him. Men and women are brothers and sisters; they make a whole family. The sin of one weighs upon all the others. One person's sin is enough to spoil everything for the rest of the people.

In this story, man and woman lead people along the way of the serpent (symbol of the false gods) renouncing living with and loving God. We all carry this orientation inside of us. But the person is free to enhance or repress this orientation.

Somewhat irritated, Adam said to Eve, "Why did you make me eat of that fruit? How on earth did you think of even touching it? The other trees offered the same or better fruit as this. Why did you have to taste this one?"

"You yourself didn't resist. I had not even finished talking to you when you had already taken a bite. Don't try to put all the blame on me."

This disobedience made them discover a new feeling which they had never before experienced: shame. They were ashamed of not obeying God after the privileged treatment they had received. They felt shame for wanting to be equal to God and defying him.

They were afraid that God would withdraw the spirit, because then they would only be earth and dust. This shame also led them to cover up their sexual organs since they feared that their desire, which until now had been good and natural, could turn into something bad.

Shame, Toil, and Pain for Humans

That same afternoon the Lord God was walking in the garden and found it strange that the people did not come out to greet him as they usually did. So God called out, "Where are you? Why don't you come out to welcome me? What are you doing?"

"We did not dare come to greet you as we are, naked, so we hid," Adam replied.

"Haven't you always come naked to greet me? What has happened today that you think you would offend me if I saw you like this? You didn't eat from the tree I forbade you, did you?"

"The woman you gave me as a wife gave me some to try, and I ate it," Adam answered sheepishly.

"Why did you do that?" God scolded the woman.

"The serpent invited me and I ate," the woman replied quietly.

"Damned serpent! Of the wild animals, you are the worst. You will creep on the earth and you will eat dust all of your life. The woman and you will be enemies from now on. She will step on your head and you will barely be able to reach up to bite her heel," the Lord shouted indignantly.

And God warned the woman, "From now on, sorrow will be a part of your life. You will have children after difficult pregnancies and painful labor."

The carefree and joyful lifestyle Eve had so recently enjoyed turned into tears in her eyes. Adam did not escape the Lord's anger either. God said to him, "Don't think you are going to go free because Eve was the one offering the fruit. Why didn't you stop her rather than imitate her?" Adam wanted to make excuses for himself, but he could not get the words out. There was no excuse. He knew perfectly well that God was right.

"How could we go back and change things?" he thought to himself.

Then the Lord God said, "You will have to work and care for everything. Even the smallest grain of wheat you will have to earn with sweat and toil. When your life ends, you will go back to the earth out of which I molded you, because you are nothing but dust, dust and nothing else."

The Lord God threw them out of paradise. Now they would not be able to eat from the fruits of the tree of life. They would die just like all the other animals. This was not easy for them to accept, but they had asked for it. From that moment on, their privileged life had ended. The Lord God placed guardian angels with swords at the gates of paradise to prevent people from ever returning to it.

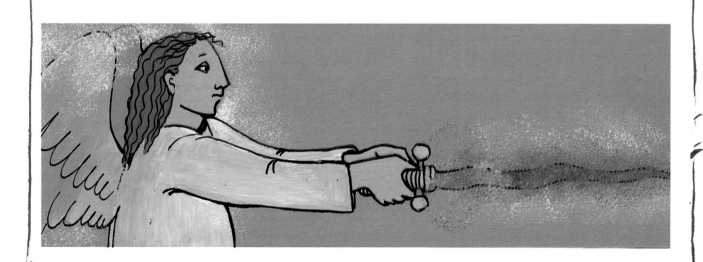

Cain Cannot Tolerate Abel

Away from paradise, Adam and Eve had two children, Cain and Abel. Cain, the older one, worked the fields. Abel was a shepherd.

The two presented to the Lord God the fruit of their work. Cain offered the fruits of the earth, and Abel sacrificed the best he had—the newly born lambs and the fattest sheep. The Lord realized that Abel's sacrifices were offered wholeheartedly, but Cain did it just to fulfill his obligation. That is why the Lord gladly accepted what Abel presented, but rejected Cain's offerings.

Cain saw that Abel was the Lord's favorite. At first he was jealous, but soon jealousy turned into hatred, which became an obsession for Cain.

One day Cain invited Abel to take a walk in the fields. When they were alone, he saw an opportunity to take revenge on his brother, since he was the cause of the burning hatred that ruled Cain's life. Cain jumped on Abel and, before he could realize what was going on, Abel was flat on the ground, dead. Cain's blows had killed him.

Cain breathed easier. He had killed Abel, so there was no one left to hate. The restlessness he had felt the previous days had disappeared. Despite this, he could only enjoy a moment of calm. He had not foreseen that, if hatred controlled him before, now remorse would be piercing his heart and causing him pain. He had gone from the frying pan into a fire that ate away at his core.

The pain of his guilt was compounded with the fear that the Lord might ask about his brother. Cain was constantly hiding so that he would not be caught. If he had to go through a field without a tree where he could take refuge, he feared the Lord might see him.

The Lord noticed Cain's strange attitude and asked, "Cain, where is your brother Abel?"

"How should I know? I am not his keeper," Cain tried to change the subject.

"Are you trying to deceive me? What relief have you found in killing your brother? If you kept the best fruits for yourself and did not give them to me, what did your brother have to do with that? You have shed innocent blood. You will be damned. The earth that used to give you fruits will no longer bear anything. You will not have a stable land or home, and you will wander from place to place," the Lord warned him.

"I will not be able to bear the crime I have committed. I will flee and wander all my life. That is, if someone doesn't find out about my crime and kill me," Cain said, quivering.

"No one has the right to take your life away from you, even if you are a murderer. I will give you a sign so that everyone knows that if they dare kill you, they will receive terrible punishment."

What Will God Do About Unfaithful Humans?

After all that, Eve had another son whom she named Seth. This child comforted her after the loss of her two other children—Abel, who was dead, and Cain, who was a fugitive.

After Seth, Adam and Eve had several sons and daughters who scattered throughout the earth, and human beings multiplied to fill the earth.

Quite a few years later, human beings had practically forgotten God. Their feelings had been corrupted and they only wished to hurt each other. Noah, a descendant of Seth, lived during that time with his sons Sem, Cam, and Japhet. Noah was the only good person in the community.

The Lord was hurt because he had created humans with such high expectations, but until then they had only disappointed him. For this reason, God decided, "Human beings were supposed to bring order to the world, conserve and guide it, but they can hardly live with each other. They attack, kill one another, and destroy things just for the sake of destruction. What good did it do to infuse my spirit in them? None. Perhaps the worst thing of all is that they have used the intelligence I gave them for evil rather than good. I will destroy them. They don't deserve to live."

But God did not want Noah and his family to pay the consequences of his anger. So God warned Noah, "Humanity is about to be exterminated and all living beings with it. You and your family can build an ark, because I will make it rain until water covers everything. There won't be an inch of dry land left. Your family and a pair of animals of each species—male and female—can go into the ark. In this way, after the deluge, the species can be preserved. Take as much food as you can too. Consider that for a few weeks, there will only be water everywhere."

Noah and His Family Are Saved

After God's warning about the rain, Noah and his family did as the Lord had told them. A heavy rain started. Day after day and week after week it rained cats and dogs. The level of the water reached the peak of the highest mountain and surpassed it. No living being was left on the earth. Only those on the ark were spared from this flood.

After forty days, God was satisfied and the rain ended. Even after the rain stopped, there was no dry land to walk upon. As far as the eye could see, everything was water and more water. In order to see if there was any dry land, Noah sent a crow. The crow returned to the ark because it had not found any place to rest.

Later on, when Noah thought there must be some dry land somewhere, he sent a dove, who returned with an olive branch in its beak. The next dove that he sent did not even return, which was a sign it had found a place to settle.

It did not take long for Noah's ark to reach dry land, thanks to the wind the Lord had sent. When the earth was quite dry, the Lord spoke, "Come out of the ark, you and your family, and all the animals you gathered together. Make them disperse throughout the earth and repopulate it. You, men and women, bear children to occupy this now-deserted land. Rule over the animals of the earth and the birds of the air, and all the fish in the water."

After this, the Lord wanted to establish a pact with those people who had been faithful, "I am making a covenant with you. There won't be another flood. I will never again try to destroy humanity. I will set a rainbow over the skies to remind you of our covenant every time it stops raining."

Population of the Earth and Dispersion of People

The earth was again populated by the descendants of Noah's sons, Sem, Cam, and Japhet. The Japhetites (descendants of Japhet) had populated Asia Minor and the Mediterranean islands. The Camites settled in Egypt, Ethiopia, Arabia, and Canaan; and the Semites included the Elamites, Assyrians, Lydians, Arameans, and the ancestors of the Hebrew people.

A few generations later, when the earth was filling up, the people decided to build a high tower to reach to the skies. The Lord God saw that they wanted to make something that was impossible for mere humans to create, so he confused their languages so they would not be able to understand one another. In this way the tower remained unfinished. In addition, those who spoke the same language joined together, and other groups went their separate ways.

The divine command to grow and multiply has been fulfilled and human beings fill the earth. Universal unity and plurality are achieved. In this way the fact of the dispersion and plurality of peoples, nations, and languages.appears in a positive light: it is not the consequence of any punishment, but rather, it responds to the will of God.

From Noah's first son, Sem, Abraham would come after many generations. The people of Israel have always considered him their father.

Stories with a Hidden Agenda

Like many other peoples, the people of Israel hoped these oral traditions would answer their questions about the origins of the world; men and women; why they should work; why there is evil, suffering, and death; what God will do with humanity. They wanted to answer all these questions with stories that blend historical events (places, traditions, people) with elements of myths adopted by the cultures of the area or created by the people themselves.

In Babylon they found themselves without a homeland, symbols, or anything: this was the punishment for their unfaithfulness to God, which the prophets had proclaimed so many times. The expulsion from paradise had been worse for Adam and Eve, and yet they had survived. The extermination of humanity by a flood had been even worse. And yet, they were still alive. The people of Israel had more reasons to keep their hope alive. With these explanations, the Jewish people found meaning in the captivity they experienced.

Babylon: An Instrument in God's Hands

God's prophet found no rest. He always had to settle people's doubts, give them encouragement, or scold them if necessary.

An old man, whose fears had been eased, asked the prophet maliciously, "You tell us we will return to our homeland, but we have heard that for years. Where will we find the strength to endure until the day of our return?"

"You have heard that the Lord created heaven and earth. God never tires. Would you like to keep your strength? Have faith in God and he will be your strength. Keep alive the hope that you will return, because the Lord has so promised. Do not expect a brief punishment, for your unfaithfulness was long and repeated. Even so, there is a king who conquers tribes and nations who will come to free you," the prophet said.

A shepherd who was concerned about feeding his animals followed, asking, "When we are liberated, where will you take us? Because if it's like the desert, perhaps it would be better to stay here."

"Don't worry about that. The Lord God will create gardens in the desert if necessary. God has done more difficult things throughout the history of Israel. You know it all too well," the prophet replied.

"I just don't understand how it is possible for the Chaldean gods to be false and powerless when the Babylonians, who believe in them, are the most powerful kingdom," a clever boy wanted to know.

"The Babylonian idols have never had power, nor will they ever have it. They have not participated in a history as rich and full of wonders as that of your people. They are nothing. The Lord has allowed Babylon to be powerful now. For God Babylon is but an instrument to punish the betrayal of the house of Judah. This Babylonian kingdom, which appears to be so solid, will fall into the hands of someone who will free you. That's the Lord God's plan."

Everyone Can Be a Part of the People of God

The prophet took advantage of the opportunity to guide the Jewish people when they asked questions. An acquaintance of his commented, "Here in Babylon there are people from all nations who were forced into exile like we were. They tell us about their gods. But we cannot tell them about ours because they are not part of the people of Israel. That's why it is easier for them to convince us than for us to convince them."

"You are the people of Israel, the servants of the Lord. God has chosen you as a people because he has willed it so. But now you have a mission—not only to remain faithful to God, but also to proclaim God's Law among the nations.

"From now on, the people of God will not be limited to those who, by origin, belong to Israel. It will be a people of believers. All those who accept and practice God's Law will belong to it, regardless of their race," the prophet said, leaving them speechless.

"But that's not according to tradition. That's new. How can we form a people out of different races? Hadn't you always told us we should stay away from those people so that we wouldn't be contaminated with false beliefs?" the friend argued.

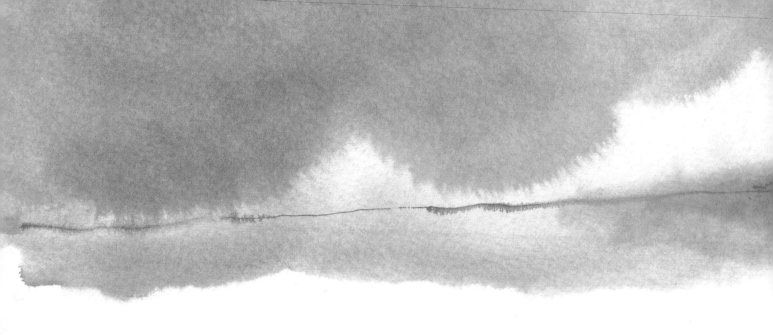

"Tradition, as we have understood it up to now, was in accordance with a situation of stability in a given country. Now everything is different: the people of God have been dispersed. It is the will of the Lord for the new people to be formed out of sincere belief and not out of race issues. I realize that accepting this new development is not easy, but the faithfulness we owe God must encourage us to do it with pleasure," the prophet responded to the objection presented.

Do We, the Conquered, Have to Spread Our Religion?

"It seems to me that explaining our God to non-Jewish people is going to be a big problem for us and for them," the friend continued.

"To explain our Law is to help them see the light. They don't know our God and find themselves in darkness. To help them move from darkness to light is to help them as persons, not to create any problem for them," the prophet argued.

"Do you know what would happen if we decided to convert our foreign neighbors to our faith? They would persecute, torture, and even kill us. We are part of a conquered people. How can we presume that our conquerors would accept our beliefs?" the friend continued to object.

"Perhaps it will indeed bring us some problems. But do not forget we are not alone. We have God on our side. God's power will protect us and help us to reach final victory. If we are convinced of this, we have nothing to fear," the messenger of the Lord concluded.

"Besides, our problem now is not converting the foreigners, but that many Jewish people have forsaken our God and have given themselves to false gods. How can they work to convince the foreigners of something they themselves do not believe?" the friend insisted.

"I realize that," the prophet agreed. "Many people of Israel seem to be deaf and blind. Even if they want to listen, deaf people cannot hear anything. Even if they want to look at something, blind people cannot see anything. Before they do hear or see, they must heal their deafness and blindness. To be healed, they need to accept the fact that their misfortunes have come because they are being punished by God. They must not forget that the Lord has not been willing to save them from the power of the Babylonian gods," the man of God said sadly.

The Rich Owner Loses Everything

A little later, the prophet was out in the fields looking at the clouds being pushed by a light wind, when he heard the word of God.

"The cities of Bel and Nebo have already fallen to the power of Cyrus, the Persian king who is threatening Babylon. Say to my people: neither Babylon nor any other people can keep power by their decision alone. This kingdom, like all things, depends on me. I have decided now that Babylon will be defeated, almost without struggle. The resistance of the small nation of Jerusalem was more than that of Babylon. Even if it thinks of itself as the most powerful kingdom on earth, it won't be able to do anything. When the time comes, it will happen as I have just said. Let my people know so that they will see that my word is about to be fulfilled and that their liberation is closer at hand."

True to his nature, the prophet of God followed the custom of the other prophets and explained things to the people through stories. This is what he told the people this time:

"There was a young Babylonian woman who had more possessions than anyone else. This made her feel secure and superior to those around her. In fact, nearly everything was hers. There were her slaves, who worked for her or depended on what she bought for them. Those who had few possessions feared her. They were afraid that she would someday decide to help herself to all their possessions, and no one would be able to stop her.

"This Babylonian woman believed that her power came from within her and that she would have it forever. She said to herself, 'I will always be the owner.' She didn't care for anything, and treated her servants as if they were animals.

"One day she woke up and saw that no one was obeying her; no one was paying any attention to her. Everyone laughed at her commands. She did not scare anyone. They even took her clothes away and forced her to walk around naked. All those who had been scorned by her could see her naked now. And she became a slave. She had to transport things in order to earn her living.

"Do you think the gods she worshiped served her well? No one could help her. They had no power. And she saw that she was made of the same clay as everyone else. Her gods were but figures made of wood; the paintings were mixtures of colors. Nothing else."

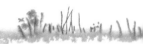

Babylon's Power Is Insignificant

"Explain to us the meaning of this story," they asked.

And he clarified, "The young woman I have described is Babylon. This kingdom believes it can hold onto its power just as the character in our story did. The Babylonians have mistreated their servants and slaves, because they think they are superhuman. The owner in the story believed the same thing. The modest owners of the story represent the small kingdoms that now depend directly on Babylon or have to pay taxes to it.

"The gods of the owner who have fallen from grace are the Babylonian gods, which you have admired as powerful. Now you see what has become of them. Now you see how they will serve you when you need them.

"Babylon will be defeated just as the woman in the story was defeated. You, the captives, will be able to return to your land and establish yourselves there. Have you understood that it is God who frees you just as it was God who made you fall prisoner? Do you understand that whether it be Babylon, Persia, or Israel, all depend on God and are subject to God's will?

"So that you know that the fulfillment of this prophecy is near, I announce to you that the cities of Bel and Nebo have already been conquered by the Persians. Their king, Cyrus, will be your liberator. Don't forget, however, that, regardless of who it is that frees you, he is only an instrument of the Lord God. The glory of the Persians will end when the Lord, our God, so decides."

Babylon Falls to the Persians

After being obligated to announce threats and punishments to the Israelites, the prophet now took advantage of telling them about the good things that Cyrus' intervention would mean regarding their return to their homeland.

The Jewish people were not sure they could believe what they were hearing. They were so used to bad news that they hardly knew how to react to good news. Perhaps they postponed their celebrating because they thought that the final liberation was still too far off.

But they did truly rejoice when they saw the Persians conquer the city; it was finally reality, not just promises.

The proud Babylonians could not even fight. The governor of the city realized that they were defeated and decided to collaborate with the Persian enemies. The river that flowed out of Babylon dried up overnight. The following day the Persians came into the city through the river bed, and the Babylonians never had a chance to defend themselves.

Return to the Land: Great Rejoicing

King Cyrus allowed all the deported to return to their homeland. At that moment, all the conditions for a rebirth of the unified people of Israel were present.

There is no need to say what the spirits of the Jewish people were like. This was the end of a long period of crisis that had started with Israel and Judah breaking the covenant with the Lord. But the hardest part of this crisis had been the Exile. The Exile was now ending. It was not a dream. No! It was true!

Gladness and joy broke forth! And the people who benefited were not the only ones to rejoice. It seemed as if the whole country wanted to share in the rejoicing; people all over were grinning from ear to ear.

Even the prophet was overjoyed and proclaimed everywhere, "We will go with gladness to the house of our ancestors. Mountains and valleys will break forth in shouts of gladness for us. We will sing until we have no voice. We will dance until our legs give out. Our slavery is over. Even the trees of the field will clap. Flowers will bloom instead of thorns; and aromatic herbs instead of weeds. Let us celebrate and exult! We have regained our freedom!"

The prophet did not need to repeat this advice to the people of Israel. The streets of the city had become a party. The households were all rejoicing. In the fields people sang and jumped for joy. A new era full of hope was now beginning, but the Israelites also realized that it would take a lot of work to rebuild the nation.

5.
The Return to the Homeland:
The Reestablishment of the People

In the year 538 B.C.E., Cyrus, king of the Medians and the Persians, conquered Babylon and, through a royal decree, authorized the return of the exiled Jewish people to their homeland.

A group of Jewish people stayed in Babylon, where they established a prosperous Jewish colony that endured until well into the Christian era. Those who returned to Palestine, however, quickly went from enthusiastic to disillusioned. Resettlement was harder than they had envisioned, since their lands had been occupied, the cities devastated, and the Temple destroyed. But the prophets were there to nourish the hopes of the people.

After fifty years of exile in Babylon, the Jewish people were returning with a single idea in mind: the rebuilding of their country. The great majority of those repatriated Jewish people had been born in Babylon and now were going to start from the beginning, in the midst of great difficulties. Those who returned from exile were of very modest means, because those who had prospered in Babylon decided to stay so as not to risk losing what they had already acquired.

There was, therefore, a small flock representing the history of Israel: the Diaspora (dispersion) of Jewish people throughout the world had started. There were families and small Jewish communities in Babylon, in Egypt, everywhere. The land and community of Palestine would always be a reference point for them, although they had their own separate lives now.

In this way, Judaism ceased to be so easily defined. Israelites are no longer anyone living in Israel, offering sacrifices in the Temple of Jerusalem, and integrated into the Jewish community. Rather, Israelites can be anyone who practices circumcision, rests on the Sabbath, keeps the Law of God in his or her personal and family lives, and identifies spiritually with Scripture (Bible) and the Jewish tradition. That can happen in any moment and place.

Return from Exile

As soon as word of Cyrus' decree allowing the Jewish people to return to their country was known throughout the land, the desert was full of caravans. The dream of returning to their homeland had finally become a reality, and the Israelites wasted no time.

It was the longest and, at the same time, the shortest of trips. It was the longest because they were anxious to get home and grew very impatient. It was also the shortest trip because the desire to get back to their land seemed to lend them wings; they moved at a rapid pace despite the fact that this was a journey through the desert.

They had arrived! They were home! It was a dream come true. But many people still did not believe it and they pinched themselves, saying to one another, "We are here. This is the land of our ancestors. This is home."

And they repeated it over and over again. So little by little, they came to believe it.

The enthusiasm of the first days soon gave way to a certain discouragement. The country they found did not look much like the prosperous country of years before. Jerusalem was like a ghost city. The Temple was totally gone and the walls of the city were almost destroyed.

Nonetheless, the people offered sacrifices to God in thanksgiving for having been allowed to return. And they soon got to work. There was a lot to be done. First, they started rebuilding the Temple, which was their most important symbol and could not be left in ruins.

Rebuilding the Temple Is No Easy Task

Their enthusiasm led them to work quickly, and very soon the foundations of the Temple were finished, which caused great happiness.

At that time, since Jerusalem was not strong enough to support itself, it was a territory of Samaria, subject to the Persians. Seeing the vigor with which the Jewish people were rebuilding the Temple and the city of Jerusalem, the Samaritans feared that the Jewish people would surpass them in power. If all Israel went back to offering sacrifices in the Temple like they used to, the Samaritans could lose the privileges they enjoyed at the time. So they went to Jerusalem to propose to the newcomers, "We would like to help you to rebuild the Temple. We also worship the same God."

All they got for an answer was, "It is our task to rebuild the Temple. You were near by all this time and have had more than enough time to rebuild it, and yet you haven't done it. And now you show an interest? No. Go back to Samaria and let us work in peace. Artaxerxes, the king of the Persians, has allowed us to rebuild. Don't you come to bother us now."

The new citizens of Jerusalem had been suspicious of the Samaritans' generous offer. And they were right to feel that way, for all the Samaritans wanted was to get control of the building to delay construction and, if possible, stop it.

The people from Samaria, however, did not give up, and tried other methods to prevent the building of the Temple. They discouraged the builders, and even wrote to the Persian king to make him believe that the Temple would represent danger for his kingdom.

Years passed in the midst of all this conflict. The Persian king was Darius. He remembered the importance that previous kings, starting with Cyrus, had given to that Temple, and he ordered, "Let no one bother the Jewish people in the reconstruction of the Temple, so that it won't be delayed any longer. May the expenses be paid with royal monies."

And so the Temple was finished.

Ezra Guides the People

Sometime earlier, a scribe by the name of Ezra had arrived from Babylon. He was very familiar with Scripture and he knew well the special powers granted to kings to govern Israel according to Jewish Law.

He read and interpreted the Scriptures so as to guide the Jewish people. In this way, the people could stay within the Jewish Law without going astray.

Ezra said, "It is the will of the Lord that you don't have contact with women from other countries. You know that in our history this has often caused people to depart from the divine Commandments. I come from Babylon, and what do I find? That many of you are married to foreign women."

"And what must we do then?" they asked.

"Dismiss all the foreign women and the children they have given you, because if you don't, the Lord will call you to task," Ezra answered. And so they did, although some more willingly than others.

There was another man who participated in an important way in the rebuilding of Jerusalem. Nehemiah lived in Babylon, where he learned of the difficulties the Jewish people who had returned to Jerusalem were going through. So he decided to go to Jerusalem and help rebuild the Temple.

These were the times of King Artaxerxes. Nehemiah had earned his trust and, thanks to this, he had the king's permission to help in this mission.

Nehemiah knew that there were people who did not want the city of Jerusalem rebuilt. For this reason Nehemiah proceeded with caution when he reached the city.

It Becomes Necessary to Defend the Wall with Weapons

Nehemiah soon realized that the wall of Jerusalem was in a shambles. He had not been very interested until he examined it closely one night. It had collapsed in some places, and was about to fall in other areas—it was in a sorry state. The following day, Nehemiah decided to make his intentions known. He gathered the most influential people in the city and told them, "We can't allow the walls of the city of Jerusalem to stay like this. We must rebuild them in order to defend the city and return to it the security and moral strength it had in the times of our ancestors."

Since the Lord was speaking through Nehemiah, he was able to convince the powerful people of the city who, without hesitation, set to the task.

It is easy to imagine the Samaritans' reaction when they heard the news. They had used every means possible to prevent the reconstruction of the Temple. If the walls were also rebuilt, Jerusalem would certainly surpass them. They had to stop that.

The Samaritans started recruiting armed men to attack the people who were restoring the walls; they thought this would stop construction. But Nehemiah had allies in addition to enemies, and somebody warned him of the Samaritans' attack. In order to prevent it, a permanent corps of guards protected the walls, and the builders had weapons to defend themselves if necessary. They even stayed by the walls at night, just in case they had to fight.

Explanations About the Law

While these things were happening, many people of the lower classes went to complain to Nehemiah. They said, "The food vendors abuse us. We had to pawn our most meager possessions to get some grain; those who don't have anything must leave their own children as a deposit so they don't die of hunger. And those who exploit us are not the enemies; they are Israelites like ourselves."

Enraged, Nehemiah went to speak to the owners; he succeeded in making them change their attitudes and treat the poor people more fairly.

After two months of intense work, the walls were restored. Now Jerusalem was a stronghold again.

Once the walls were finished, it seemed like a good time to read the books of the Holy Law—a perfect job for Ezra, the scribe. In the end, the people represented by the leaders confirmed the covenant established with the Lord in the time of their ancestors. In this way the union between God and the people of Israel was reinforced.

But many Israelites realized that sinners and evildoers, who did not keep the Law of the Lord, were having a great time and often died without being punished for their wrongdoing. Then they began to think that respecting the covenant according to the Law of the Lord did not put them at any advantage—especially when you consider that many times it involved danger and going without some of life's necessities.

Seven Exemplary Short Stories

The following stories were written after the Babylonian Exile. It is a series of short teaching stories based on historical characters. The stories contain a message for leading a good life.

For instance, the story of Jonah ridicules the Israelites who despised foreigners and believed that God only loved and took care of their own people.

In the story of Ruth, which is a wonderful account of faithfulness, the author protests racist attitudes that excluded those who were not Jewish. Although Ruth was of Moabite origin (not Jewish), she was the grandmother of Jesse, David's father.

In the stories of Tobit and Job, two good people who face the same question: Why do virtuous people have to suffer?

The stories of Judith, Esther, and Daniel present a vision full of hope. In times of difficulty and persecution, and with very dark perspectives for the future, the authors of these books, speaking in the name of God, want to reawaken and reaffirm the faltering hope of the people.

Will Jonah Successfully Escape God?

The story of the prophet Jonah was told for those who were not convinced of the need to accept people from other races in the religion of Judaism.

The Lord spoke to Jonah and told him, "Jonah, go to Nineveh, the great city, and preach its destruction, because I am tired of its evil ways."

But Jonah realized that bad things awaited him in Nineveh. If he preached about God there, he would be persecuted and perhaps even killed; so he decided to get on a boat and head in the opposite destination, to Tarshish, and get as far away from the Lord as possible.

The journey started out all right until, out in high seas, a violent storm spread panic among the passengers. All of them believed they were going to die. The storm was so bad that the waves were tossing the boat as if it were a nutshell.

Then the passengers decided to cast lots to decide who was responsible for such a horrible storm. Jonah was selected as the guilty one.

"Why do you bring this disgrace upon us? How can we calm the rain and the wind?" they asked him.

"I am fleeing from the Lord God. He has entrusted me with a mission that I don't want to carry out. If you want the wind to die down, throw me into the water," Jonah answered.

No sooner said than done, Jonah was cast out and the storm ceased.

By the decision of the Lord, Jonah found himself inside the belly of a great fish who had swallowed him. Several days passed before the fish threw Jonah out on the beach.

Jonah's Surprise in Nineveh

During those days, Jonah had had some time to reflect on his behavior. He realized that escaping from God was not all that easy. After the reflection and prayers he said in the belly of the fish, when the Lord suggested again that he go to Nineveh, he went there immediately.

Nineveh was a very large city; it took three days to cross it. Jonah started preaching, "Repent from your evil ways. The city will be destroyed in forty days."

Jonah, who was expecting indifference, was surprised when he saw that people started to do penance. The first one was the king of the city, who dressed in sackcloth and sat in ashes.

The Lord saw that the citizens had heeded Jonah's preaching and decided not to destroy the city. But Jonah felt that a few days of penance was not enough to make up for their past bad behavior. Jonah told the Lord, "I suspected this would happen. Wasn't I right in trying to escape to Tarshish? I knew you were too kind and you would change your mind about the pending doom."

Then the Lord said, "Have you noticed the tree by your hut that gave you shade? It has dried up."

"I have noticed. After forgiving the city, you have dried up the tree. Why have you done that?" Jonah complained again.

"See, Jonah, you are complaining about the death of a tree and yet you are asking me to exterminate a city of over one thousand people. Aren't the people of Nineveh more important than your tree?"

And so Jonah had to admit that such a large number of people was not to be taken lightly.

The Lord had sent Jonah to preach to Nineveh, a foreign city. This was a clear sign that people of other races should be accepted into Judaism.

Despite Threats, Tobit Abides by the Law

When the Israelites had not yet been freed from the domination of the Assyrians and lived in exile far from their homeland, there was a man named Tobit, of the tribe of Naphtali, who lived in Nineveh. He was a just man who abided by all the precepts of the Law—no matter the risks.

Before being deported, his lands had fallen into Assyrian hands. Everyone else was worshiping idols to ingratiate themselves with the invaders. Tobit, still free, traveled to Jerusalem to offer some of his possessions and a sacrifice in the Temple—just as the Law prescribed. He risked being found out by the invaders and put his life in jeopardy, but he kept faithful to the Law.

When he was in Nineveh, he helped poor people by giving them clothes and food. He also buried the dead that he sometimes found in the streets, although the Babylonian king, Sennacherib, had forbidden it. Some even betrayed Tobit when they saw him doing this. He had to go into hiding to escape the soldiers, and he lost everything he had. He only had Anna, his wife, and his son Tobias.

A little later, one of his nephews got a position close to the new king and interceded on behalf of Tobit. He could finally return home. However, through all the difficulties and tribulations he never rejected the commandments of God's Law.

Once again at home, with enough food and comfort, he was informed that an Israelite had died in the public square. Without finishing his food, he got up and went to fulfill his duty of burying the dead, despite the scorn of his neighbors who said, "Look at him; he had to flee from home because he buried the dead, and now he is back at it again. Let's see if he himself doesn't die, too."

Not paying any attention to them, Tobit buried the dead man.

Tobit Loses His Sight

When he finished burying the dead man, Tobit sat near a wall to rest. He did not realize that there were some birds above him whose droppings fell on his eyes. He tried all kinds of remedies to fix his eyesight, but it was too late: he was blind.

Anna, his wife, had to find work weaving and knitting because Tobit could no longer support his household because he was blind. She blamed Tobit.

"What good were your prayers and good deeds? See how much good they did you."

Tobit's relative Raguel lived in Ecbatana, another city far from Nineveh. He had a daughter named Sarah who lived in deep sadness. She had tried to get married seven times, and each time her husband had died on the wedding night. If this kept happening, she would not be able to have children, and, in those times, a childless woman was considered useless. Even her maids made fun of her.

Realizing that his blindness was not improving, Tobit was growing discouraged, and he felt the weight of the years more and more. He thought his death was at hand and did not want to leave his family unprotected and in need of money. He then remembered that he had loaned some money to Gabael, who lived in a city near Ecbatana, and wanted to go collect his debt.

Since he was in no condition to make such a long journey, he called his son Tobias and told him, "My son; I don't know how much longer I have left. Before I die, I would like you to go and get back the money I lent to Gabael. He will give it to you with this receipt." And he gave the document to his son. "You have to go to the city of Rages in Media, which is quite a distance from here. Be prudent. Avoid dangers. Keep the Law of the Lord I have taught you. Look for a traveling companion and I will pay him to accompany you."

"I will do so, father," Tobias answered.

Tobias Goes on a Journey with Raphael

When Tobias met Raphael, a young and trustworthy person, they started on their way.

After many days they grew tired and hot and decided to take a swim. So they went swimming in the Tigris River. While they were splashing in the water and rejoicing in the coolness they had found, a great fish jumped out of the water.

Raphael said to Tobias, "Catch it, open it, and take its guts out; they will be very useful to you."

Tobias did as Raphael had said. But he could not resist asking, "And what use would the guts be?"

"Look, Tobias," Raphael said, "we are close to Raguel, who is a relative of yours. Tonight we will sleep in his house. His daughter is looking for a husband. Many have tried to marry her, but they all have died on the wedding night. We will go there and you'll marry her."

"You want to kill me? Why do I have to marry her if all of the others have ended up dead? Besides, all I did was ask you about the guts of the fish, and you come up with this scheme?" Tobias protested.

"Calm down. You haven't let me finish. The other husbands have died because a demon killed them on the wedding night. Why? Because they were not Israelites. You know that the Lord doesn't want marriages between Israelites and foreigners. But you are a relative. Listen to me closely because I will now tell you what to do with the guts of the fish. Once you are married to Sarah and you are in the room, burn the heart and the liver of the fish. The smell will make the demon flee, and you will be safe and sound."

"And the bile, what do I have to do with it?"

"Don't worry. For the time being, just keep it."

Will Tobias Survive the Demon?

Raguel received them with open arms, as a good relative should. All cried for joy, and Raguel prepared a wonderful meal. Then Tobias spoke to Raguel about his daughter.

"Raguel, I would like to ask you for your daughter's hand."

"That gives me great joy. No one is more entitled than you, but I don't want to deceive you. She has had to bury many new husbands, and I wouldn't want the same to happen with you."

"Don't worry. The Lord will protect me. Give me your daughter as a wife, and tomorrow morning you will still have a son-in-law."

Since Tobias insisted, Raguel accepted. He joined Sarah and Tobias's hands and blessed them. They wrote and sealed the document of their wedding and then they had dinner. When the dinner was over, Sarah went to her room and cried. She thought Tobias would suffer the same fate as all the previous husbands, and she did not want to see him dead.

When Tobias went into the room, he burned the heart and liver of the fish, comforted Sarah, and they both went to sleep.

The following morning, Raguel was ready to receive the bad news of Tobias's death. He had a tomb prepared to bury him. So when the maid told him that the newlyweds were alive and peacefully sleeping, he could not believe his ears.

Joy in Raguel's House; Happiness in Tobit's House

The party was starting at Raguel's house, since it had not been done after the wedding. There were cries for joy and congratulations everywhere. The celebration lasted twice as long as usual. Raguel did not want to let Tobias go, because he wanted to continue celebrating.

But Tobias was concerned about his parents. It had been too long since he had left and he knew they must be worrying about him. So, he said goodbye to his relatives. After getting payment for Gabael's debt, he started on his way back to Nineveh, taking his wife with him.

When they were almost there, Raphael told Tobias to go ahead with these instructions: "Go to your father's house and rub the fish's bile on your father's eyes. As soon as you have done so, he will regain his sight."

Tobias did not need to hear anything else. Because he was now so anxious to see his parents he traveled even faster than he had been, as though he had wings on his feet.

So much time had passed that his parents had almost lost hope of seeing him return. When they saw him arrive, they hugged him tight and did not want to stop kissing him.

As soon as he could, he rubbed the bile on his father's eyes. The burning sensation made Tobit rub his eyes. As soon as Tobit took his hands away from his eyes, he regained his sight. Tobit praised God as jubilantly as Raguel had over the marriage of his daughter.

But Who Was Raphael Really?

Tobit and Anna were marveling at the young woman Tobias had brought along and all the goods he was carrying with him. Raguel had been so excited that he had given Tobias half of his possessions.

"And where is Raphael, the young man who accompanied you?" Tobit asked.

"Here he is," Tobias indicated. "Thanks to him I have a wife, riches, and my father has regained his sight."

And he explained how much Raphael had helped. Father and son agreed that what Raphael had done for them was priceless. Even so, they said to him, "Take half of all our goods, although we know we will never be able to repay you for what you have done for us."

"That is not necessary. I am Raphael, an angel of the Lord. I have come to reward you, Tobit. Now you know that whenever you helped a poor person or buried a dead man, it wasn't in vain. All your good deeds have been taken into account, as well as your courage in keeping the Law of the Lord. So both you and your daughter-in-law have been healed."

All fell on their knees, not daring even to look at him.

And Raphael continued: "I am returning to the place from where I came. Continue keeping the Law of the Lord as you have done up to now."

And he left. Tobit and his whole household continued to keep the commands of the Lord as they had always done.

Misfortunes Start for Job

The priests of Israel tried to explain the suffering of good people to the Israelites by telling them that God tested them to see how faithful they were. Here is another story they used to explain God's plan:

Job lived in the land of Uz. He was an upright and religious man who followed faithfully the Law of God. In addition, he was very rich and powerful, the wealthiest man in the region. God had granted him three sons and seven daughters. He could not be happier.

One day the Lord was meeting with his angels, and Satan was there, also. The Lord said, "Have you noticed, Satan, how faithful Job is? There isn't anybody like him; he keeps the Law and stays away from evil."

"If I were in his place I, too, would have reasons to be faithful to you. He has everything. He lacks nothing. He only has to move one finger and he has whatever he wants. It is easy to be good, fair, and faithful if you are wealthy like that," Satan answered maliciously.

"Fine. So that you see that Job's faithfulness does not depend on his goods, I'll let you do whatever you want. But don't lay a finger on him," the Lord granted.

Job was resting when a messenger arrived and told him, "The enemy has attacked and has taken all the oxen, donkeys, and camels. They have killed all your laborers."

He had not finished speaking when another messenger arrived and said, "Lightning struck us. All the sheep and shepherds have died. I was the only one saved."

Another messenger came in breathless: "Lord, your ten sons have died. They were eating in the house of one of your sons, as usual, and a tornado destroyed their house, which collapsed on top of them. No one has survived."

Will Job Endure the Pain?

All this bad news dealt a painful blow to Job, but the death of all his sons went straight to his heart. He needed some more time to react to this terrible news. The messengers of doom expected him to start screaming and crying in desperation.

With great effort, Job stood up. Then he fell on his knees and said, "Naked I left my mother's womb, and naked I'll return to earth. The Lord gave me everything I had and the Lord has taken it away. Blessed be the name of the Lord."

Another day, when the Lord met Satan, he reproached him, "What good was taking everything away from Job? He continues to be as faithful as before. His faithfulness did not depend on his goods."

"Because as long as their bodies are not touched, men put up with anything. Let me make him ill and we'll see whether or not he rejects you," Satan asked.

"Very good. Let us see if his perseverance goes together with his health. But don't put his life at risk."

Suddenly Job found his whole body full of sores that itched and burned. But that did not hurt him as much as the scorn of his wife, who said to him, "Look at the just man. Curse God before you die!"

But he answered saying, "Don't say stupid things. If we accept the good things from God, why shouldn't we also accept the bad?"

Are Misfortunes the Result of Sin?

Three of Job's friends wanted to comfort him in his misfortune. They told Job, "You know God sends misfortunes to sinful people. Think carefully how you might have offended God, so that you can repent and God may take pity on you. Don't be too proud to think that you haven't done any wrong. You cannot possibly think God is mistaken in sending you this grief."

Job answered, "If I had committed any wrong, I would have to thank you for your insistence in making me recognize my sin, but I am not aware of having hurt anyone. My suffering is not because of the sores, but because God is allowing this after I have always been faithful to the Law. I will have to think, perhaps, that God is not as fair as I had thought. Don't try to make me say what is not true.

"If I had sinned and knew what I had done, my suffering would be less, since I would understand the cause of my misfortune. But it isn't that way. Then, what is happening to me? Is it an injustice, a game, something entertaining to God? If that is the case, my life of faithfulness to God has been meaningless."

The Lord intervened in the discussion saying, "Who is this man who wants to understand things just as God does? Because if he does, I'll come to him for lessons. Where were you when I created the heavens, the earth, and all living beings? Perhaps you were there and knew what I was doing?"

Job answered, "My God, I don't want to challenge you. The priests have always told us that misfortunes came as a consequence of our own sins. Since I have always followed these teachings, I am not able to understand what is happening to me. Until now I only knew what others said about you. But now I have heard you and I ask you to forgive my mistake. I regret it."

The Lord was considerate toward Job, since Job had not meant to challenge God, but was just trying to understand his own situation. His human intelligence could not comprehend divine decisions.

Then the Lord gave Job everything he had before and twice that.

Those Who Are Not Jewish by Race Can Profess the Jewish Religion

Hearing the story of Job, the Israelites understood that people should not criticize the decisions of God, even if they sometimes seem impossible to understand.

During those times there was a much discussed question: Was the Jewish religion only for people of the Jewish race, or for all those people who accepted it in their hearts even if they were not Jewish? Could one marry a person of another race if their spouse accepted the Jewish religion?

When people chose a literal interpretation of the Law, they sometimes cut off all relations with those who were not of the Jewish race (as Ezra did.) At any rate, the idea that anyone who accepted God's Law had to be welcomed into the religious community of the Jewish people was gaining ground. People tried to extend that notion, explaining the following story:

A long time ago, when the judges governed, there lived in Bethlehem of Judea a man called Elimelech. He and his wife, Naomi, settled in the country of Moab, where they lived for a few years. Their two sons, who grew up there, married two Moabite women.

A little later Elimelech died, and his two sons followed him shortly. So Naomi and the two Moabite daughters-in-law were alone. Naomi spoke to them and said, "I have no more sons whom you could marry, and I have no husband to have more sons. You have a right to look for another husband to give you children. Go then to the house of your parents and may God bless you."

How Will Naomi and Ruth Live?

One of the daughters-in-law returned home, but the other one—called Ruth—did not want to abandon her mother-in-law. Naomi's insistence was to no avail, for the young woman had made up her mind. They returned to Bethlehem together.

Their financial situation was very unstable. They had nothing. So, during harvest time, Naomi went to the field of Boaz, a rich relative of her father-in-law. She would gather a little wheat grain that the harvesters left behind. She used the flour she got to bake some bread.

Boaz saw Ruth and said to her, "Come to harvest here anytime you want, and if you are thirsty, ask the laborers for water; they have been instructed to give it to you."

In addition, Boaz told the laborers to leave more wheat behind so that Ruth could gather it.

"Why do you treat me so kindly, since I am a stranger to you?" Ruth asked him.

"I have heard about how you have dealt with Naomi, the way in which you have taken care of her and accompanied her when she was by herself. So, not only can you drink water, you can also share my food."

Ruth stayed in Boaz's fields all day, gathering wheat. In the evening, she went to her mother-in-law's house and they ate together.

From Ruth the Moabite Will Come King David

A little later on, Naomi advised Ruth: "Look, my daughter, you need a man by your side, and Boaz seems to be interested in you. Go today where he works and see where he goes to sleep after dinner. When you find out, lie down at his feet, and he will tell you what you have to do. Come on! Tidy up and put on your best clothes!"

At midnight, Boaz turned over and realized there was a woman at his feet.

"Who are you?" he asked.

"I am Ruth, your servant. You, who are my relative, should marry me according to the Law. Remember that the closest relative has to take as a wife the woman who is widowed and without children."

"I am glad you came to me. Everyone knows you are a good woman. But rest now until dawn. If someone who has more right to you than I do does not take you as a wife, I will do it."

It was still dark when Ruth received a good handful of barley from Boaz, and she went to her mother-in-law's and told her what had happened. Naomi said to her, "Now wait at home. Boaz will do what is best."

Just as Naomi had predicted, Boaz looked for a relative who had more rights than he did to take Ruth as a wife, and asked him, "Would you like to take Ruth, Elimelech's daughter-in-law, as a wife, for she is widowed and without children?"

"No, I cannot take her as a wife," the man answered.

"Very well then; tell the elder witnesses that you are giving up your rights to marry Ruth and give them to me."

It was done that way and Boaz married Ruth. From this union came Obed, who would be David's grandfather.

Holofernes Wants to Conquer the Jewish People

The story of Judith clearly manifests God's intervention.

Nebuchadnezzar, king of the Assyrians, sent general Holofernes to conquer Israel. During the long journey from Assyria to Israel, Holofernes did not find any nations who dared to confront him. Rather, they all sent messengers to say, "We declare ourselves to be servants of Nebuchadnezzar. We are his slaves. Do with us as you will."

The Jewish people learned that the temples of those who surrendered to Holofernes were desecrated and robbed, and they could not allow that to happen to them. They then prepared to resist.

Holofernes was furious to find out that the insignificant people of Judea planned to put up a resistance, and he wanted to learn more about them. So he asked Achior, a Canaanite and therefore a neighbor of the Jewish people, to explain things to him.

Achior said, "These Jewish people have the power that comes from their God. Throughout their whole history it is shown that, as long as they keep the covenant with their God, they are victorious over their enemies. Only when they have gone astray from their Law have they lost the battle. So, we should find out if they are presently separated from their God. If that's the case, we can go and attack them. But if not, we will pass them by and leave them alone, lest the power of their God rise against us and defeat us."

Holofernes replied, "All the people we have conquered until now also had their gods. If we stopped short because of the gods, we would never start any campaign. On the other hand, you seem to be thoroughly convinced that this God can defeat us. If you are so sure, we can send you with the Jewish people so you can be with the victors," Holofernes said sarcastically.

Achior was taken to the gates of Bethulia, the first Jewish town they would have to conquer to get the whole country. When Achior told them his reason for coming, the Jewish people welcomed him and considered him their guest.

Will Judith, a Woman, Defeat the Assyrians All by Herself?

After a few weeks of siege over Bethulia, the situation of the city was becoming desperate. The enemies had taken control of the fountain that sprang from the city, and food was scarce. So the population of Bethulia was putting pressure on the governors to surrender to the invaders.

Judith, a widow from the city, had heard of the intentions of the leaders to surrender the city. So she asked them, "I have heard you want to give the city up. Is that true?"

Uzziah, the chief of the city, answered, "Many people have died of thirst. The reserves of water have run out. Only abundant rain could save us. You are a good woman; pray for us so that the Lord sends us rain."

"I'll do more than that. Before the five days you have set as a deadline to surrender the city, the Lord will send salvation through my hands. Wait for me tonight in front of the city gates because I will go to the enemy camp and bring you victory," Judith promised.

Judith was very pretty. She dressed up in her best clothes to appear before Holofernes and prayed to the Lord, "My God, protect me and give success to my mission, so that I can liberate this city and my own people."

Then, accompanied by a maid, she went to meet with the leaders by the gates of the city. They were all impressed with her beauty. Judith crossed the gates and headed toward the Assyrian camp saying, "I will return before five days and, with God's help, we will be able to free the city."

Will the Assyrian General Trust Judith?

Judith came before Holofernes, who asked her, "How come you, a Jewish woman, came to me? What has made you leave the city and come to my camp?"

Judith knelt before Holofernes and answered, "I have come because my God has entrusted me with this. Achior already explained to you that our God does not abandon us if we don't sin against him. Well, the Jewish people of the city, pushed by their hunger and thirst, are about to take the sacred foods reserved for God alone. I will go out to pray each night. When they eat from those foods, God will let me know and I will tell you. Then you will be able to go not only into Bethulia, but right into the very city of Jerusalem without meeting any resistance."

"You have spoken wisely. Pray to your God and tell me when they sin. If you do so, I will fill you with honor and riches," Holofernes promised.

The Assyrians gave her a tent to rest in and at midnight she went out to pray. Since the soldiers had orders from Holofernes to let her go out, they did not stop her. She did this for three days.

What Will Judith Do?

On the fourth day, Judith dressed up to go to a banquet Holofernes was giving in her honor. Everyone ate and drank a lot. Holofernes was very drunk and at her side. When the dinner and party ended, Holofernes, who had fallen in love with Judith and wanted to spend the night with her, stayed with her. But, since he had abused food and drink, he fell asleep.

Judith asked the Lord for strength, and with Holofernes' own sword she cut his head off and put it in a sack. Then she and her maid left the camp as if she were going to pray, like all the other nights.

But, instead of doing that, she went to Bethulia and showed Holofernes' head to the Jewish people.

All broke out in cries of joy and awe.

"Hang Holofernes' head on the walls so that his soldiers will see it at dawn," Judith told them.

When the Assyrians went to wake Holofernes up, they found him beheaded and realized Judith was not there. Then, seeing Holofernes' head hanging from the walls of Bethulia, they were frightened and fled in every direction. The Jewish people of Bethulia and other cities, who had been warned by Ozziah, pursued them.

The enemy army had been dispersed and victory belonged to Israel. Through Judith, the Lord had saved them from their enemies. The leaders of the Jewish people recognized it and said to Judith, "You are the pride of Israel and the glory of our people. Through your hand, God has saved the people of Israel. You will be blessed forever."

Esther Never Imagined She Would Be Queen of the Persians

God also intervened in the story of Esther, though in a different way.

In the Persian court, King Ahasuerus invited everyone to a banquet. During the banquet he ordered the queen to present herself so all could admire her beauty, but she did not want to please him.

The queen's attitude angered the king, who decided to throw her out of the palace. Then the servants of the king went out looking for young women for the royal harem. Perhaps one of them would please the king so much she would replace the rejected queen.

In the same city of Susa there lived a Jewish man named Mordecai, who had adopted Esther when she was a small child. Now Esther had become a beautiful young woman. The king's servants noticed her and took her to the palace.

Mordecai, who really loved Esther, walked in front of the palace each day to see if she was being treated right. After a time, Esther was brought before the king, who was fascinated with her beauty and sweetness. Showing herself just as she was, Esther won the heart of King Ahasuerus, and he made her his queen. The crown on her head made her even more beautiful.

One of the days when Mordecai had gone to the palace to inquire about Esther, he heard two servants plotting to kidnap the king. Mordecai told Esther and she told the king. The king immediately set out to see if the plot was true. The two servants confessed and were condemned to death. The discovery of the plot against the king was recorded in the palace books to be remembered.

Haman Wants to Exterminate the Jewish People

A little later, the king appointed Haman as the second most powerful person in the kingdom. All servants knelt before him, but Mordecai refused. Then Haman, to retaliate, thought of a way to exterminate the Jewish people. He spoke to Ahasuerus and said, "Scattered all throughout your kingdom there are people who do not obey your commands, but rather live by their own laws. This people will end up being a danger for you. So I believe it would be better to exterminate them and get rid of the danger."

"You have my permission to do whatever you think is suitable," the king answered.

A royal decree was then published that stated that all Jewish people would be exterminated and their goods confiscated on a given date, a few months later. The Jewish people were desolate. Mordecai was concerned not only with his own fate, but also because he thought he was the cause of his people's tragedy, since he knew this was Haman's way of retaliating.

Mordecai informed Queen Esther about the edict and asked her to intercede with the king so that it would not be carried out. Esther reminded Mordecai that, according to custom, if the king did not call for the queen, she could not go before him. If she did so, she could be condemned to death.

But Esther also realized that her intervention was the only hope for salvation that her people had. So she decided to risk her life and go before the king without being called. After praying and placing herself in God's hands, she went to meet the king.

Esther Tries to Prevent the Extermination

Esther appeared before the king without having been called for, and he looked at her in anger. This look made Esther faint and fall at his feet. When she came to, the king calmed her down.

"Don't worry, Esther. You can come before me without danger. Tell me, what made you come?" the king asked affectionately.

"I would like you and Haman, your trusted man, to come to a banquet I am preparing," Esther said in a weak voice.

"We will gladly go. But you ask for little. You know I would give you anything you ask for," the king said pleasantly.

Haman was honored to receive the queen's invitation, but when he was leaving the palace, he saw Mordecai sitting by the gate and showing no fear of him, and he was filled with anger. So, he ordered a high pole to be prepared from which Mordecai was to be hanged.

That night the king could not fall asleep. To entertain himself, he asked that the book of the palace chronicles be read aloud. The reader came upon the passage that described the plot Mordecai had uncovered. The king realized that Mordecai had not received any reward for denouncing the plot against him, and he thought that was unfair. Just then, Haman was coming to the palace to ask for the king's permission to hang Mordecai.

But before Haman could open his mouth, the king asked, "Listen, Haman. What must a king do for a man whom he wants to honor?"

Haman, thinking the king was talking about him, replied, "He should dress him in splendor and make a minister of the king parade him on a horse through the city saying, 'This is the man the king wants to honor.'"

"Very well," the king answered. "Go out and do what you have suggested with Mordecai, the Jewish man you will find sitting by the gate of the palace."

Haman Had Gotten Too Many Ideas

Haman could not respond, but he did not like the order one bit. He had to honor the man he had wanted to kill. When he was done, he returned home embittered. As soon as he arrived, the servants of the king called him to the banquet.

At the banquet, the king asked Esther again, "What would you like to ask from me, my queen?"

"I would like you to grant my life and spare the lives of my people, because someone has conspired against us so that no one in the whole kingdom will survive," Esther said resolutely.

"What are you saying? Who is the villain who has done that?" the king asked.

"He is right in front of you. Haman wants to exterminate my people," the queen accused.

Haman realized he was lost and asked the queen for mercy, but someone had informed the king that Haman had prepared a pole in his house from which to hang Mordecai.

"Hang Haman from that pole," the king ordered, angered by Haman's deceit.

Before long the decree against the Jewish people was changed; the new one was very different from the original. In the new one the Jewish people were granted the right to organize and attack their enemies. The date fixed for the extermination of the Jewish people became one for extermination of the enemies.

Thus through Esther the Lord had saved the people again.

Who Will Explain King Nebuchadnezzar's Dream?

In the old times, when Nebuchadnezzar conquered Jerusalem, he had taken some captives to his court. Among them were four young men who would be trained to serve the king later. Their names were Daniel, Azariah, Mishael, and Hananiah. Although they were away from their country, the four of them made an agreement with the king's steward that they would not have to eat the foods of the king's table that were forbidden by their religion. Since they looked well nourished, the steward did not object.

A little later, Nebuchadnezzar had a dream that left him very anxious. Many wise men from all over the kingdom came to the court, but none of them could solve the mystery of that dream, and the king could not regain his peace of mind.

He was on the verge of despair when Daniel, one of the four young men, came before him and explained, "In your dream, you are the head of gold, the silver represents the kingdom that will come after you, and the bronze represents a third kingdom which will dominate over all the earth. The fourth kingdom will be as strong as the iron in your dream. And what you saw at the foot of the statue, a mixture of iron and clay, is a kingdom with a weak and a strong part.

"Without anyone pushing it, the rock you saw made the mountain fall and broke the statue into pieces, with all its parts, the clay, the iron, the bronze, the silver, and the gold. It means that the Lord, the King of Heaven, will destroy all these kingdoms and create one that will never be destroyed."

After this interpretation, the king promoted Daniel and gave him an important position in the court.

Not Even Fire Can Handle the Three Young Men

Some time later the big statue that King Nebuchadnezzar had commissioned in his likeness was finished. By royal decree, the statue was to be adored by everyone. Daniel's three companions were denounced because they refused to do it. Brought before the king to answer for their actions, they explained, "We can only adore our God, as it is written in the law of our ancestors."

The king could not bear to be contradicted by these three young men, so he ordered them to be thrown into a furnace. Then he listened in to hear their cries or moans. Instead, all that could be heard from inside the furnace were songs of praise to God. Nebuchadnezzar could not believe his ears.

When the furnace door was opened, the three men emerged safe and sound. Seeing that, the king praised God and promoted the young men to positions of high authority in his kingdom.

A while later, the king had another dream that tormented him because he could not find an explanation for it. Trusting that Daniel would be able to interpret his dream, the king called him in.

Daniel said, "The huge tree you have seen in your dream is you, King Nebuchadnezzar. The fact that the tree was cut down means that you will be separated from the people and will go to live with the beasts of the field; you will eat herbs like they do, and your whole life will be like theirs, until you recognize that God is the one who rules the kingdoms of human beings. When you accept God, your power and glory will be returned to you."

Just one year after the interpretation, everything that Daniel had predicted was fulfilled, and the king did not return to his throne until he had recognized God.

Lions Do Not Attack if God Does Not Want Them To

Some years went by and Belshazzar, the new king, organized a feast and ordered the wine to be served in the sacred cups that had been stolen from the Temple of Jerusalem years before. While they were drinking, there appeared a huge human hand that wrote on the wall of the king's palace. They called Daniel in to interpret it.

When Daniel was before the king, he said, "King Belshazzar, you know what happened to King Nebuchadnezzar, for he was your father. Until he accepted God he couldn't leave his life with the beasts of the field. You knew about it. Why, then, have you profaned the holy cups of the Temple to drink wine and toast your gods?

"The writing on the wall tells your future. God will end your kingship. You will die and the kingdom will be divided between Medians and Persians."

King Belshazzar died the same night, thus fulfilling Daniel's words which had been inspired by God. Then the Median Darius became king.

Daniel became highly respected in the eyes of the king. A group of courtiers around the king became jealous and sought a way to get rid of Daniel. Since they could not find him guilty of any wrongdoing, they managed to get the king to sign an edict saying, "Whoever takes on a god who is not Darius himself will be thrown to the lions."

In this way, they could accuse Daniel before the king and he had no choice but to fulfill the decree he himself had signed. Daniel did not renounce God, and he was thrown to the lions' den.

The following day, when they opened the den, Daniel came out of it alive. From that time on, Darius recognized the power of God and ordered Daniel's accusers to be thrown into the lions' den. They were immediately dismembered.

Had It Not Been for Daniel, Susanna Would Have Suffered a Bad Fate

Susanna, a virtuous woman who was married to Joakim, lived in the city of Babylon. Two elderly judges often visited her house, which was one of the most respected in the city. But the true reason for their visits was Susanna's beauty, for they had fallen in love with her.

One day Susanna was bathing in her garden and the two elders came before her and said, "We are in love with you and want to take you into our arms. The garden gate is closed; no one will see us."

"Are you mad? I won't have anything to do with you," Susanna replied.

"You'd better satisfy our desires or we will accuse you of making love with a young man and you will be condemned," they threatened.

"I will not commit that sin," Susanna said firmly.

Since the elders had not succeeded in making Susanna sin, they accused her of wrongdoing. Everyone believed their testimony, since they were older. Susanna was found guilty and she waited to be condemned to death.

They were leading her to her execution when Daniel intervened. He had the two elders separated and asked the first one, "Under what kind of tree did you see Susanna with her young lover?"

"Under a sycamore," the first one said.

When Daniel put the question to the second one, he said, "Under an oak tree."

So, everyone realized that the two elders had given false testimony about Susanna. They were the ones to be executed instead of the woman.

The Maccabees: Eleazar Does Not Want to Pretend

The Persians, who were then the conquerors of the Israelites, allowed them to practice their religion without any obstacles. But things were to change. Alexander the Great, king of Macedonia, defeated the Persians and therefore took over Israel. His successors treated Israel in a very different way. During the first period—under the rule of Egypt—they were respected, but when Israel fell into the power of Assyria, the people were persecuted for their religion.

Antiochus Epiphanes was the king of Syria. When he had conquered Egypt, he went to Jerusalem, profaned the Temple, and pillaged as much as he could from it. He sent a letter to every part of his kingdom in which he forced all the Jews to forsake their laws and religion and adopt the one he ordered. He also ordered his soldiers to kill anyone who did not follow his commands.

Many Jewish people conformed to the demands of the king and worshiped the idols for fear that they would be executed if they were discovered practicing their Jewish religion.

They were also forced to eat pork, which was forbidden by their religion. Many ate it, but others only pretended. There was an old scribe, Eleazar, who refused to eat it. Some people advised him, "You don't have to really eat it; only pretend that you are."

And Eleazar answered, "I cannot pretend because if a young man should see me, he might imitate me. I must be an example of faithfulness to young people. The Syrian soldiers won't be able to kill my trust in the Lord."

Neither blows nor threats of death would make Eleazar change his mind.

The Seven Brothers: Now, That's Courage!

Eleazar was not the only hero. Seven brothers and their mother were taken before the king to force them to eat pork. One of them spoke on behalf of all, "We don't know what you want from us, but if you want to make us forsake the religion of our ancestors, we'd rather die."

This courage enraged the king. He gave the order to have huge cauldrons with boiling oil prepared. The child who had spoken was tortured and killed.

Their mother encouraged them not to betray their religion and to prepare for death.

Since the second child also refused to try to taste pork, he was also put to death. He still had the strength to say to the king, "You are making us die like this, but the God of heaven will raise us to eternal life."

One by one they were tortured and killed, but they refused to give up their beliefs. The soldiers demanded that the mother ask her sons to save their lives. On the contrary, she encouraged them and gave them strength to face death with dignity. After all the brothers were killed, they killed the mother, who showed the same courage.

Nothing infuriated the king more than the courage that the young men had shown. Anger ate him up inside because he had not been able to bend the will of some simple young men.

Mattathias Fights the Invaders

After these events, royal messengers came to the house of Mattathias, a priest who had settled in Modein, and they said to him, "You are a great leader of this city. If you offer sacrifices just as the king has ordered, the rest of the people will follow your example."

For an answer, he said, "Even if the whole country should leave our religion, neither I nor anyone in my household will."

And, seeing that a Jewish man was approaching to offer a sacrifice against God's law, Mattathias could not help himself and he killed the man.

Then Mattathias, his children, and anyone who wanted to join them went into the desert to prepare their resistance against the Syrian invaders.

Other groups of people also went into the desert to fight the oppressors. Syrian troops attacked one of those groups. Since the Jewish religion forbade any activity on the Sabbath, they did not fight. Up to one thousand men, women, and children were killed.

Mattathias' group heard what had happened and decided, "Even if it is on a Sabbath, we will fight. If we didn't, they would soon exterminate us."

Mattathias' men were joined by all those who were unhappy and who had escaped from the disasters of the invaders. With the army they made, they conquered the Syrians many times.

Mattathias was already old and his hour of death arrived. Before dying, he said to his children, "Do not abandon the Law and, if necessary, give your life for the covenant of your ancestors. Simeon, who is more experienced, will be your counselor and your father. Judas Maccabeus, who is the stronger, will be your military leader."

So the brothers organized according to their father's wishes and were to be known as the Maccabean brothers. Mattathias was buried with full honors and the Maccabean brothers continued the struggle against the oppressors.

The Hour of the Maccabeans Has Arrived. Will They Be Successful?

Seron was a general of the Syrian army who wanted to gain glory by defeating Judas Maccabeus, who had waged many battles against him. So, Seron prepared a huge army and went to meet Judas.

Judas also came out to meet Seron. When Judas' men saw how numerous Seron's army was, they said to Judas, "There are fewer of us. How do you plan to defeat such a huge army?"

"We don't win the wars. The strength comes from God in heaven. God protects us and, if he is on our side, numbers are irrelevant," Judas replied.

They attacked Seron, who was totally defeated, and his army dispersed. Antiochus, the king, was angry and sent another army, much larger than the first, with orders to destroy the country of Judea so that he would never have to hear of it again. Judas knew Antiochus' intentions. He found out all the moves the king planned, and, when the army was encamped just outside the country limits, Judas attacked. In the same way he had finished Seron, he defeated Gorgias, the new leader sent to fight him.

Hearing the news of Gorgias' defeat, Lysias wanted to destroy the Maccabean army. If Gorgias' army was big, Lysias' was enormous, but it was no match for the Maccabeans. When Judas saw the power of the enemy army, he prayed to the Lord, "Lord of heaven, protect us and help us defeat the army of the invaders, just as we overcame them in other battles because of your intercession."

When they defended their religion, the Lord gave them support and they were victorious. This time, too, the enthusiasm and strength with which the Maccabean men fought, together with God's intervention, were instrumental in Lysias' defeat.

After defeating Lysias' army, the Maccabeans were able to reach the Temple of Jerusalem. They restored worship there and appointed priests to care for it. They rebuilt the altars of sacrifice and all the other rooms that needed it. Honor was restored to the Temple of the Lord.

Judas, a Famous Warrior

The victories over the Syrians and the countries neighboring Judea gave Judas a fame that many officers of the Syrian army would have wanted for themselves.

King Antiochus Epiphanes, who was in a military campaign in Persia, was informed that all the armies sent against Judas Maccabeus had been defeated. He then became ill and was near death. Seeing that his hour was near, he confessed, "I remember the evil I have committed against Judea for no reason; that's why I am ill with sadness, and I will die in a foreign land."

Antiochus Eupator, his son, succeeded him. Just like his father, he decided to attack Jerusalem. In order to do that, he gathered such a number of soldiers, cavalry, archers, and elephants that this new army surpassed in number the three previous ones put together.

This time, too, the Maccabean men fought with courage, and one of them, Eleazar, even sacrificed his life. In the midst of battle he pierced with his sword an elephant that appeared to be the king's. Although he killed the elephant, it trampled Eleazar to death.

After this battle, the Jewish people had to withdraw to the walls of Jerusalem. The city was besieged. The Jewish people did not have much of a chance for victory, but the danger of a civil war in Syria forced the invading army to withdraw after making peace with the Jewish people. Before the Syrian withdrawal, however, King Antiochus ordered the wall to be brought down without honoring the peace accord they had reached.

Jonathan Takes Judas' Place

Demetrius, who had been a captive of the Romans, returned to Syria to claim his rights to the throne. He defeated Antiochus and Lysias in a battle. Both Antiochus and Lysias died for their treason.

Judas decided to make a covenant with the Romans so that he would not always have to fight alone. He knew that they were a courageous people and faithful to their commitments.

It did not take Demetrius long to decide to conquer Israel. He sent a powerful army that greatly outnumbered Judas' army. When Judas' soldiers saw the huge army, the majority of them deserted. Only eight hundred men remained to fight an army of over twenty thousand. Although the men who were faithful to him advised him to withdraw and regroup, Judas did not pay attention. The two armies waged war and the invading army defeated them. The Jewish people lost the battle and Judas was killed.

Jonathan, Judas' brother, continued the resistance against the invaders. Bacchides, an enemy general, found out about Jonathan's leadership and sought to defeat Jonathan with a great army. But Jonathan was not impressed and encouraged his people, who attacked Bacchides' men with great determination. Victory was the reward for their courage. Defeated, Bacchides had to withdraw.

After this victory, there was a time of relative calm. But the peace was interrupted because some Israelite traitors warned Bacchides that Jonathan had let his guard down and was not prepared for war.

Jonathan's Incredible Victories

Jonathan found out about the betrayal before Bacchides could carry out the attack. The traitors were executed. The rest of Jonathan's army started preparing for the defense.

They divided up the tasks: Simon stayed in the city and Jonathan went out to fight the approaching enemies. Neither Bacchides' powerful army nor all his weapons of war could conquer the Jewish people.

Bacchides returned empty-handed. Those who had encouraged him to go to war had to pay the consequences of his fury: they were murdered for encouraging a campaign that had ended in defeat.

Jonathan decided to take advantage of the situation and proposed peace to Bacchides. Bacchides saw the opportunity to return to his country once peace was made, instead of returning defeated, and he accepted Jonathan's offer.

So, Israel could live in peace under Jonathan's leadership.

In the invading country of Syria, however, a civil war had broken out. Both sides asked Jonathan to fight for them. Alexander received Jonathan's help and was the victor—but not for long, for he was soon betrayed and then murdered.

Demetrius was the new king. Once peace came, Demetrius discharged his troops. This was the opportunity Trypho, the traitor, was waiting for, and he sent his army to attack the vulnerable king. Demetrius then asked Jonathan for help, and he lent it. Jonathan's three thousand men defeated Trypho's one hundred thousand. Demetrius thus kept his life and his throne.

Trypho = Treason

As soon as Demetrius was safely sitting on his throne again, he forgot he owed his life to the Jewish people. So Jonathan supported Antiochus VI, the king who was supporting Trypho.

Demetrius, who had been helped by them, now became the main enemy of the Jewish people. Demetrius' generals were preparing to fight. But when the soldiers found out that Jonathan knew of their intentions, they were afraid because of the fame of Jonathan's men, and they fled and left the fires burning to make others believe they were still there.

Trypho and Jonathan were now on the same side. But Trypho did not want anyone interfering with his plans. He met Jonathan in the city of Bethzur and said to him, "We are not at war with each other. Why have you come with such a numerous army? Send the troops away and keep only a guard, since there is no danger in sight."

Jonathan trusted Trypho and did as he had said.

When he came back into the city with the few men he had kept as guards, the gates were closed to prevent them from escaping. All of them, starting with Jonathan, were massacred.

Then Trypho attacked the Jewish people, thinking that he could easily conquer them now that they did not have a leader. But Simon, Jonathan's brother, regrouped the army and stopped the fatal blow that Trypho wanted to inflict.

When Jonathan, his main threat, was dead, Trypho only had to get rid of Antiochus in order to reign. He murdered the king, who was only an adolescent. It was clear now that the Jewish people would no longer help Trypho. They changed sides and pledged their allegiance to Demetrius.

Antiochus Is Ungrateful to Israel

King Demetrius was able to get control of the situation in his kingdom and earn the respect of the Jewish people. Simon conquered Gazara, which was a threat to his people, and Jerusalem was totally liberated and rebuilt. Then there was a period of peace in Israel.

After a time, the Persians imprisoned King Demetrius. Antiochus, his brother, asked Simon for help, which Simon agreed to give. Antiochus conquered Trypho, who had taken advantage of Demetrius' misfortune and proclaimed himself king.

Once again the support of the Jewish people was forgotten. Instead of being thankful and sending them riches and rewards, Antiochus sent an army to control them.

At that time Cendebeus was the leader of the enemy army. Simon said to his children, "I am too old to defend Israel, and my strength is failing. My children, fulfill my obligations for me."

Simon's children fought courageously and defeated Cendebeus. They won both in war and in peace.

One day some time later, when Simon and two of his children were together, Ptolomy, Simon's son-in-law, appeared and murdered them. Ptolomy did not want to be just an important general in Simon's army; he wanted to reign over all of Israel.

Despite his attempt, Ptolomy's plot to assassinate John, Simon's other son, failed. John, with his followers, started the fight against Ptolomy.

As we have seen, the whole period of the Maccabees—and the whole history of Israel—is characterized by invasions and threats to the chosen people. In those times, the stories in which God's intervention liberated the people were necessary to inspire trust in the Lord and to encourage the people not to lose their spirited disposition.

What Happened from That Moment until the Birth of Jesus?

The story we have seen so far is known as the Old Testament or Old Covenant. The last book of the Old Testament was written about fifty years before Jesus' birth.

Jesus' birth starts the era of the New Covenant or the New Testament. Some years go by, however, until the writings of the New Testament start. We have no written account during those years.

Jesus was born, grew up, and received his religious education at home and in the synagogue—where both Jesus and his disciples learned the language, history, and spirit of the people of Israel.

Also during these years the Jewish people wrote books that help us understand the background of the books of the New Testament. This is called rabbinic literature (from the rabbis, who were the teachers and interpreters of the Law written in the Bible). All these writings express a great hope: that the old world is ending and a new, different one is beginning. Enough evil and injustice. God wants the world to be just as he had planned in the beginning: a world of peace and justice known as the "Reign of God."

Around the year 28, Jesus starts proclaiming: "God is preparing to rule! The reign of God is among you!"

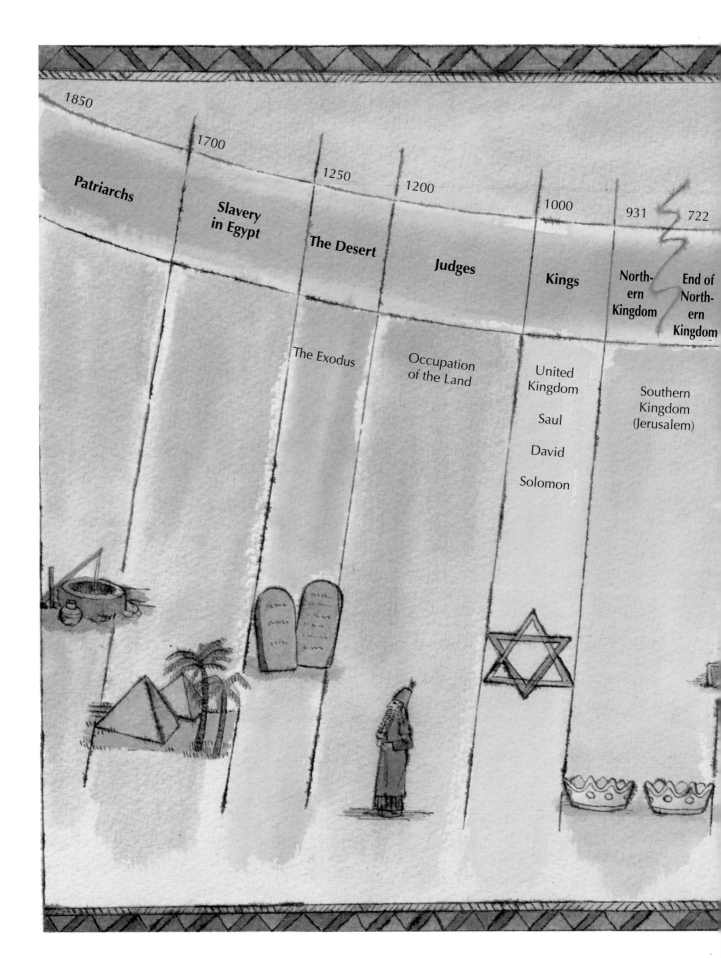

1850

1700

1250

1200

1000

931

722

Patriarchs

Slavery in Egypt

The Desert

Judges

Kings

North-ern Kingdom

End of North-ern Kingdom

The Exodus

Occupation of the Land

United Kingdom

Saul

David

Solomon

Southern Kingdom (Jerusalem)

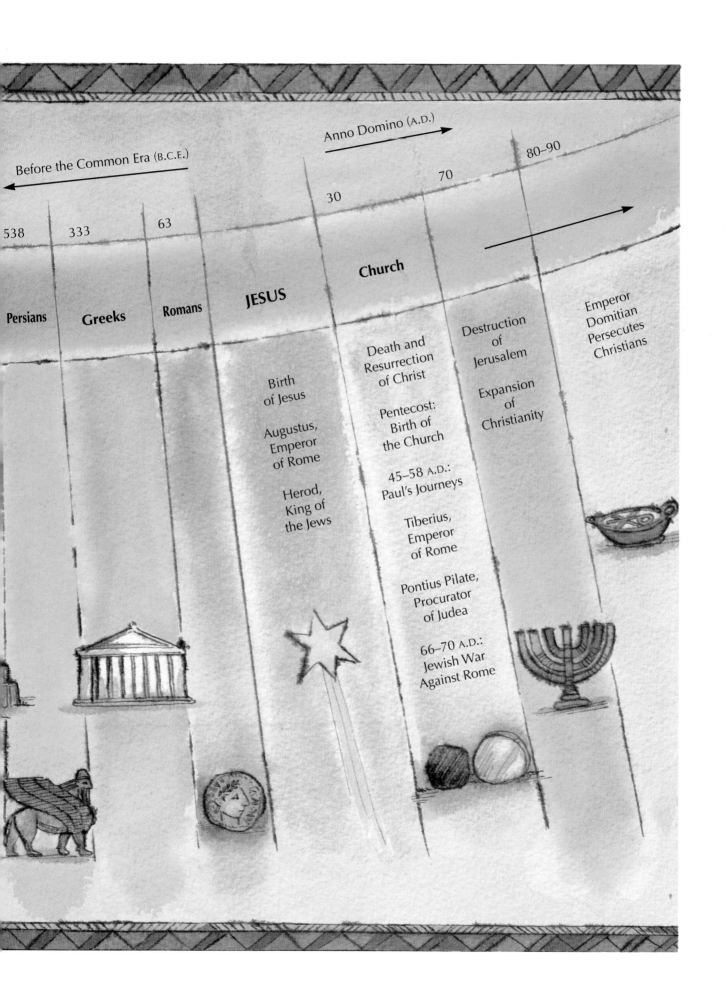

Before the Common Era (B.C.E.)

Anno Domino (A.D.)

538   333   63   30   70   80–90

Persians   **Greeks**   **Romans**   **JESUS**   **Church**   Emperor Domitian Persecutes Christians

Birth of Jesus

Augustus, Emperor of Rome

Herod, King of the Jews

Death and Resurrection of Christ

Pentecost: Birth of the Church

45–58 A.D.: Paul's Journeys

Tiberius, Emperor of Rome

Pontius Pilate, Procurator of Judea

66–70 A.D.: Jewish War Against Rome

Destruction of Jerusalem

Expansion of Christianity

II
New Covenant
(New Testament)

We are now in the second part of the Bible, which contains twenty-seven books: the four gospels, which tell about the life and teachings of Jesus; the Acts of the Apostles, which tells the experiences of the followers of Jesus and the spread of the gospel throughout the world; the letters of the apostles to the different Christian communities; and the Book of Revelation, which contains a series of revelations to encourage the persecuted church.

From Jesus to the Gospels

About thirty years passed between the time Jesus lived, died, and rose until the gospels were written to tell of Jesus' life, death, and resurrection.

The apostles traveled the world proclaiming what they had seen and heard from the Lord Jesus, their friend. They passed around written letters to the Christian communities so that their words and actions would not be forgotten. Later, they gathered all the information they had in the gospels. All this was accomplished in three stages:

Stage 1: Jesus proclaims the Good News: the Reign of God. He said that God is coming to rule the earth and wants to work within it, especially on behalf of the outcast, the sick and possessed, children and women, sinners, and simple people. With his words and actions Jesus proclaims the merciful love of God. Those who held the political and religious power crucified him, but God the Father raised him again.

Stage 2: Begins after Jesus' death. The apostles experienced the presence of the risen Jesus and proclaimed the Good News: the reign of God arrived with Jesus, who died and rose from the dead for us. Saint Paul and other apostles wrote their letters around that time. At the same time, some small collections of words and actions of Jesus were written and sent to the new Christian communities.

Stage 3: The four gospels Mark, Matthew, Luke, and John—are written. The evangelists gathered together what they found in oral and written tradition in the communities and shaped it according to what each of them wanted to convey to the community for which he was writing. In fact, the final writers of the four versions of the gospel (the evangelists) do not attempt to explain the life of Jesus in detail, but rather want to transmit to us the meaning of his life. They wrote manuscripts on papyrus leaves or parchment. In the Christian communities there were people who very carefully copied these texts, trying not to make any mistakes in transcription.

Documentation About Jesus' Times

Jesus was born in the Jewish world that was under Roman control. Israel had almost always been dominated by foreign powers, or were warring against those who wanted to subject it. So in Jesus' times the people were anxiously awaiting the arrival of a Messiah who would return their freedom.

The following were the different groups and organizations that operated in the times of Jesus and the apostles:

The priests were in charge of the worship in the Temple of Jerusalem. They were quite numerous. The high priest, or chief priest, led all of them. The high priests were members of the priestly aristocracy of Jerusalem. Prominent, for instance, were Annas and his son-in-law Caiaphas, who were great priests in the times of Jesus. They had control over the market at the Temple and the animals for sacrifices; they also enjoyed riches and the good life. Those who were simple priests had to work in the towns and villages and traveled to Jerusalem when they had to serve in the Temple and during important feasts.

The Levites—descendants from the tribe of Levi—were in charge of the auxiliary services of the Temple.

The Sadducees were a conservative and opportunistic group mainly made up of high priests and rich families. They were directly responsible for Jesus' death.

The Pharisees (which means *separated*) formed separate groups where they lived according to the tradition and Law of Moses: they prayed, gave alms, offered sacrifices, etc. Their main fault was their pride, for they thought they were better than others. They seldom practiced charity toward their neighbors. Saint Paul had been a Pharisee until Jesus befriended him on the way to Damascus.

The scribes were those who knew and taught the sacred books. When they completed their studies they were called doctors or teachers of the Law, with the honorable title of rabbi. They were Jesus' main opponents, since he claimed that the Law is made for the person and not the person for the Law.

The publicans or tax collectors were at the service of the Roman invaders or of Herod. They were not popular, and were considered public sinners—every good Jew despised them. Jesus did not hate them since he ate with them and even called one of them, Matthew, to be his follower.

The Zealots were partisans of a guerrilla movement who wanted to expel the Roman invaders. They expected a Messiah to free them from the Romans and from the rest of their enemies.

The Herodians were supporters of King Herod's family.

The synagogue was the place of gathering and the house of prayer for the Jewish people. They gathered there every Saturday to listen to and discuss the Law of Moses and the Prophets. The synagogue was also used as a school.

The Sanhedrin, or Great Council, was the council of the elders, the supreme authority for the Jewish people. A high priest presided over it. It had seventy-one members: elders (representing the illustrious families), priests (priestly aristocracy), and the scribes (doctors of the Law).

The Samaritans, the people of the region of Samaria, were excluded from worship in Jerusalem due to the animosity and hatred between Jews and Samaritans. Each group avoided contact with the other, which is why people were amazed at Jesus' welcoming attitude toward the Samaritans. The new church sowed the gospel in Samaria, and continued to spread throughout the world.

Jewish Festivities

The established feast day among the people of Israel was the Sabbath. Just as the Creator had rested on the seventh day, the Jewish people had one day of rest, after six days of work. Sabbath practices became increasingly regulated with numerous laws that forbade many activities on that day. The activities of people were limited. That is why Jesus—who was criticized by the Pharisees because he healed many people on the Sabbath—said: "The Sabbath is for the person, and not the person for the Sabbath." We Christians celebrate the first day of the week, that is, Sunday or the day of the risen Lord.

In addition to the Sabbath, the Jewish people had many annual feast days. The most important was Passover, celebrated in the springtime in remembrance of the liberation of the people of Israel from slavery in Egypt. During the Passover meal and for the entire following week they ate unleavened bread in remembrance of the hurried exit their ancestors had made from Egypt on their way to freedom.

The week of the unleavened bread ended with the feast of the First Fruits, in which they offered the first barley harvest to God.

At the end of the wheat harvest the feast of Weeks was celebrated. This was also known as the Greek word Pentecost (fifty), because it took place fifty days after the Passover. It commemorated the time when Israel was formed as a people at Sinai, where it received the Law.

At the beginning of autumn, the new year was celebrated ten days before the feast of Atonement (Yom Kippur), in which the people asked God for forgiveness for their sins. This was the only time at which the high priest would enter the "holy of holies," the innermost and most sacred part of the Temple.

A few days later came the feast of the Tents or Tabernacles, celebrated at the end of the harvest of fruits and grapes; it lasted a week. This was a very popular feast during which people lived in tents or little huts set up in the fields, in remembrance of the time that the Israelites lived in tents on their way to the Promised Land.

The feast of the Dedication was celebrated in winter to commemorate the new dedication of the Temple made by Judas Maccabeus after the desecration carried out by the king of Syria, Antiochus Epiphanes.

In the last month of the Jewish year there was the feast of the Purim, which lasted two days. It commemorated Esther saving the people from extermination during the reign of the Persian King Ahasuerus.

The Language of the Books of the New Testament

While practically all the books of the Old Testament were written in Hebrew, some in Greek, and a few in Hebrew with certain chapters in Aramaic, those of the New Testament were all written in Greek. There was probably a first edition in Aramaic, but as soon as the first church started preaching the gospel outside of Palestine, Greek was used to update and translate the tradition of Jesus words and actions. Greek was the international language of trade and communication throughout the Roman world.

6.
Jesus of Nazareth:
The Proclamation of the Kingdom

As it so often happens, those who years before were the allies became the oppressors. The Romans had taken control over Israel and they named a governor who exercised power in the name of Caesar, the leader of the Romans.

Six or seven years before our era, the birth of Jesus—the fundamental event for Christianity—took place in Bethlehem. After Jesus' death his disciples continued his mission. It was around the year 70, when those who had lived with Jesus were either dead or getting very old, that the accounts of the life and teachings of Jesus were written. The first Christians believed that Jesus was the Messiah, the Savior, the Son of God in human form, but they wanted to know him well; they wanted to understand his life and his words. They would tell each other the few details they knew about Jesus' birth and childhood and, in the light of their faith in him, they tried to find the meaning behind it all.

They enhanced the simple acts that Jesus' mother Mary had told them with amazing stories.

By adding to the stories, they did not want to give exact details, but rather to emphasize the significance of the events they had experienced and to underline the importance of everything that happened around Jesus' birth. For instance, with those tender stories of the birth and childhood of Jesus, the first Christians wanted to express that with "Jesus, God entered this world and will not abandon it," or also that "on the holy night of the birth of Jesus there rose a sun that will never set."

Promises About John

At that time Zechariah, a priest of the Temple, went into the sanctuary of God to offer incense. When he was inside, an angel appeared to him and said, "Don't be afraid, Zechariah. Your prayers to the Lord have been heard. Elizabeth, your wife, will be pregnant and you will have a son and you will name him John. The Spirit of God will be upon him and he will come before the Lord preparing the people for his coming."

Still startled by the appearance of the angel, Zechariah asked, "How could that happen? Elizabeth and I are already old. How is she going to get pregnant?"

"I am Gabriel, the one sent by God. You are a priest. You know well all the cases explained in the Scriptures in which God has given children to women who could not have them. Maybe another person would not know this, but you do. Your doubting deserves a punishment: you will be struck mute from now until all that I have said to you is fulfilled."

Leaving the sanctuary, Zechariah realized he could not talk and had to make himself understood through signs. A little later his wife Elizabeth conceived a baby. For her this was an extraordinary event which filled her with joy. She could hardly believe it and said, "God has wanted to save me from the shame of not having had a son. No one will now be able to say I am a useless woman. Praise be to God."

Mary, Chosen for the Prodigy

A few months later, the angel Gabriel was sent to Nazareth, a town in Galilee, to the north of Israel. He entered the house of a young virgin named Mary and said to her, "Rejoice, Mary. You are full of grace. The Lord has looked upon you."

Mary could not have been more surprised and hardly understood what the angel was telling her, but he continued, "God has chosen you from among all women for a wonderful mission. You will have a son and will name him Jesus. He will be the son of God. He will come from King David, and will have more power than the king. His reign will change the hearts of people and it will never end."

"And how could I be pregnant?" Mary asked. "I haven't been with any man."

"You will be pregnant by the power of God. For this reason the child born of you will be called the Son of God. Your cousin Elizabeth, who was barren, now carries in her womb the one who will prepare for the coming of your son."

"Elizabeth is pregnant? I can't believe it! I am glad for her; she must be very happy. I must go to visit her, to see how she feels. At any rate, I am about to marry Joseph, and I don't know if he'll get mad at me, no matter how well I explain this to him . . . ."

"Don't be afraid. Joseph will be informed of this miracle," the angel assured her.

"If God has decided that this extraordinary act should happen to me, I am available for this and for anything else God may want of me."

Joseph's Doubts

And so it was: Mary got pregnant and Joseph, her fiancé, found out. He, who knew Mary well and loved her, was very surprised. He did not think Mary would be capable of going with another man while she was engaged to him. He could not understand what was happening.

After confirming the news, he realized he had no choice but to leave her. He felt very sad. What was he going to do now with the great love he felt for Mary, if she did not feel the same? His head was pounding and he lay down to rest awhile.

While he was sleeping, and still concerned about Mary's pregnancy, he saw an angel in his dreams who told him, "Joseph, do not be afraid to accept Mary in your house as your wife. She is pregnant by God's action. She is still a virgin. You will name the baby Jesus. He will save the people from their sins."

Suddenly, Joseph's sleep was calm and relaxed. He no longer felt anxious and could rest. When he woke, he ran to Mary's house to take her into his home.

Mary and Elizabeth Meet

Once everything was clear between Joseph and Mary, she set out on a journey to visit Elizabeth, her cousin, who lived in a small town of Judea. When she arrived at Elizabeth's house, Mary greeted her with a big hug. Elizabeth said to Mary, "God has decided to work wonders for the people through the son you have in your womb. Blessed you are among women. What an honor that the mother of my Lord should come to visit me! As soon as you greeted me, the child in my womb jumped for joy."

"Don't you realize, Elizabeth, the wonder that has happened in us? Who am I that the Lord has chosen me for such an important mission?"

"The God of our ancestors, Abraham, Jacob, and David, who has taken down the most powerful kings from their thrones, has dispersed the proud-hearted, has filled the poor with good things, and has left the rich empty-handed. The God who has protected our people since the beginning of time has looked upon me, who am nothing. Truly we have a great God who favors the humble."

The two cousins talked about their situation over and over. They were not that sure what was really happening to them. Mary stayed with Elizabeth for a few weeks. Afterward she returned to Nazareth with Joseph. Soon the time arrived for Elizabeth to have her baby; eight days after the birth, they took him to the Temple to be circumcised. Elizabeth insisted he be named John and, still unable to speak, Zechariah confirmed it in writing.

As soon as they had named the baby, Zechariah was able to speak again and he prophesied, saying, "Blessed be God, who has sent this Savior. This child will go before the Lord to prepare his coming and will be called Prophet of the Most High."

As the child grew up, he also grew in intelligence and kindness.

Journey to Bethlehem

It was then that Caesar of Rome wanted to know how many people there were in his empire. So the head of every family had to travel to the city of his parents' origin in order to be counted in the census. And Caesar issued an edict for everyone to do exactly that. This was the least convenient of times because Mary was almost due to give birth, and it would not be good for her to travel at that time.

Nonetheless they set on their way to Bethlehem, a town of Judea, to register in the census there. Joseph's parents, descendants of David, were from that town.

The journey was not easy for Mary but, after much effort and toil, they arrived in Bethlehem. Now they could rest and refresh themselves.

Bethlehem, however, was full of people who had gone there for the same reason as Mary and Joseph. They went to several shelters and an inn, but it was all in vain: there was no room. Then Mary started feeling labor pains and Joseph quickly looked for a solution: he took her to a shepherd's shelter and, as soon as they got there, Jesus was born.

Angels and Shepherds

This was not exactly how Mary had imagined that Jesus—the Savior of the world—would be born. But the joy of his birth surpassed any inconvenience. Joseph went to fetch water to wash the baby. Once he was clean and wrapped in swaddling clothes, they put him in a manger they used for a cradle.

There were shepherds in that region who spent the night outside watching their flock. Suddenly, in the midst of a great light, an angel of God appeared to them and told them, "I bring you good news. Today in Bethlehem was born the child who will save the people. It is Jesus, your Lord."

The sudden apparition in the middle of the night surprised the shepherds who were half asleep, and they were afraid. The angel realized and said to them, "Don't be afraid. I am an angel of the Lord. You will find the newborn baby wrapped in swaddling clothes and lying in a manger."

And then a group of angels joined the first one, proclaiming, "Glory to God! Glory to God! May the people favored by the Lord be filled with peace."

The shepherds hurried to look for the baby and, among the swaddling clothes, they saw Jesus placidly sleeping. After seeing him, they went to communicate the great news to the rest, praising the power of God.

The Wise Men from the East

To show how Jesus was born for all peoples, the following account is given:

In the meantime three wise men coming from the East arrived in Jerusalem. They wanted to find out where Jesus had been born, so they went to ask King Herod.

"We have followed a star from the East to worship the king of the Jews, who was born today. Where was he born? Tell us."

Herod went to consult the priests and informed the wise men of what they had said.

"It must have been in Bethlehem of Judea. Go, and when you find him, come back and tell me so that I can also go to worship him."

The wise men thanked Herod. It was not difficult to find Jesus in Bethlehem, for the star led them from Jerusalem to the place where Jesus was born. Arriving, they adored Jesus and presented their gifts: gold because he was a king, incense because he was God, and myrrh because he was human. Through a dream they were warned not to go back and tell Herod where Jesus was, so they took another route to return home.

The Children, Innocent Victims

As soon as the wise men had left, Joseph fell asleep. He needed to rest from the many emotions of the night, more than from the long journey. But he did not rest long. In his dream God spoke to him saying, "Flee to Egypt. Herod wants to kill the child."

Immediately, Joseph took Mary and the baby and fled to Egypt.

When Herod found out that the wise men had gone another way without telling him, he was enraged. He was upset because he feared that a certain king of the Jews was living and could take his throne away from him. So, to be on the safe side, he made a decision. He ordered his soldiers, "Kill every child under two years old from Bethlehem and the surrounding areas."

The bloodiest of cruelties came upon Bethlehem. Cries, excuses, and explanations were all for naught.

Jesus' family stayed in Egypt until God appeared again in Joseph's dreams to tell him they could return home because Herod was dead. Happy to be able to return home, they got on the road back to Nazareth.

Jesus Is Taken to the Temple

It was normal to consecrate the first-born male of each family to God. Jesus' parents took him to the Temple to present him to the Lord and so fulfill the Law.

When they were entering the Temple, they met old Simeon. He took Jesus in his arms and proclaimed, "Now, Lord, I can die in peace, because I have seen the child who will be the salvation of Israel and will show the truth to other nations."

And he addressed Mary saying, "Your son will be a sign of struggle and contradiction. And the pain will pierce your soul as with a sharp sword."

Jesus' parents were surprised to hear that of their son. But the people in the Temple had not finished speaking. Anna, a prophetess who was also in the Temple at that time, did not cease praising God. She told everyone that the child would be the liberator of Israel.

As he was growing up in Nazareth, Jesus combined his love for studying with learning his father's trade as a carpenter. This allowed Jesus to learn the trade well enough to be able to manage the workshop later on.

What Was Jesus' Language?

Jesus normally spoke Aramaic, which was the language used in Palestine at the time. He also knew Hebrew well, the language in which almost all the books of the Old Testament were written. By the time he was twelve, Jesus was able to have discussions with the teachers of the Law in the Temple, quoting texts from sacred Scripture. But it seems that Jesus also knew and expressed himself in Greek, the international language of the times spoken by the people in some of the regions Jesus would later visit—such as the Decapolis (east of Jordan) and some of the lands on the Mediterranean coast. Perhaps he even knew Latin, the language of the Romans who dominated the country. On his cross there was a sign that read: "Jesus, king of the Jews," written in Hebrew, Greek, and Latin.

Jesus, Lost

Each year, for the Passover feast, the family went to Jerusalem. And so they went when Jesus was twelve years old. On the return to Nazareth, both Joseph and Mary thought that Jesus was with the family, somewhere in the procession; but he was not. That night they began searching for him, but they could not find him; he was not with anyone in the caravan returning to Galilee. So, they decided to return to Jerusalem immediately. However, traveling at night was not advisable because they were in danger of being attacked by bandits, so they camped for the night.

They looked everywhere for Jesus, but could not find him anywhere. Nor did they find him the following day. However much they asked—and they searched for him high and low—they did not find him. They were worried. Perhaps something bad had happened to him. Would they ever see him again? Everyone had their hearts in their hands. On the third day they passed by the Temple, and they found him inside, amidst the teachers of the Law, discussing the sacred Scriptures with them.

Mary hugged him.

"My son, why have you done this to us? Don't you realize I was worried to death?"

Jesus responded, "You shouldn't have worried about me, or concerned yourselves with looking for me. I have passed the time conversing with the priests and studying the Scriptures."

Then he returned home with them to Nazareth, where he continued to grow into an intelligent and good person.

The School in Palestine

According to the Old Testament, there were no formal schools in Israel. Children were taught at home, especially about religion and the history and traditions of Israel. The male children learned a trade from their fathers, while the female children learned domestic chores such as cooking, weaving, and sewing.

After the Exile in Babylon synagogues were born, primarily in places where people lived too far from Jerusalem to frequently travel to the Temple. Each Sabbath they would gather in the synagogue to listen to Bible readings and to pray. Lessons were also offered in the synagogue for children older than six. They were modeled after the old nations, such as the Sumerians and the Egyptians, who almost always had schools in the temples where the young people studied grammar and literature, natural sciences, mathematics, geography, and astronomy.

In the synagogue schools, the principal teachings were the Law of Moses and the Torah, from which they studied history, geography, and language, but without forgetting other ideas. The teachers were those in charge of the synagogue, although they also taught the scribes, who were also called teachers of the Law or rabbis.

John Begins to Preach

Twenty years had already gone by. John the Baptist lived in the desert, where he wore camel's skin and ate honey and locusts. He prayed and meditated in the desert until one day he received a divine summons that he should begin preaching.

And he did so in this way: "Repent from your sins. Don't think that just being descendants of Abraham will be enough to save you. In the same way that a tree that does not bear fruit is cut down, you will be punished if you do evil."

The tax collectors at the time were called publicans. They asked, "What should we do to be saved?"

"Collect what is due and don't take advantage by keeping part for yourselves," John answered.

And the soldiers asked, "And we, what do we have to do?"

"Do not denounce those who don't deserve it. Be satisfied with your wages and don't make anybody give you money in exchange for protection."

Then he addressed everyone, "The rest of you, share what you have—clothes and food—with those who need it."

Many wanted John to baptize them as a sign of repentance and purification. Others asked, "Are you the Christ, the savior of Israel, or do we have to wait for another?"

"I am not the Christ. I only baptize you with water. But the one coming behind me will have more power than fire or lightning. I am so insignificant by his side that I wouldn't even dare to undo the strap of his sandals," John answered.

The Baptism of Jesus

Then Jesus went to the River Jordan, the place where John was baptizing, to receive baptism. Jesus had listened to and learned a lot from John because, in addition to being his cousin, Jesus recognized him as a prophet. They were close. Jesus asked to be baptized, fully aware of what he was doing.

And John exclaimed, "Behold the man I was speaking about."

Jesus went into the water to be baptized, but John refused to baptize him, saying, "You should be baptizing me, and you come to be baptized?"

"Do it, John. God wants it this way," Jesus told John.

Overcoming his hesitation, John baptized Jesus. The Spirit of God, through baptism, came into Jesus. Even his expression changed and his face shone. All were looking at Jesus because of the way John had spoken about him. After the baptism, Jesus went to the desert to pray.

Jesus Is Tempted

Jesus had been fasting for over forty days. This was a hard trial, and Jesus, like any other man, also knew times of discouragement, in which he must have even thought of giving up his mission. This doubt is presented as a dialogue with the devil:

The devil came before Jesus and, resolved to make him sin, proposed, "Don't you claim to be God's son? Then you must have some kind of power, right? Besides, you are hungry. Why would a powerful man like you need to go hungry? Tell this rock to become bread," he said, pointing to one, "and then we will believe in your power."

But Jesus wanted to show that there are more important things than the need for food, even after so many days of fasting.

On the other hand, the devil was pushing him to make a show of his power. But that was not Jesus' mission; he would only do it when it was absolutely necessary. So he said, "It is written in the Scriptures: 'Man does not live by bread alone.'"

Then the devil took him to the highest tower in the Temple and said, "You must surely have made up that story about being the son of God. If you were, you wouldn't hesitate to throw yourself from this tower, since Scriptures also say that God will protect you from all harm."

"Do you think I am an acrobat to entertain you? You will not tempt the Lord, your God," Jesus cut him off abruptly.

The devil still insisted a third time. From the highest point in the region he showed Jesus all the kingdoms of this world, and said, "I will give you all these kingdoms you see, and the glory of being the most powerful in the world. You only have to do one thing: kneel before me."

"Do you really think I will bend before the evil you represent for any material possession? Let me remind you of another Scripture verse that you have forgotten: 'Adore the Lord, your God, and serve him alone,'" Jesus warned him.

Then the devil left ranting and raving, because he had not been able to trick Jesus.

Jesus' First Disciples

A little later the prophet John, who continued to baptize, saw Jesus passing by and, unable to control himself, proclaimed so that everyone could hear, "Behold the Lamb of God. He will teach you the way to go to the kingdom of God."

Two of John's disciples who were there followed Jesus until he turned around and asked them, "What do you want? Why are you following me?"

"Teacher, where do you live?"

From these words Jesus understood that those two men wanted to learn and, with a kind smile, he said to them, "Come with me and you'll see."

They stayed with him all day, listening to his teachings. At the end, Andrew, one of the two young men, went to look for his brother Simon, and explained to him, "We have found the Messiah, the one sent by God."

And he introduced Simon to Jesus, who said to him, "Your name is Simon, but from now on your name will be Peter, which means rock, and you will be the surest support, hard as a stone, for my teachings."

Then they all went together to Bethsaida, the brothers' hometown. Jesus met Philip there, and he said to him, "Follow me!"

And Philip did so.

Mary and Jesus Go to a Wedding

A few days later there was a wedding in Cana of Galilee. Jesus, his mother, and his disciples were among the guests.

It so happened that, halfway through the banquet, the hosts ran out of wine. Mary, who realized what a hard time the bride and groom must be going through, said to Jesus, "They have run out of wine."

"Providing wine is not our responsibility. I don't know why you are telling me this," Jesus replied.

But, without paying any attention to Jesus' reluctance, Mary said to the servants, "Do as he tells you."

There were six empty jars and Jesus ordered the servants to fill the jars with water. When they did so, Jesus told them, "Take the wine to the steward to be tested."

When the steward tried it, he said to the groom, "Don't you ever do this again; you have served the worst wine first and you have saved the best for last. Don't you realize that, if you serve the best wine first, the guests are happier? When they are already filled, you serve the worst."

When people realized what Jesus had done, many believed in him.

In the Synagogue of Nazareth

One Sabbath, Jesus happened to be in Nazareth and he went to the synagogue, the place where the Scriptures were read and interpreted.

After reading a passage, Jesus explained its meaning. But the congregation was not listening because Jesus was not a wise scholar; he was only the son of Joseph, a simple carpenter.

Jesus noticed their attitude and said to them, "No one is a prophet in his own land. Those who should believe in him most, since they have always known him, turn their backs on him. There are examples in Scriptures of foreigners who accept the prophets who have been rejected in their homeland, as is the case here today."

These words were not well received by the people of Nazareth. They felt hurt and wanted to grab Jesus and throw him from a high mountain, but he stole away quietly.

Jesus had begun a period of preaching which forced him to leave the carpenter's workshop, his home, and his town.

His family did not quite agree with his decision. He was the son of a carpenter and had to take his father's place, for Joseph had died. They did not like the fact that, instead of working at home, Jesus would go around the land preaching.

The Prophets or Jesus?

Jesus' disciples did not quite understand his words, and so they asked, "Teacher, you say things that are very different from what the prophets had said. What should we do? Do we have to forget the words of the prophets?"

"I haven't said any such thing. I have not come to abolish the sacred Law or the prophets. I have come to improve them. All the details in Scripture will be carried out as planned. Those who explain the meaning of the Law are the scribes or teachers of the Law. According to the Pharisees, they themselves are the ones who follow the Law more faithfully. Both the former and the latter say they defend the Law, but they adapt it as they see fit if they think it will benefit them. You must not imitate them. You must be more honest than they. If you are, you will know the Law as it should be understood," Jesus explained.

First Healings by Jesus

After this, they went on their way to Capernaum, a Galilean city where Jesus taught in the synagogue. In that synagogue there was a man possessed by the devil, who, upon hearing Jesus, cried out, "Away, get out of here! There is nothing between us, Jesus of Nazareth! I know who you are. You are the Holy One of God."

"Quiet! Come out of this man!" Jesus commanded.

With great convulsions, the devil came out of that man without harming him. Those present were amazed and said, "We realized that, when he was interpreting the Scriptures, he did so with authority. But, who is he that even the devils obey?"

The news spread like wildfire and Jesus gained fame in that area. Then, they went to the house of Peter's mother-in-law, who was sick in bed, and the word of Jesus made her fever go away. The woman rose and gratefully began to serve them. In the evening, all those who had sick people at home brought them over so that Jesus could cure them; Jesus laid hands on them and they were healed. Seeing this, people believed in Jesus.

Catch Anything?

Jesus' fame was growing. On a certain occasion, they were by Lake Genesareth. There were so many people that there was not any more room, and the only way to prevent people from crowding around him was for Jesus to preach from a boat a few yards off shore. From the boat he was teaching the Word of God.

When he finished speaking, he told Simon, who was the owner of the boat, "Row in and cast your nets to fish."

"Master, we have worked all night and we haven't caught anything; but we will do as you say," Simon replied.

After a while, Simon wanted to take the nets out of the water, but he could not lift them and had to ask the fishermen on the other boat for help. They were more and more amazed because they filled both boats with fish until the boats were about to sink with the weight.

Then Simon—or Peter if you wish—who had hesitated to cast the nets, knelt before Jesus and said, "Lord, don't get near me, for I am a sinner."

The Paralyzed Man's Ingenuity to Reach Jesus

Jesus had disembarked when he saw two brothers, James and John, sons of Zebedee, who were repairing their nets: then he called them over and immediately they left their boats and their families and followed him.

In one of the cities where Jesus was preaching there was a man sick with leprosy—an incurable disease at the time. This man bowed before Jesus and said, "Jesus, if you choose, you can cure me."

A few words from Jesus were enough to heal him. Full of happiness, the man went to the Temple to present the offering that the Law commanded, as Jesus told him to do.

In another city people were anxiously waiting to hear Jesus. There were Pharisees and scribes—teachers of the Law—from all over the country. The room was packed and there was no way to reach the place where Jesus stood. A few men were carrying a paralyzed man to be cured; unable to find a better solution, they removed some tiles from the roof and lowered the stretcher with ropes, thus placing the man in the middle of the room.

Jesus realized that the man had overcome many obstacles to reach him, and, because at that time people believed that physical disabilities were consequences of sins, he said to the man, "Your sins are forgiven."

Immediately a disapproving murmur rose in the room. The Pharisees said to one another, "This is an insult to God, a blasphemy. No one can forgive sins but God alone."

Hearing them, Jesus insisted, "What do you think is easier: to forgive sins or to make this man walk? So that you know I can forgive sins," he said to the paralyzed man, "rise, take your stretcher, and go home."

The man did as Jesus told him and everyone was astonished to see him walk.

Jesus Changes Meaningless Customs and Norms

After these events, Jesus saw Levi, a publican, or tax collector, who was sitting in his office. Levi was not a Jew. His job was to collect taxes for the emperor. In that society, he was considered an undesirable person because, in addition to helping the Roman oppressors, he did not practice the Jewish religion. Even so, Jesus asked Levi to follow him; immediately Levi left everything and went with Jesus.

Although some of the important persons of that time thought that Jesus associated with unsavory characters, Jesus wanted to include a pagan among his followers, since his message was for everyone who wished to hear it.

The tax collector offered him a great banquet attended by many non-Jewish people. For this reason, the Pharisees criticized Jesus, "Why do you eat with sinners?"

And Jesus answered, "I am a doctor, and the sinners are the sick people. In the same way that healthy people do not need a doctor, it is sinners, not good people, who need me."

A few days later, on the Sabbath—the day on which the Law imposes absolute rest—Jesus was teaching in the synagogue. There was a man there whose right hand was paralyzed. The teachers of the Law and the Pharisees—the important men of the times—were waiting for Jesus to do something against the Law so they could catch him and accuse him of something.

Despite this, Jesus asked them, "Is there anyone among you who, having one of his sheep fall into a well on the Sabbath, wouldn't take it out just because it is a day of rest?" Silence was all he got for an answer. "Therefore, good can be done on the Sabbath."

Addressing the man with the paralyzed hand, he said, "Stand and stretch out your hand."

The man did so, and his hand regained movement. The faithful people thanked God, while the Pharisees wanted Jesus to disappear. The Pharisees met and discussed how to get rid of him—for Jesus' teachings, which they did not accept, were popular among the people.

The Group Closest to Jesus

A few days later, Jesus went to the mountain to pray. The following day, after praying all night, he called the disciples—those who considered him their teacher—and chose twelve from among them—the same number as the tribes of Israel—whom he called apostles. Jesus chose the brothers Peter and Andrew; the brothers James and John; Philip; Bartholomew; Matthew—who was the tax collector Levi, who had changed his name—Thomas; James, the son of Alpheus; Simon the Zealot; Jude, the son of James; and Judas Iscariot.

The apostles combined their work with the task of following Jesus. Only Matthew quit his job because it was not respectable.

Some rich women who believed in Jesus' teachings also collaborated with the cause, providing the means for the preacher's survival.

Then Jesus went to the people who were waiting for him. It was a huge crowd, hailing not only from Israel but also from beyond the borders. They brought sick people to him and he healed them; they presented people possessed by the devil, and he expelled the evil spirits from them.

The Main Objective: Happiness

Raising his arms, Jesus said, "Don't be sad about your situation, for happiness doesn't come from material goods.

"Happy are the poor in spirit because they are poor in their hearts and make the effort to be sincere. Happy, also, are those who are persecuted for defending kindness. All those people will have a place near God. Happy, also, are the humble, who don't think themselves superior to anyone; those who honestly accept their mistakes.

"If you follow my teachings—and this will place you in difficult spots at times—the comfort you will receive will make you forget the bad times, and you will be happy.

"Happy are those who are straightforward, those who don't accept the mediocrity of their environment and struggle for justice. They are thirsty for justice and will be satisfied.

"Help those who suffer, those who are going through hard times. When you need it, you will also receive the necessary support.

"'Happy are those who show goodness and are good of heart because they will reach the presence of God.

"Happy are those who work for peace, because they will be considered God's children.

"You will be happy when they insult, persecute, and speak evil of you because you uphold my teachings, because all your sufferings will be rewarded in heaven."

People were amazed to hear him because these were new ideas, different from what the teachers had told them up to that time.

The Law, but Also the Heart

On another occasion, Jesus was teaching his disciples, "Your ancestors have been told: 'Do not kill.' But I tell you: do not get angry or insult each other; let there be peace among you. Even if you want to present an offering to the Lord and you know that someone is mad at you, you have to go and make peace first, so that the offering will be well received by God.

"'Do not break your promises and fulfill what you have promised to the Lord,' is another one of the old commandments. But I tell you, do not swear. Do not put God as witness of your statements; pronouncing God's name is not something to be taken lightly. Simply affirm or deny what you believe.

"'An eye for an eye and a tooth for a tooth,' your ancestors said. This meant that an aggressor had to pay according to the harm he had committed. It is easy to do good to those who have done good to you, but I tell you: Love your enemies and pray for those who speak ill of you. If someone slaps you on one cheek, offer the other one. If you love those who love you, what merit is there in that? Sinners do as much. Do good and love everyone without expecting anything in return and you will receive a reward from God.

"When you do good, or give alms, don't do it so that others can see and praise you. Only God, the Father in heaven, is interested in your good works.

"Do not accumulate treasures on earth, because wherever your treasure is, there will your heart be, too. The true treasure is the one you store in heaven with your good deeds. No one can serve two masters: you cannot serve both God and money. Love for money may make you miss the most important thing: to live according to God's teachings."

A Solid Household

As the prophets had done in times past, Jesus told brief stories—parables—so that the people who listened to him would better understand. He told them this one:

"There was a sensible man who wanted to build himself a house. Since he wanted it to last, he built it upon a rock. The rains came, storms raged, and the winds blew. The house resisted everything because its foundations were solid. Another man, however, decided to build his house on sand. A strong wind and the waters of a flooded river came against it and it immediately collapsed, becoming just a pile of ruins. The man was homeless.

, "Those who listen to my words and practice them are like the man who built his house on rock. Those who listen but don't put them into practice are like the man who built his house on sand."

The Lines Between Good and Evil Are Unclear

He also explained to the people the parable of the weeds and the wheat:

"The kingdom of heaven is like a man who sowed good seeds on his field. While everyone was sleeping, his enemy sowed tares—a poisonous plant that looks like wheat—in the same field. When the plants grew, the servants realized there were weeds among the wheat and told the master, 'There are weeds growing among the wheat. Do you want us to pull them out?'

"'No; don't pull them out yet. You could mistake them and ruin the wheat. When the harvest time comes, you will first gather the weeds to burn, and then the wheat to keep in the barn.'

"I am the sower, and the field is the world; the good seeds are those who do good and the bad seeds are those who do evil; the enemy is the devil. The harvest comes as the end of the world will arrive, and my angels will be the harvesters. All the wrongdoers, separated by the angels, will go to the fire, but the good people will be welcomed in the Father's house.

"So, be merciful—forgive, help, aid—as your Father is merciful. Do not judge, and you will not be judged; do not condemn, and you will not be condemned; forgive and you will be forgiven; give, and much will be given to you. Know that you will be measured with the same measure you use for others. Much will be demanded of you if you have been very demanding, and you will receive generosity if you have been generous."

How Easy It Is to See Faults in Others!

On another occasion, the disciples were accusing one another of not following the word of God correctly. Jesus warned them, "Do not do like the one who wanted to remove a speck from his friend's eye and did not realize he had a beam in his own. It is easier to see the faults of others than one's own. First remove the beam from your eye, your own faults, and then you will be able to help others take the specks from their eyes.

"Good deeds come from a good heart; but evil deeds come out of a bad heart. A tree is known by its fruits: no good tree gives bad fruits. A bad tree gives bad fruits and the good tree gives good fruits."

When he finished all these explanations, he dismissed the crowds.

Conversation with a Samaritan Woman

Jesus and his disciples started on their way from Judea to Galilee, and they had to go across Samaria. When they reached the Samaritan town of Sychar, Jesus, who was tired, sat down by Jacob's well while his disciples went to buy some food. Then a woman came to draw water from the well. Once she had done it, Jesus asked her for water. She was surprised because Jews and Samaritans did not talk to each other.

She asked, "How come you, a Jew, are asking me, a Samaritan, for water?"

"If you knew who I am, you would be the one asking me for living water. Such is the word of God, like water that satisfies so you would never be thirsty again. If you drink of your water, you will be thirsty again. But if you drink of my water, you will have a spring inside you and will never be thirsty again."

"Give me some of that water," the Samaritan requested, "so I will not need to come back to this well."

"Go and fetch your husband and come back," Jesus told her.

"I don't have a husband," the woman replied.

"You are right, because you have had five husbands and the one who is with you now is not your husband," Jesus said.

"I see that you foretell things. Are you a prophet? If you are, you must know where we have to worship God. Our parents did it on this mountain, but you, Jews, say that God must be worshiped in Jerusalem."

"The time has come when you will not worship God on this mountain or in Jerusalem. God is a spirit, and wants to be worshiped, as a spirit, within the heart of each person."

The woman said, "I know the Messiah, the Christ, is to come and he will reveal everything."

"I am the one," Jesus revealed.

We Had to Get Along with These People?

Then, nervously, the woman left behind her jug and went into town crying out, "Come, come. You will see a man who is the Christ."

At that time the disciples returned and offered food to Jesus. But he told them, "I have food that you don't know about."

The disciples were puzzled and said to one another, "Perhaps someone has brought him food."

Jesus clarified, "My food is doing the will of my Father, who sent me from heaven to carry out his work of salvation. Do you think the harvest time is still far away? Raise your eyes and you will see the time to harvest has come."

The Samaritan woman then arrived with a group of people who believed in him from what she had told them. Those people were like the wheat to be gathered; that is why Jesus had spoken about the harvest.

The Samaritans invited Jesus to stay with them and he taught them for two days. After that time, the Samaritans told the woman at the well, "We no longer believe because you told us, but because we have heard him and are convinced that he is the Messiah."

From the Invading Army—A Person of Faith

Afterward, Jesus continued on his journey until he was near Capernaum. In that city there was a centurion—a Roman army officer—whose dearly beloved servant was about to die. In order to prevent this from happening, the centurion sent a group of elders to Jesus to tell him, "Lord, come to save the centurion's servant. He deserves it for he is a good man. He himself has had a synagogue built."

Jesus agreed and went to the centurion's house. When they were near, some of the centurion's friends came running and said on his behalf, "Lord, it is not necessary for you to come to my house. I am not worthy enough for you to enter. I have not come out to meet you because I don't believe I'm worthy of coming before you. Just say a word and my servant will be healed."

Even Jesus was amazed at the centurion's trust. Then he addressed those who were with him and said, "Never, in all of Israel, have I found anyone with such a strong faith."

When they returned home, the messengers found the servant healed.

Messengers from John

Some time later, Jesus and his disciples were about to enter Nain when they ran into a funeral procession. A widow was about to bury her only son. Jesus felt compassion. He went near the coffin and said, "Boy, I command you. Rise up!"

Then the dead boy rose and started to talk. Jesus gave him to his mother, who was now crying harder than before, but she was weeping with joy. In the meantime, people proclaimed that God had visited his people.

All of Jesus' works had reached John's ears, and he decided to send two of his disciples to Jesus to ask him, "Are you the one who is to come, or should we wait for another?"

At that time, Jesus healed many sick people, and he said to John's messengers, "Go and tell John what you have seen: the blind recover their sight, the lame walk, the lepers are healed, the deaf hear, the dead rise, and the poor are given the Good News."

The disciples told John what they had seen and heard.

In the House of Simon, the Pharisee

After these events Simon, a Pharisee, invited Jesus to dinner. A woman who had a reputation as a sinner lived in the city, and, hearing that Jesus was at Simon's house, she went there. She was carrying a flask with perfume. Crying, she began to bathe Jesus' feet with her tears, wiping them with her hair. She kissed them and anointed them with the perfume.

The Pharisee was thinking, "If Jesus knew this woman is a sinner, he wouldn't allow her to touch him."

Then Jesus addressed Simon, "Look, Simon. There was a lender who had two debtors. One owed him five hundred days in wages and the other owed fifty. But since they couldn't pay, he forgave the debt. Which of the two do you think would be more grateful?"

"The one who was forgiven more."

"That's right. This woman has done for me what you hadn't done. She has welcomed me better than you. She deserves forgiveness for her sins because she has loved much."

And he told her, "Woman, your sins are forgiven. Go in peace."

The Seed and the Good Ground

On another occasion, he was in front of a great crowd and explained this parable:

"A sower went to sow his seed. A part of it fell by the wayside, but it was trampled upon and the birds ate it. Some seed fell on rocks, and they dried up for lack of moisture. Others fell on thorns, and, growing near them, they choked. The rest fell on good ground and produced a great amount of fruit.

"The seed is the Word of God. The ones that fall by the wayside are taken by the devil, so that they won't believe or be saved. The ones that fall on rock are those who at first believe, but they have no roots; after practicing the Word of God for a while, they quit. The ones that fall among thorns represent those who have heard, but they feel trapped by the riches and pleasures of life. Those that fall on good ground are those who have accepted the Word of God and put it in practice; their deeds are good, like the fruit of the seeds."

The Mother and the Brothers of Jesus

Then Jesus' mother and some of his relatives came forward. They wanted to take him home because they did not like his lifestyle or the news they were receiving about him. But they could not get close to him because of the crowds.

Then he said, "Who are my mother and my brothers and my sisters? Those who listen to the Word of God and put it in practice."

Jesus meant that the bonds created by believing in the same God are as important, if not more so, than blood ties among brothers and sisters, or even one's own mother.

A few days later, Jesus was on a boat with his disciples, and he asked them to go to the other shore. While they were sailing, Jesus fell asleep. Suddenly there was a big storm over the lake, and the waves were so big that it seemed the boat was going to sink. The disciples woke Jesus up and said, "Teacher! Teacher! We are sinking!"

He Has Control over the Wind, the Water, and Demons. . . . Who Is He?

Waking up, Jesus spoke to the waves and the wind. Instantly, everything calmed down. His disciples were astonished when they saw that the waters and the wind obeyed him.

Later, they came to the region of Gerasenes. Coming on land, a man possessed by demons came to meet them. He was homeless and practically naked, and wandered among the tombs in the cemetery. Nothing could hold him back. He broke through chains, shackles, everything.

The demon spoke to Jesus from inside the man, saying, "Don't bother me, Son of the Most High. If you make me leave this man, let me at least go into that herd of pigs."

Jesus allowed it, and the pigs threw themselves down a cliff to the lake where they drowned. Everyone in the city heard about this event. They went to see what had happened and found the man who had been possessed. The man was now calmly speaking to Jesus.

This change shocked them, and, instead of believing in Jesus, they asked him to leave. Jesus went on to the boat and began his homeward journey.

There Are Different Ways to Touch

Reaching the other shore, a crowd was waiting for him. At that time Jairus, the chief of the synagogue, came to him and said, "Lord, come to my house. My only daughter is dying. Save her!"

Jesus then went to Jairus' house. He was surrounded by so many people that they were pressing on him and he could barely walk. Suddenly Jesus stopped and asked, "Who has touched me?"

"Lord, people are pushing all over, and you ask who has touched you?" the disciples asked.

"Yes, I have felt the power come out of me."

There was a very tense moment, but it did not last long. A woman fell to his feet and confessed, "Lord, I am suffering from hemorrhages. No remedy has done me any good, and I thought to myself, 'If I could only touch his garment, I would be healed.' That's why I touched you."

"Your faith has saved you. You can go in peace."

The woman left healthy and happy.

Has Jairus' Daughter Died?

Then some servants from Jairus' house came and said to him, "Your daughter is dead. Don't bother the master any more."

Jesus said to him, "Don't worry. You only have to have faith and she will be saved."

When they got to the house, everyone was weeping and sobbing, but Jesus said to them, "Why are you crying? The child is only sleeping."

Those who were there, who had seen her dead, laughed at him when they heard those words.

Jesus took the girl by the hand and said, "Little girl, rise up!"

Her spirit came back to her, and she rose immediately. Then Jesus told her parents to give her something to eat. Her parents were astonished and at the same time very grateful to Jesus for having returned their only daughter to them.

Jesus Sent His Apostles

After the apostles had experienced so much with Jesus, he decided to send them off to proclaim the Word of God. He gave them powers to cure sick people and to expel demons.

He gave them advice, saying, "Don't take anything for your journey: no bread, no walking staff, not even a change of clothes. When you go into a house, stay there. If they don't want to receive you, shake the dust off your feet as a testimony against them. Go and preach the Good News."

Some Clarifications for the Pharisees

On another occasion, the Pharisees went to Jesus and asked him, "How come your disciples do not keep the Law and don't wash their hands before eating?"

Jesus took advantage of this question to teach the crowds gathered, "You, Pharisees, try to decide between what is pure and what is not according to the Law. It is not what goes into the mouth of a person that contaminates him or her, but what comes out of a person. Everything that goes into the mouth ends up in the stomach and then goes out; the words that come out of a mouth, however, come from the heart. From the heart can come bad wishes leading to evil actions, hatred, robberies, murders, adultery. This contaminates a person. Eating without washing one's hands doesn't contaminate anybody."

Another time he was speaking with the Pharisees about the bread from heaven during the time of Moses. Jesus declared, "I am the bread of life. Whoever comes to me will not go hungry and whoever believes in me will never be thirsty."

With these words Jesus meant that faith and the practice of God's word cause such a feeling of fullness that it is comparable to being satisfied by food and drink. That is why one cannot feel hunger or thirst: whoever is full does not need anything else.

Some Leave

The Pharisees were scandalized when they heard Jesus speak this way, and it confirmed their decision to get rid of him. They did not care if Jesus explained his words, since they were only looking for excuses to condemn him.

Right after the scandal caused by Jesus' words, some left his company. Then Jesus asked his apostles, "Do you also want to leave me?"

Simon Peter asked, "Lord, where would we go? Only you have words of eternal life and we believe you are the holy one of God."

The People Have So Much to Learn from the Canaanite!

Then Jesus withdrew into the region of Tyre and Sidon. There he met a Canaanite woman, who cried out to him, "Have pity on me, Lord, Son of David. My daughter is possessed by a demon. Help me, drive the demon out from her."

Jesus did not pay attention, but, since she would not keep quiet, the disciples said to him, "See what she wants since she comes shouting after us."

"I have only been sent to the sinners of the house of Israel," Jesus answered.

Meanwhile, she had arrived, and kneeling before Jesus she said, "Help me, Lord! Help me!"

"It is not right for me to help you instead of helping my own people. That would be like throwing the bread of the children to the dogs," Jesus replied.

"But dogs also eat the crumbs that fall from their masters' tables. Couldn't I just get a little of your people's surplus?" the woman insisted.

"You are persistent and have a great faith. Let it be done as you wish," Jesus granted.

And from then on, the demon never again bothered her daughter.

Marriage and Divorce

Another day the Pharisees wanted to put Jesus in a bind. They said to him, "Is it right to send a wife away for any reason?"

"Haven't you read that God made them man and woman, and said, 'The man will join his wife and both will be just one?' So, what God has joined, let no one tear apart," Jesus explained.

"Why then, did Moses command an act of divorce in order to send a wife away?" they insisted.

"Moses allowed it because of the hardness of your hearts, but it wasn't that way in the beginning."

When the Pharisees left, the disciples said to him, "If such is the situation of the man with a woman, isn't it better not to get married?" they asked.

"Whether or not to get married is each person's decision. Each person should be free to do as he or she wishes. And those who decide to give up marriage to dedicate themselves fully to extending the kingdom of God should be free to do so, also."

Equality in the Reign of God

Jesus told this parable to explain the kingdom of heaven:

"What happens with the reign of heaven is similar to what happened to the owner of a vineyard. The owner went out early to hire workers for his vineyard. After finding them, they agreed he would pay them a daily wage. He went out at noon again and hired more workers and said to them:

"'You too can go to my vineyard and I will pay you fairly.'

"The owner went out later and again hired more workers for his vineyard. Even in the afternoon he did the same with some who had not worked the whole day.

"At the end of the day, he paid the workers. He started with the last ones and gave them a daily wage each. Afterward, he paid the same to those he had hired a few hours earlier. And then he paid the ones before them. When he got to the first ones, they thought they would be getting more, but they only received the daily wage, just like the rest.

"Then the first workers complained, saying, 'The last ones only worked for an hour, and they have gotten the same as us, who have endured the heat and the effort all day.'

"The owner said, 'Didn't we agree that I would pay you a daily wage? I am just giving you what we agreed on. I am not committing any injustice. If I want to give the last one the same as the first, that is not your business. Can't I do as I please with my money?'"

Jesus concluded, "In the reign of God the first ones will receive the same reward as the last ones, just as in the vineyard of the parable."

Loving Above External Norms

On another occasion, a Pharisee asked Jesus, "Teacher, what is the greatest commandment of the Law?"

Jesus answered, "Love the Lord, your God, with all your heart. This is the first and the most important. The second is very similar: Love your neighbor as yourself. These two commandments summarize the Law and the teachings of the prophets."

The presence of the Pharisees allowed people to realize the way the teachers of the Law and the Pharisees acted.

"Woe to you, teachers of the Law, hypocrites! You will neither go into the kingdom of heaven nor let others enter. You are like blind guides who manipulate the Law to suit your needs. You fulfill the external precepts of the Law, pay your dues to the Temple, but forget the most important things: faithfulness, justice, and mercy.

"If one of you doesn't fulfill the slightest detail of the worship as the Law prescribes, you don't allow it. However, you don't care if workers are swindled, the poor are despised, or the Commandments of God are ignored.

"It is like straining a mosquito out of your water but then swallowing a camel.

"You act like one who cleaned the outside of his cup but left the inside dirty: you only want your outside to appear clean, but inside you are full of corruption.

"You seem to be good in the eyes of others, but inside you are full of hypocrisy and evil. You are like whitewashed sepulchers, nice on the outside, and full of rottenness and death inside.

"You are like vipers; you are in charge of keeping the tombs of the prophets clean and nice, but when someone comes before you in truth, you don't waste any time in sending him to the tomb. But I will have my Father in heaven hold you accountable for all this when you ask to enter the kingdom of heaven."

Always Watchful

Then, addressing his disciples, he explained the following parable:

"Look. There were ten girls who went out with their lamps to wait for the bridegroom. Five of them were careless and the other five were careful. The first ones did not take oil for their lamps, while the others did. Since the bridegroom did not arrive on time and it was late, they fell asleep.

"At midnight, they heard him coming and woke up. The neglectful ones realized that they did not have enough oil and asked the prepared ones to share. But the careful ones thought that no one would have enough if they shared, so they sent the others to buy some.

"While they were gone buying more oil, the bridegroom arrived. The ones who were prepared went into the wedding with him, and the door was closed. When the others arrived, the bridegroom wouldn't even let them come in.

"You must always be watchful, because you don't know the day or the hour in which you will be called to go into the kingdom of God. If death arrives and doesn't find you ready and clean of heart, as happened to the careless girls, you will be left out of the kingdom of heaven."

The Children and the Neighbor

A little later, Jesus realized that the disciples were arguing among themselves. He got closer and heard them discussing who would be the most important among them. Jesus joined the conversation.

"Anyone who welcomes this child," and he took one who was near by, "welcomes me, and whoever welcomes me, welcomes the one who sent me. The one among you who is as pure of heart as a child, that one will be the most important. The one who becomes the most humble among you and serves the others, that one will be the most important."

A few days later, a teacher of the Law went to look for Jesus and asked him, "Lord, I know I must love my neighbor as myself. But, who is my neighbor?"

Jesus answered him with a parable:

"A man was coming down from Jerusalem to Jericho. Some robbers attacked him, took everything from him, and left him naked and half dead by the wayside. A priest of the Temple went by and did not pay attention. A Levite also went by, looked at him, and kept on going.

"A little later, a Samaritan—one of those foreigners you despise— passed by and nursed his wounds, picked him up, and took him to an inn where they could take care of him. When the Samaritan had to leave, he gave the owner of the inn two silver coins, saying, 'If you have spent more than this, I will pay you when I return.'

"Which one of the three do you think is the neighbor of the attacked man?" Jesus asked.

"The one who showed compassion, picked him up, and took care of him," the teacher of the Law answered.

"You are right," Jesus affirmed. "Go and do the same."

Jesus turned the teacher of the Law's question around because he had only wanted to test Jesus. Jesus explained that one does not have to wait for the neighbor to show up in order to love; you must take on an active attitude and reach out to those neighbors in need.

One Must Leave Time for the Spirit

On another occasion, Jesus had been walking for a long time. He stopped at his friend Martha's house to rest. Martha had a sister named Mary. While Martha was busy trying to serve Jesus, Mary, sitting at Jesus' feet, was listening to his words. Martha complained, "Lord, do you think it is fair that while I am busy preparing everything, Mary is sitting down doing nothing? Tell her to help me."

"Martha, sometimes work doesn't leave any time to listen to the Word of God. It would be better for you not to be so busy serving so you can care for the needs of the spirit. Mary has decided to listen to me. I cannot tell her not to do it, for she has chosen the best part."

Prayer to the Father

Another day, when Jesus was resting with his disciples, they asked him, "Lord, John the Baptist has taught his disciples to pray. Teach us, too."

Jesus told them, "When you pray, don't do like the pagans, who talk and talk. They think they'll be listened to that way. But God already knows what you need, even before you ask. So, do it like this:

"'Our Father in heaven, may all recognize you as God. May your will be done on earth as it is done in heaven, that we may be able to get what we need. Forgive our faults, as we forgive the faults of others against us. Do not place us in a situation where we could do evil, and take us away from what is bad.'"

"And with this prayer, God will grant us whatever we ask?" one of the apostles asked.

"What kind of father among you would give a stone to his son when he asked for bread? Or a serpent instead of a fish, or a scorpion instead of an egg? And if you, who are sinners, give good things to your children, even more so will my heavenly Father give the Holy Spirit to those who ask."

Concern for the Reign

Each one of his actions and words raised great expectations among the simple people. More and more people came to him. One day when he was with a large crowd, he said, "The day will come when acknowledging me as the Son of God will be dangerous. Those who defend me before people will be defended before God, and those who deny me will also be denied before God. Don't be afraid of those who can take away your life but can do nothing against the spirit. You should only fear God, who can condemn the spirit."

When he said that, a man in the crowd presented a problem of inheritance. Jesus answered with a parable:

"There was a rich man whose fields yielded such a huge harvest that he didn't have any space in his silos to store it. Then he thought, 'I will pull my silos down. I will build bigger ones, where I will store the grain. And once I have stored everything, I will enjoy my riches and say to my soul: My soul, you have riches in store for many years: eat, drink, and enjoy life.'

"But that same night, God claimed his soul. And all his goods were good for nothing."

Jesus continued, "The same happens to those who store up material treasures instead of becoming rich in good deeds, which are the riches that God cares about. So, sell all your possessions and give alms to the poor. And you will have a treasure in heaven. If you spend your time storing up treasures, you won't have any time to follow my word.

"May your main concern not be what you will eat or what you will wear. Look at the birds: they don't sow or reap, and God feeds them. Have you seen the lilies of the field worry about how they are going to dress? And yet, not even Solomon in all his splendor was dressed like them. Work for the kingdom of God and all these things will be given to you. Your Father knows what you need.

"I haven't come to bring peace to this earth, but to set it afire. People will be divided against each other: parents against children and children against parents. It is not easy to accept my word or to practice it, but it is inevitable to have problems in a world that behaves badly."

7.
Jesus of Nazareth:
Death and Resurrection

Any Day Is a Good Day to Do Good

After a time, Jesus was teaching in the synagogue. One day there was a sick woman there who had been hunched over and unable to stand up straight for eighteen years. When Jesus saw her, he said to her, "Woman, your illness has left you."

At that same moment, the woman straightened up and with her heart filled with joy and praise for God, she left. But the chief of the synagogue, who was furious with Jesus for healing on a Sabbath, said to those who were present, "There are six days to cure them in. Come then, and not on the Sabbath."

And Jesus answered, "Who is among you who, even on a Sabbath, does not take his donkey to drink? Hypocrites! Can you untie your donkeys and I cannot get Satan out of this woman, who had been held bound for eighteen years?"

As on other occasions, the chief of the synagogue did not have an answer for this, and kept quiet, while the simple people rejoiced over these unusual events.

Inviting the Poor

A few days later, Jesus was invited to dinner at a Pharisee's house and, seeing that all the guests were choosing the places of honor, he said to them, "When they invite you to a dinner, do not choose the places of honor, because those could have been reserved for someone more important than yourselves and then you would have to go through the embarrassment of having the host move you to a lower place. But if you sit in the last places, your host will have a reason to take you up to a better place and you will be honored in the sight of others. As in this case, whoever exalts himself or herself will be humbled, and those who humble themselves will be exalted."

Addressing his host, he said, "When you prepare a meal, do not invite family, friends, or rich neighbors. They will certainly invite you back some other day, and, thus, they will have repaid your invitation. Rather, invite the poor, the lame, and the blind. Since they cannot repay you, you will receive your reward in heaven."

Cleverness to Do Good

Through the following parable, Jesus used the same reasoning as the Pharisees to convince them of the uses of money:

"A wealthy man's steward was accused by his master of misspending his money:

"'I have found out that you are pilfering my money. You will have to close your accounts because you will no longer administer my goods.'

"The steward kept quiet since what he was accused of was true, and he started to think about a plan to survive should his master fire him. He thought, 'I am too old to do any kind of work that would require any physical labor, and I cannot beg.'

"So he had an idea that when his master fired him, he would find open doors in other households. He called his master's debtors one by one. He asked the first one, 'How much do you owe my master?'

"'One hundred barrels of oil,' the debtor answered, worrying that perhaps the steward would want payment right away.

"'Sit down; let's change your document. Write down fifty, and I will honor it,' the unfaithful steward told him.

"'With pleasure,' the debtor thought. He made the change the steward proposed, and happily went on his way.

"The steward did the same with another one:

"'And you, how much do you owe?' the clever steward asked.

"'One hundred sacks of wheat,' the debtor replied.

"'Look, we will make a change that will please you. Let us make a new receipt that says you only owe eighty,' he proposed.

"The debtor, of course, accepted gladly. Once he had changed it, the debtor left very satisfied.

"And the steward did the same thing for all the debtors.

"The steward was fired but he was well received by those he had favored.

"Eventually, however, the master was bound to find out about the steward's plot, but he couldn't do anything since the receipts were valid.

"When his anger at the steward's last swindling had subsided, the master praised the steward who had so ingeniously obtained a reward from the creditors when he could no longer live off his own money."

By this parable Jesus hoped to explain that evil doers are often more clever than the followers of the reign of God and that occasionally we can learn something from them. Forgiving part of the debt, the steward would get compensation later. If we learn from this clever man and forgive the poor their debts, they will later intercede for us before God so that we can enter God's kingdom. Doing good, therefore, is also a good investment.

Opportunities Should Not Be Missed

Jesus also explained the following parable:

"A man prepared a big banquet and told his servant to inform those he wished to invite. But they made excuses such as: 'I am sorry, I have just bought a field and have to go and see it,' or, 'I have bought five pairs of oxen, and I have to try them out; excuse me,' or, 'I have just gotten married and I cannot come.' The servant returned to the house and explained this to the master.

"Bothered by his friends' indifference, the master told his servant, 'Go into the streets and public squares. Invite all those who are poor, lame, or blind, until the house is full. No guest who was invited to my dinner, even if he wanted to, will now get a single morsel of my feast.'"

Through this parable Jesus taught that, if God's messenger was inviting people to God's house, there was no acceptable excuse for not fulfilling his word after having heard it. Their places would be taken by the people who were more receptive to the Good News.

"What must we do to follow you?" they asked.

"Anyone among you who does not renounce your goods cannot be my disciple. In addition, in order to follow me you must leave your father, mother, and any other relative, because my disciples must be preoccupied with God's things, not with issues of family business."

All the publicans and sinners came closer to listen to Jesus, but the Pharisees mumbled and said, "Look, he is with sinners and eats with them."

Jesus had explained in the past why he did this. This time, so that they would understand it better, he told another parable:

The Lost Sheep Are the Ones that Are Found

"There was a shepherd who had one hundred sheep that were growing healthy and fat. One day when he was counting them he realized that one was missing. Without giving it a second thought, he left the ninety-nine behind and went looking everywhere for the lost one until he found it. Full of joy, he carried it home. Then he called his friends together and they celebrated the return of the lost sheep.

"So in heaven there will be more joy for one sinner who converts than for ninety-nine good people who do not need conversion."

Since the people did not appear satisfied with this explanation, he told another parable:

"There was a man who had two sons; one day the younger son said, 'Father, give me the part of my inheritance that belongs to me.'

"Then the father divided his property between his sons. The younger son went to a far away country and squandered his inheritance. When he had spent everything, the whole country went

through a period of famine, and the son did not have anything to eat. He then got work watching pigs in the mountains. He was so hungry he was tempted to eat the pigs' feed but that wasn't allowed.

"Then he said to himself, 'My father's servants have whatever they want, while I go hungry.'

"He decided to return to his father's house and ask him to at least let him work as a servant if he could no longer accept him as a son. After many trials and tribulations, he arrived at his father's house. His father, who had been waiting for him to return, saw him in the distance, ran to him, embraced him, and covered him with kisses. The son said, 'Father, I have sinned against heaven and against you. I am not worthy to be called your son.'

"Without letting him finish, the father called the servants and ordered, 'Bring the best clothes, put a ring on his finger, and sandals on his feet. Kill the fatted calf and let us have a banquet, for this son of mine was dead and has come back to life; he was lost and now we have found him.'

"Returning from the field, the older son heard the music and asked a servant what was going on in the house. The servant answered, 'Your brother has come back and we are celebrating.'

"Hearing that, he got angry and refused to come to the party. When his father found out, he went to talk his eldest son into coming. Before he could say anything, the son expressed his anger.

"'I have served you for so many years and you never gave me a goat to celebrate a feast with my friends. But now this son of yours who has squandered his fortune comes back and you kill the best calf for him.'

"Then the father explained, 'My son, you have always been with me and all I have is yours. But my other son has come back and I had to celebrate; it is as if he were dead and had come back again anew.'

"Sinners who repent and return to God will be treated the same way that father treated his lost son. See how the return of a sinner gives more joy than a good person."

Is Helping the Poor an Obligation?

A wealthy man concerned about his own future asked Jesus, "Lord, is it an obligation to help the poor, or are you simply giving advice about something that's good to do, but not essential?"

A parable helped Jesus dispel any of this man's doubts:

"There was a man who was so rich that he always wore very expensive clothes. He dined sumptuously every day and indulged in other luxuries and, even then, he did not know what to do with all his riches. There was a poor man at his door by the name of Lazarus, who did not have a morsel of bread to feed himself. He only wanted to eat the crumbs that fell from the table of the rich man, but he wasn't allowed to do that. As if this weren't enough, his body was totally covered with sores that no one dressed. And that wasn't all: dogs, who are impure animals, did not leave him alone, and licked his whole body.

"The poor man died and went to heaven with Abraham. A little later the rich man died and went straight to hell. In the midst of the flames and the torment of hell, the rich man saw Lazarus at a distance in the company of Abraham. His suffering was such that he said, 'Father Abraham, tell Lazarus to wet the tip of his fingers and refresh my tongue; I can't bear this torture.'

"But Abraham answered, 'My son, remember that you received all your goods on earth during life. What did you do with them? Lazarus, instead, got all evil. Now he is consoled and you are tormented. In addition, even if I wanted to, I wouldn't be able to help you because there is an impassable abyss between the two of you and those who want to pass to the other side cannot do so.'

"The rich man insisted, 'If that cannot be, at least send Lazarus to my house to warn my family, so that when they die they don't end up in this place of torment.'

"'They have Moses' word. Let them hear it,' Abraham answered.

"'No, father Abraham, they will not listen. But if a dead man appears to them, they will pay attention and repent.'

"'If they don't listen to Moses and the prophets, they will not pay attention even if a dead person rises,' concluded Abraham.

"Imagine how the rich man had wished at that moment that he would have shared his riches with poor Lazarus when he was alive."

The man who had posed the question realized that Jesus' story referred to him.

Forgiveness and Faith

One evening the following week, the apostles were sitting around Jesus and asked him, "You always say we have to forgive those who offend us, but up to what point? Because, by that system, people could spend their whole lives bothering us. If we forgive them every time, there is no reason for them to stop doing wrong."

"When people ask for forgiveness it is because they are sorry; otherwise they wouldn't do it. Whether they bother you a few times or repeatedly is really their own problem! They would be the ones who don't behave like decent people.

"If you do not forgive, your heart will harden and you will end up being like them. So, forgive them every time they apologize, regardless of the number of times."

"And how should our faith be? We try to have faith, but many times we cannot avoid doubting. Perhaps if we were clear on what faith should be like . . ."

"Being faithful means that you are convinced that the path you are following is the right one, that all the steps you take seem simple. It is the energy that allows you to easily do what previously had seemed impossible. If you really believe, you can do whatever you set out to do."

As darkness fell, the apostles took Jesus' words in and mulled them over to understand their full meaning.

Foreigners Are More Grateful Than Those from Town

The following day they set out for Jerusalem and, in a town between Galilee and Samaria, ten lepers came out to meet him. Since in those times people with leprosy could not approach healthy people, they shouted from afar, "Teacher, heal us from this illness. If you want to, you can do it."

Jesus told them, "You can go before the priests and show them that you are cured."

They did so. But one of them, realizing what had happened and that he was healed, stopped halfway and returned to look for Jesus. Finding him, he knelt down and thanked Jesus, his eyes full of tears.

Jesus answered, "Weren't ten of you cured? Only you, who was not born in Israel, has thought to come back to thank me? It is clear that faith does not depend on where you were born, but on the will to believe. Go, good man, your faith has saved you."

The cured leper went away with his heart filled with joy and gave praise to God.

Why Should We Pray?

Days later, Jesus realized that the disciples were not quite sure why they should pray. To explain it to them, he told them the following story:

"There was a judge who had received his high position through his friends' influences rather than through his own efforts. His only concern was to work as little as possible and earn as much money as possible. He left his case load unattended.

"In the same city there was a widow who did not stop asking for justice. Since he knew he wouldn't make any money with this case, the judge did not even want to hear her out.

"At the beginning he refused to budge, but because the woman insisted, he told her clearly that he had other cases to attend to and could not waste his time with a case as insignificant as hers. But she did not lose hope and kept going back to him every day to ask for justice.

"Her perseverance was so great that the judge said to himself, 'I will have to solve this case, even if I couldn't care less, so that she leaves me alone.'

"A few days later, the widow's case was resolved.

"Do you think God will turn his back on you if you ask for what you need? If the judge of this story, as evil as he was, ended up listening to this woman, God, who is good, will do much more. In any case, follow this woman's example: continue praying so that you will get what you need."

I Feel Pity for Evildoers

That same afternoon, after lunch, Jesus lay down in a field to rest awhile, but he could not fall asleep. Two apostles were with him to watch over his sleep. In the meantime, they were commenting between themselves.

"We are so lucky to have met the Master! Now I feel like a new man. I sometimes feel pity for those who don't want to listen and continue to live in sin," one said.

"Yes, I feel the same way. Sometimes I think we should help, but their evil is rooted deep inside. I even wonder whether they are able to understand us. After all, they don't want to have anything to do with virtue."

Jesus heard them and, getting up, he explained to them, "Listen, two people—a Pharisee and a publican—went to the Temple to pray. When he prayed, the Pharisee said, 'I thank you, God, because I am not like the rest of the people; I fulfill what the Law says. Nor am I like that sinner the publican.'

"The publican, instead, didn't even dare to raise his eyes and only murmured, 'Lord, forgive me, for I am a sinner. Help me.'

"Do you know which of the two was more pleasing to God? The sinner who repented rather than the Pharisee who was so self-righteous. So, don't think yourselves superior to others. Think that those who brag about their own qualities will be humbled and those who are not proud will be recognized and exalted."

The apostles did not say anything, but they knew that Jesus' warning was a result of their previous conversation.

Simplicity of Children, Complexity of Rich People

Afterward he went to rejoin the other disciples and the rest of the people. Some mothers took their small children to Jesus so that he would touch them and they would be protected.

But the apostles wanted to prevent them from bothering Jesus and did not let the mothers get closer. When Jesus realized this, he scolded them, "Why don't you let them bring the children to me? Don't stop them. You should try to be like them. You wish your entrance to heaven was as secure as theirs. You must wait for the reign of God with the same spirit as children and then you will have a place in heaven."

A little later, someone approached him and asked, "What should I do to obtain eternal life?"

"You know what to do. Do you know the commandments of the prophets? Keep them," Jesus answered.

"I have observed everything since I was a child," the man replied.

"One thing is missing. Go and sell what you have, divide it among the poor, and follow me," Jesus advised.

But the young man's expression suddenly changed. He was very rich and Jesus had probably asked for more than he was willing to give. He could only say, "My riches are already a sign of God's favor. Why should I have to sell them, since God has given them to me?"

But he left without waiting for an answer. Everyone knew, himself included, that he was only trying to justify his position, since he felt incapable of doing what Jesus had asked.

Jesus commented, "How difficult it is for rich people to recognize God as Lord! Their material goods caused them to feel superior to all. Because they are accustomed to this, they refuse to feel inferior to anyone, including God. That's why it is so difficult for rich people to enter heaven."

Illness Is Not a Consequence of Sin

"We," Peter cut in, "have left everything to follow you."

"All of you who have left something to follow me will receive much more in this life than what you have left. You will have eternal life," Jesus promised.

On another occasion when they were entering a city, they met a beggar who had been blind since birth. In those days people believed that illnesses were a punishment for sin. So, the disciples asked Jesus, "Who caused this man to be born blind? Did he sin, or did his parents?"

"His blindness is neither his fault nor his parents'. His blindness symbolizes the fact that I am the light of the world for you just as I am for this blind man," Jesus clarified.

Then, with a little saliva, he made some mud, rubbed it on the blind man's eyelids, and told him, "Go and wash yourself in a fountain."

The man did as he had been told and he could immediately see. Joy drove him to go everywhere proclaiming what had happened to him. Those who had seen him begging could not believe it was really the same person.

The Pharisees Are More Blind Than the Blind Man

Since it was a strange phenomenon, people took the blind man before the Pharisees. He explained to them, "I am the blind man who used to sit by the wayside. Jesus put mud on my eyes, told me to wash, and now I can see."

"A man who cures on the Sabbath cannot come from God," the Pharisees said.

"But a sinner could not work wonders like this one," others said.

They asked the former blind man, "And you, who do you say he is?"

"I only know that I couldn't see and now I do. For me he is a prophet."

But the Pharisees did not want to believe him. So they called his parents in to confirm he had been blind since birth.

"Our son is old enough. Ask him," the parents answered, fearing that their answer would displease the Pharisees.

The Pharisees then called the former blind man in again and asked him to explain once more how things had happened.

"I have already told you. It is obvious that I couldn't see before and now I can," he repeated.

"We know that the man who has cured you is a sinner," they said.

"I don't know whether he is a sinner. Even so, giving sight to the blind is only possible with God's help, and we all know that God wouldn't be helping sinners to perform this kind of miracle."

Going out, he met Jesus, who asked him, "Do you believe I am the Son of God?"

"Yes, I believe," the cured man said resolutely.

"I have come to give sight to those who don't have it and to blind those who see," Jesus commented.

The Pharisees, who were on the prowl, said sarcastically, "Are you trying to say that we are blind?"

"If you were blind, you would not be responsible for what is going on, but since you see, you are to blame. All will be held accountable according to their abilities. Whoever has more will have to give more, and whoever has less won't have to give as much," Jesus replied.

Those Who Have More Must Give More

Jesus then saw that a parable could help them understand better what he had just said, and told them the following:

"There was an owner who had to go abroad for a time. Before his journey, he called his servants in and entrusted his money to them until his return.

"He gave the first five coins—a whole fortune. The second received two, and the third got one.

"His business kept him abroad longer than expected. Returning home, he called his servants and asked for the state of his affairs. The first one returned ten coins to him, the second returned four, and the third said, 'Lord, I know you are very demanding and you would have been very upset if I had lost your money in a bad business deal. So, I placed my coin in a secure place. Here it is, just as you gave it to me.'

"'You couldn't at least invest this money so that I could make a small profit? That didn't involve any risk. What good are hidden riches? They are good for nothing!' he said indignantly.

"Without allowing him to say anything in his defense, he took the money away from the servant, gave it to the one who had turned his five coins into ten, and threw the third servant out of the house, leaving him to his own devices.

"All those who have will receive more; but those who don't have will lose everything, even if it is little."

Do We Always Have to Share with Those Who Have Less?

"Taking away from those who have less and giving it to the ones who have more seems very unfair. Wouldn't it be more fair to take from the one who has more and give it to the one who doesn't?" a person asked Jesus.

Jesus looked at her. He realized she had asked the question in good faith, in order to understand him, and he answered her, "A person must be accountable for all he or she has. Those who have one gift must use it to improve their lot; those who have five gifts must take advantage of all of them. Whether it be money or qualities, all must make the most of what they have.

"People are not rewarded for what they have, but rather for what they do with what they receive. Those who show that they are able to produce receive a reward, not because they have a lot, but because they have wisely used what they have.

"In this parable, if the servant who had five coins had limited himself to hiding them, and the one who had received one had made it yield another one, the five coins from the first would have been taken away from him and given to the latter; the one with the five coins would have been fired."

Assignment: Listen to Jesus

When he had finished speaking, Jesus wanted to go with his apostles to Bethsaida, but a multitude of people found out and went there too. Jesus' fame caused many people to gather around him. The Zealots, the Jewish patriots who struggled against the domination of the country by the Romans, also believed that Jesus could lead them to victory over the Romans. They agreed on many aspects of his teachings. So they had spread the word to go to Bethsaida to listen to Jesus. They wanted to force him to become their king and start a revolt against the Romans.

As was his habit, Jesus was healing those who needed it and speaking about the reign of God.

He was teaching for a long time and it grew late. The disciples advised him, "Take leave of the crowd so that they can go to the towns to buy food."

Jesus answered, "You give them something to eat."

"But teacher," they replied with surprise, "how are we supposed to find food for so many people?"

"What food do we have?" Jesus asked.

"Only five loaves and two fish," the disciples answered.

"Ask them to sit in groups of fifty."

Then Jesus took the loaves and the fish and, raising his eyes to heaven, blessed the loaves, broke them, and gave them to the disciples to share them among the people. There were more than five thousand people.

When all had had their fill, they collected the leftovers and filled twelve baskets. Everyone imitated Jesus' action of sharing his food, so those who had plenty shared it like good brothers and sisters with those who had not brought anything. It was a greater miracle that people gave up what was theirs to share it with others. No one had ever accomplished anything like it before.

Realizing this wonder, and prodded on by the Zealots, people started acclaiming and proclaiming Jesus as king. But those were not Jesus' plans; he did not want any political power. He stole away, disappointing the Zealots, who were left without a leader for their rebellion.

Jesus Walks on the Water

They had already gotten away from the people when Jesus asked the apostles to go ahead, get on the boat, and row to the other side of Lake Gennesaret.

They did so. Halfway through the trip, a strong wind rocked the boat. Seeing that it was getting late, Jesus decided to go and meet the disciples by walking on the water. Seeing him walking on the water, the disciples were alarmed. Then Jesus told them, "It is I; don't be afraid."

But the disciples were not quite sure if they were seeing him or a ghost. Then Peter said, "Lord, if it is really you, ask me to come to you on the water."

"Come!" Jesus said to him.

Peter was walking toward Jesus but, seeing that the power of the wind was increasing, he was frightened and began to sink.

"Lord, save me!" Peter cried out.

Jesus stretched out his hand to Peter and took him out of the water, saying, "Man of little faith. Why did you doubt?"

They got on the boat and the wind died down. All the disciples knelt before Jesus, saying, "Truly you are the Son of God."

Herodias's Revenge on John

At the request of Herodias, his brother Philip's wife, King Herod had thrown John the Baptist in prison.

John the Baptist had been constantly recriminating Herod for living with his brother's wife. Herodias had wanted to take revenge by putting him in prison and was looking for an opportunity to kill him.

A few days later it was Herod's birthday. During the party in his honor, Herodias's daughter danced in public. She did so well that Herod said to her, "Ask me whatever you want and I will grant it."

Persuaded by her mother, the girl requested, "I want John the Baptist's head on a platter."

King Herod wished that she would have asked for something else. But he had given his word in front of all the guests and he could not go back on it.

He sent the executioner to the prison to behead John the Baptist, and they gave Herodias's daughter his head on a platter, just as she had asked.

Then his disciples asked for John's body to bury it.

A Strategic Withdrawal

It was not a good time for prophets. John was dead, and Jesus could no longer count on the Zealots, who had supported him until then. If he did not want to start the fight against the Romans, it was dangerous for him to continue captivating the people. If Jesus did not push people to rebel against the Romans, in a certain sense he was helping to keep them in power. In the Zealots' minds that amounted to collaborating with the enemy. The Zealots alone could not convince the people to rise against the Romans, and Jesus had not wanted to get in the middle. Since he was no longer their ally, Jesus was an obstacle in the Zealots' quest to liberate Israel from Roman rule. It would be better if he were not there at all; it would be easier to motivate people to rebel. It would be better for him to disappear.

The environment was ripe for this. So Jesus and his disciples went to Syria, far from the threats, to wait for a better time to renew their preaching. In that remote place, Jesus asked them, "Who do people say that I am?"

They answered, "Some say you are John the Baptist risen; others say you are a prophet."

"And you, who do you say that I am?"

"You are Christ, the Son of the living God," Peter responded without hesitation.

"Happy are you, Peter, because my Father in heaven has revealed that to you. You are the rock upon which I will build my Church, and the devil will be helpless against you. Whatever you decide will be accepted by my Father in heaven."

But he told them not to tell anyone about this.

Concerns: Death, Emptiness

At times the disciples grew discouraged.

"I just don't understand what Jesus is saying about having to suffer and die. Sometimes I can't help thinking we are wasting our time following a man who doesn't want people to proclaim him king and accepts the fact that he will have to die without defending himself. Won't we be vulnerable and deceived if he dies?" one of them said to his most trusted friend.

"That is true. We have changed our whole life: our land, the fishing, and our families have suffered for it. If he dies, we will have made all these sacrifices in vain. Even if he doesn't mind dying, he should try to avoid it for our sake."

To clarify their doubts they asked Jesus, "If you are not afraid to die, Master, you should at least avoid it for our sake, for we are your followers. If you die, these past years of our lives would be meaningless. We may end up agreeing with our families, who thought we were crazy to follow you."

"Don't you think you are not important to me. For you I am willing to go to the bitter end. I don't want to die, but I will accept it if necessary. Look, I am guiding you; I lead you, my sheep, and I am your shepherd. A good shepherd must be willing to give his life for his sheep. Look at what a shepherd does."

The Good Shepherd

And he explained a parable to them:

"A shepherd went to see his sheep. When he arrived, he entered through the gate, which the gatekeeper opened because he recognized the shepherd's voice. Another person wanted to enter the sheepfold, but broke the fence rather than entering through the gate. This man was a thief. Then the shepherd scattered his sheep to protect them.

"When it was time to leave the shelter, the shepherd had only to call his sheep, each one by its name. They, who knew the voice even better than the gatekeeper, came out trustingly. The shepherd stood before them and they all followed him.

"But a group of bandits had decided to steal the sheep, and they threatened him. There were ten of them, so the shepherd couldn't do anything. He knew that if he confronted the thieves, he would get killed. And yet, he didn't hesitate to confront them.

"This attitude annoyed the robbers, who became enraged and attacked him. They beat him up and he was badly wounded. While the shepherd was recuperating from his wounds, a man hired to take his place was attacked by two robbers; he didn't waste any time in running away and fleeing, leaving the sheep to their own fate at the hands of bandits.

"What did the real shepherd do for his sheep? He risked his own life, even though sheep are just animals. The one hired as a shepherd, what did he do? He ran away. I am not a hired shepherd. I am the good shepherd. If he has risked his life for the sheep, wouldn't I do the same for you? Don't ask me to run away, because then I would abandon you to your own fate. Perhaps I wouldn't die, but your lives would have no meaning. Since I would have to stop proclaiming what I have taught you so as not to die, wouldn't that be worse than death? If death comes, it would be for you and for all those sheep who want to join my fold."

While he was explaining this story, some other people joined them; one of them observed, "So, you don't give up your life freely. You cannot save your life in front of your enemies. It is as if some bandits attack a person in the desert and, since they are stronger, he says he has given up his life. He has not given it up; the assassins have taken it away from him."

"That would be true if I didn't have the power to keep my life, but I do. I just don't want to use my power to protect it. That's why no one is going to take away my life: I offer it freely."

The one who had asked did not say anything, but from his bemused expression it was obvious that he was not quite convinced of Jesus' power over life and death.

Jesus in His Glory

Some time later, Jesus took Peter, James, and John, up to the top of a mountain. When they were there, Jesus was transfigured: his face shone like the sun and his clothes became a dazzling white.

Moses and Elijah appeared to them, and they were talking to Jesus. Immediately, a bright cloud covered them and a voice came out that said, "This is my beloved Son, who has all my support. Listen to him."

Hearing this, the apostles fell on their knees, frightened. Jesus approached, touched them, and said, "Rise up, be not afraid. Do not tell anyone about this vision until the Son of Man is risen from the dead."

And, when they looked around, Jesus was alone. They did not see Moses and Elijah any longer.

Is Lazarus Sick?

When they came down from the mountain, a messenger from Bethany, the city where Martha and Mary lived, came to Jesus and said, "Lord, your friend Lazarus, the brother of Martha and Mary is very sick. We fear he will die."

"Don't worry. Lazarus' illness will not end his life, but it will give people a reason to believe in my teachings," Jesus assured him.

So, Jesus stayed in that place for two more days. Then he decided, "Let's go and see Lazarus."

The disciples were afraid that sufficient time had not passed for the anger to subside. Bethany was close to Jerusalem, where the priests and Pharisees were plotting their revenge against Jesus, who no longer had the Zealots' support.

When they arrived in Bethany, Lazarus had been buried for four days. When they heard Jesus was coming, Martha came out to greet him. She embraced Jesus crying and said, "Why didn't you come earlier? If you had been here my brother wouldn't have died. But I know that everything is possible with you."

"Your brother will rise. I am the resurrection and the life. Those who believe in me even if they have died will be saved, no matter how impossible that seems to the people of this world. On the other hand, those who live believing in me will never die, since when you die your life only changes form. This limited life changes into eternal life. Do you believe in me?" Jesus asked.

"Of course, Lord. You are the Messiah, the Son of God, who has come to this world to save it."

Not long afterward, Mary came weeping, accompanied by a group of Jewish people.

"Lord, if you had been here my brother would not have died," Mary repeated.

Is Lazarus Dead?

Jesus saw the pain of the two sisters and of the friends who were sobbing. He also felt a deep sadness because Lazarus was his friend. Jesus' eyes filled with tears, but he made an effort to suppress them and said, "Where have you buried him? Take me there."

When they arrived, he ordered, "Remove the stone from the entrance."

"Lord, it has been four days since he died. It smells bad in there," Martha objected.

The resolute look on Jesus' face made her understand that it should be done as he said. Once the stone was removed, Jesus cried out, "Lazarus, come out!"

No one was expecting to remove the stone or that Jesus would ask Lazarus to come out. Everyone was astounded. But that was nothing compared with what they saw next: Lazarus emerged from the tomb on his own two feet and with his whole body in bandages (as it was the custom to bury the dead in those times).

"Unbind him and let him go."

His sisters took Lazarus home to take care of him. Seeing that he had power over death, many people believed in Jesus. One of them was the heckler who had looked amused when Jesus told him he had power over death and life.

The Pharisees Are Enraged: Jesus Is in Hiding

Right after Lazarus' resurrection, Jesus' reputation became a source of high expectation for the people. The Pharisees and the priests felt threatened; they could not allow more and more Jewish people to follow Jesus because of this event.

They were afraid that the followers would cause confrontations between the Jewish and Roman authorities. If that ever came to be, the immediate response of the Romans would be to take power away from the priests and to provoke a massacre of the people.

So they decided to arrest Jesus and kill him.

Caiaphas, who was the high priest, said, "Better for a man to die for the people, than all the people because of a man."

They also wanted Lazarus dead, so that he would stop telling what had happened to him.

For a time Jesus did not show up in public.

Passover, the great feast of the Jewish people that commemorated their liberation from Egypt, was still six days away. Jesus took advantage of the time by going to Bethany to see his friends. He was in the house with the three siblings when Mary, after washing his feet (as was the custom with honored guests), anointed them with a very expensive perfume. Judas Iscariot, the disciple, said, "Wouldn't it have been better to sell this perfume for three hundred days' wages and share it among the poor?"

Hearing that, Mary was embarrassed, but Jesus said, "The poor will always be among you, and you can give them alms. Mary has done this sincerely. When she pours such an expensive perfume on my feet she shows that I am very important to her; by giving me importance, she gives it to all my teachings. That's what matters."

The Passover: Jesus Is Acclaimed

During the days before the Passover, there was speculation in Jerusalem about whether or not Jesus, as a good Jew, would dare to go to the city even though his life was threatened.

But Jesus had already decided to go into Jerusalem and, for once, to allow people to acclaim him. So he said to his disciples, "Go to the next village. When you get there, you will see a donkey tied down. Untie it and bring it to me. If anyone asks you, say, 'The Lord needs it. We will return it soon.'"

They did just as Jesus had told them; the owners of the animal did not object.

They covered the donkey with some blankets and Jesus rode to Jerusalem. His followers were spreading their cloaks on the path, making a carpet. They waved olive and palm branches and cried out, "Blessed are you, Jesus, who comes in the name of God!"

"Make them be quiet. Don't you see they are blaspheming?" some Pharisees told Jesus.

"If they kept quiet, the stones would shout. Let them be."

They were already close to Jerusalem. The joy of that moment did not prevent Jesus from crying, as he said, "Jerusalem, now you are carefree and happy; but you will be destroyed and not a stone will remain standing because you did not want to recognize the Messiah among you. I wish that things were different."

Jesus' entrance in Jerusalem was triumphant. The followers of Jesus, not as numerous as before but more enthusiastic, sang and praised Jesus and thanked God for having sent him. A deep joy overcame them.

Away with the Merchants of the Temple

Immediately after Jesus went to the Temple, which he found full of merchants and vendors. There was a great racket going on and continuous activity.

He was going there to pray, and he had found a marketplace. Who would be able to pray in such an environment? Perhaps the Passover had become a commercial feast. Where was the religious meaning of the feast?

These thoughts irritated him, and, overturning the merchants' tables, he expelled the sellers from the Temple, saying, "My house is a house of prayer, it is the house of God. It is not a place to sell, buy, trade, bargain, exchange, run, or shout. I have come to a Temple, and I find a den of thieves. Every one of you, get out of here now! Away!"

He stayed in the Temple speaking to the crowds:

"A man planted a vineyard and rented it out to some workers. When the harvest time came, he sent his servants to collect the fruits. The servants went out three times, and all three times they came back beaten up and empty-handed. The owner started losing his patience; but he controlled his anger and decided to send his son to the vineyard, convinced that they would respect and listen to him. But the workers killed him so there would not be an heir for the vineyard and it would be theirs. Do you think the owner of the vineyard would be compassionate with these people? No! The workers will die and the vineyard will be given over to other people who will fulfill their obligations."

It did not take much for them to understand that the son in the parable was Jesus himself and that the workers were the Pharisees. So, the followers kept shouting, "May that never happen!"

The Pharisees, who were also listening, were totally enraged that Jesus had gone to Jerusalem even though they had threatened him because he was revealing their true intentions to the whole world.

Even so, and for the same reason that the Temple merchants had not reacted against Jesus, the Pharisees did not dare arrest him right there because the people were captivated by him and, if they tried to harm Jesus, everyone would rebel against the Pharisees.

They Want to Outwit Jesus

The Pharisees then tried to find a riddle to trick Jesus so that he would lose his prestige before the people and they would stop supporting him. Then they could arrest him. They sent some men to ask Jesus, "Teacher, are we supposed to pay taxes to Caesar or not?"

The Pharisees who had sent the men thought, "If he says yes, it will seem as if he agrees with the Romans, the invaders, and when people realize, they will lose trust in him. On the other hand, if he says no, he will seem to be as a person who doesn't respect the laws. We will say that a person who doesn't keep the existing laws is ill equipped to lead others. In either case, he will lose his influence over the people."

Jesus looked at the men who had asked the question and said, "Do you have a coin?"

"Yes, here it is," they answered, giving him one.

"Whose is this image and inscription?" he asked them.

"Caesar's," they replied.

"Very well then," Jesus concluded. "Give to Caesar what is Caesar's and to God what is God's."

Jesus had found an answer to undo all their plans. They could do nothing but go back the same way they had come.

What Courage, Giving from Our Own Want!

From where he stood, Jesus could see how wealthy people were dropping money in the offering basket of the Temple. At this time, a widow approached and she put in two cents.

Jesus commented on this with those present and said to them, "It would appear as if the wealthy people have given much more than this woman, but that's not so, because the wealthy have given a part of their excess. But this woman has given the two coins she needed to live on. It is much more valuable to give your whole livelihood than from a surplus of your wealth."

In those days there was a lot of talk about how decorated and beautiful the Temple was. So, Jesus warned them, "The day will come when not one stone will remain standing on this Temple we now see. Before that, you will be persecuted, tortured, and mistreated if you declare yourselves to be my followers. This will be an opportunity to be my witnesses. Your adversaries will not be able to contradict your words but you will suffer for my cause. Even your parents and brothers and sisters will denounce you. So, remain firm in faith; for each hair you lose for my sake you will receive a reward."

Judas Wants to Precipitate the End

Judas Iscariot, the treasurer of the apostles, was a Zealot and had shared with the Zealots the hope that Jesus would free Israel from the Romans. Like the Zealots, Judas was disappointed at Jesus' firm refusal to lead a rebellion. However, Judas kept hoping that, when Jesus saw himself in a desperate situation, and at the end of his rope, he would take up arms against the Roman oppressors. So, in secret agreement with the rest of the Zealots, he visited Caiaphas, the high priest, and said to him, "I am one of Jesus' apostles. Give me money and I will find a way to hand him over to you, so that you can do with him as you please." Since the priests and Zealots were enemies, Judas asked them for money so as not to arouse suspicions about the revolt he was planning.

"Here is the money," they said, handing him a bag with coins. "As soon as there is an opportunity to arrest him, let us know and we will go to capture him."

The Passover Supper

It was the day before the Passover. As on so many other occasions, Jesus and the twelve apostles were preparing to eat together, this time to commemorate Passover. Jesus poured water in a basin and washed his disciples' feet, one by one. When the Master got to him, Peter argued, "You, Lord, want to wash my feet? I will not allow it!"

"If you don't let me wash your feet, you cannot be my follower," Jesus answered.

"Then, wash my hands and head too. I want to be with you."

"The one who is clean only needs to wash his feet. You are clean, although not all of you."

When he finished, he sat at the table again to tell them, "If I, who am your teacher, have washed your feet, it is so that you will do the same for one another. The servant is no less than the master, nor the master more than the servant. Do like this and you will be happy." He continued, "One of you will betray me."

Then Peter signaled to John, who was by Jesus' side, to ask him who it was. John asked in a low voice, "Lord, who is it?"

Jesus whispered back, "The one to whom I give this morsel of bread I will dip in the dish."

He gave it to Judas Iscariot and said to him, "Do soon what you are going to do."

It was night. Judas left immediately, resolved to do it. Had he perhaps interpreted a certain agreement on Jesus' part from the words he had just said?

280

Jesus Bids His Disciples Farewell

As soon as Judas left, Jesus said, "Where I am going you cannot come. But I leave you a new commandment: Love one another as I have loved you. In this they will recognize that you are my disciples."

"Lord, where are you going? Why can't I go with you?" Peter asked.

"Where I am going you cannot come now; you will come later."

"Why can't I? I would give my life for you."

"No, Peter; before the rooster crows tomorrow morning, you will have said three times that you don't know me."

"Never, Lord. I will never deny you," Peter argued.

"I am going to my Father's house to prepare a place for you. Then I will come for you. Then where I am you can be, too. You know the path I have to take."

"Lord, if we don't know where you are going, how can we know the way?" Thomas asked.

"Listen to my teachings, Thomas. They are the way, the truth, and the life. You remember them, don't you?" Thomas nodded. "Then you know all that is necessary."

The apostles remained silent while Jesus spoke of his departure. They were confused and sad. Jesus wanted to encourage them.

"I have told you I am leaving, but I will come back to you. What is the reason for your sadness? If you really loved me, you would be happy about it. Do not be troubled or afraid. I leave you the peace of mind, the calm of spirit that results from following my will. My peace will be with you forever."

Then Jesus took bread, broke it, and gave it to his disciples, saying, "This is my body, given up for you. Do this in memory of me."

When they had finished dinner, Jesus took the cup filled with wine and said, "This is my blood, the sign of a new covenant between God and people; it will be shed for you."

And he passed the cup to all the disciples so they could drink from it. When he finished, he prayed, "Father, the hour has come! May all people have eternal life. May all recognize you as the only God and me as your Son and Messiah. I accept what is to come."

Jesus Is Arrested

They then left the house and went to the Garden of Olives, where Jesus often went with his disciples. He said to them, "Stay here and pray. I will go a little further."

Reaching the place, he knelt down and started to pray.

"Father," he said, "if it is possible, save me all this pain, but don't take my human wishes into account, but your will as God."

He prayed there for a long time, thinking how to avoid suffering. He did not want it to happen, but at the same time he wanted everything to be over.

He then went back to his apostles and found them sleeping.

"What are you doing sleeping? It is time to pray, not to sleep," he said to them.

He had not finished talking to his disciples when he heard voices approaching. A group of men were getting closer, and he recognized one of them in the darkness: Judas Iscariot. Judas went to Jesus and kissed him on the cheek.

Jesus said, "Judas, you are handing me over with a kiss?"

Wanting to defend his Lord, Peter drew his sword and cut the ear of a Temple guard.

"Peter, put away your sword," Jesus shouted. "Don't make my course even more difficult."

Reluctantly, Peter did as his Master had told him.

The End: Judas Is Desperate

The whole world collapsed around Judas: he had handed over his Master, whom he deeply loved, and there would not be any uprising. Jesus did not authorize the use of weapons to defend him. He hardly noticed the events that followed, although he knew well what was coming.

They tied Jesus' hands and took him to the house of Annas, the father-in-law of the high priest Caiaphas, whom Judas Iscariot was visiting at that precise moment. Judas wanted to return the coins so that they would free Jesus; of course, Caiaphas and his friends laughed at him. Then desperation seized Judas: he was helpless both to initiate the revolt and to free his Master. Without realizing how, he suddenly found himself on a field looking for a high tree. After mechanically tying one end of his belt to a branch and the other around his own neck, he jumped. Death freed him from the unbearable emptiness that his treason had caused him. His betrayal had been for nothing.

Peter Does Not Know Jesus

Peter and another disciple followed Jesus. The gatekeeper of the house addressed Peter and asked him, "Aren't you one of the disciples?"

Peter was in a territory dominated by priests; if anyone recognized him something bad would happen to him, so he replied, "You are wrong. I don't know the man you are speaking about."

Inside the house, Annas was interrogating Jesus.

"What is your teaching? Who are your disciples?"

Jesus answered, "I have always spoken openly and haven't hidden from anyone. Whoever has listened to me can tell you what my teachings are."

As if he had said some awful thing, the guard by his side slapped him, saying, "Is that any way to answer the high priest?"

Calmly, Jesus asked, "If I have spoken wrongly, show me how. But if I have said the right thing, why do you strike me?"

Outside, Peter was warming himself up by a fire with the guards of the priests. One of them asked him, "I think I know you. Weren't you in the garden when they arrested Jesus? Yes, I think so."

"You must be mistaken. I don't know who that Jesus is."

They still insisted a third time: "You are one of the followers of Jesus, the preacher!"

"Are you kidding? What would I be doing with such a man?"

Immediately, the rooster crowed, announcing dawn. At that time, the guards were taking Jesus before Caiaphas, and, passing near Peter, Jesus looked at him lovingly. Peter went out and cried bitterly, disconsolate for having denied Jesus.

Jesus Before Caiaphas

While they were waiting for dawn, those who were watching Jesus mocked him. They blind-folded him and struck him from behind, saying, "Aren't you a prophet? Guess who struck you."

In the morning they took Jesus before Caiaphas, the high priest, and the Sanhedrin (the council made by the elders, Pharisees, and Sadducees). They asked Jesus, "Are you the Messiah?"

"If I tell you, you won't believe me. What good is it to say?"

"Then, you are the Son of God?"

"Yes, I am."

"We don't need any more testimonies. We have heard him blaspheme with our own ears."

They Must Ensure Pilate's Condemnation

They wanted to condemn him to death, but they needed the order of execution to be signed by Pilate, the Roman governor at that time. So, they led Jesus before him.

"Of what are you accusing this man?" Pilate asked.

"He is instigating people—from Galilee to Judea—saying we don't have to pay taxes to Caesar. And he says he is the Messiah, the king we are expecting. If he is proclaimed king, and taxes are not paid to you, the Roman power will be weakened," the priests answered.

"Are you the king of the Jews?" the Roman governor asked Jesus.

"You have said it," Jesus answered.

Once the interrogation was finished, Pilate said to the priests, "I don't find any fault with this man."

"And you will set a man free who is calling the people to rebellion? This is not an appropriate decision for a Roman governor," they insisted.

Pilate did not know what to do and wanted to get rid of the problem, so he said, "Is this man a Galilean? Then take him to Herod, who governs in Galilee."

He had said this because during those days, Herod was also in Jerusalem.

Round of Judges: Now Herod

The Galilean king was surprised at first. He was passing through Jerusalem and had not expected that anyone would be sent to him to be judged, especially not by Pilate, since they did not have a good relationship.

After the initial surprise, he was glad to meet Jesus to satisfy his curiosity. He had heard so much about him!

"So you are a king, also? You don't look like one," Herod said.

Everyone broke out laughing.

After being arrested, Jesus had not slept the whole night. His face showed the lack of sleep and the bad treatment he had received.

The Scribes and high priests who had come along took advantage of the opportunity to speak ill of him.

"He is a sorry-looking king!"

"He is only a madman, but we can assure you that what he says is true: a crowd follows him and listens to him. One signal from him would be enough to start a revolt and you wouldn't have enough soldiers to repress it."

"Speak. Don't you see what they are accusing you of?" Herod said to Jesus.

But Jesus kept silent. He knew that regardless of what he said, they would condemn him.

"See, he keeps quiet. He doesn't know what to say because we have thousands of testimonies," the priests lied.

Before Jesus' silence, Herod continued, "They tell me you know how to perform miracles. Do one, and perhaps I will free you. Turn someone into a frog, or make fire come down from heaven."

Then everyone laughed. They were having fun, as if Jesus were a clown.

They wanted to make sure that he was condemned, so they were adding fuel to the fire.

"It is dangerous for this man to stay alive. He poses as the Messiah and yet he does not respect the words of our ancestors because he says different things than our ancestors did."

"And he is not satisfied with being king; he says he is the Son of God."

They would not stop making fun of him.

"It must be easy for God to work miracles. Show us your repertoire, Son of God," Herod insisted.

But none of the accusations made Herod accept responsibility for Jesus' death. So the accusers brought Jesus back to Pilate.

Pilate Again

The priests made sure that they had a good number of Jesus' enemies gathered before the palace of the Roman governor, so that they could ask for Jesus' death.

"Look here, I am not Jewish. Why are your compatriots so insistent that you are impersonating the Messiah, the king of the Jews? Are you that king?" the Roman delegate asked once again.

"My kingdom is not like the kingdoms of this world. If it were like those, my supporters would have fought against you to defend me, and they haven't done it. I have come to this world to proclaim the truth; whoever believes in the truth is part of my reign," Jesus explained.

Then Pilate went out to speak to the people gathered there and said, "This man is not guilty of anything. I cannot condemn him to death. I will have him scourged and I will set him free."

"No! Crucify him! Crucify him!" they shouted, because it was customary for criminals to die on a cross.

Meanwhile, the soldiers placed a crown of thorns on his head, knelt before him, and said, "Hail, king of the Jews," and they would slap him, mocking and laughing at him.

It was not easy for Jesus, who had only done good, to endure that torment. And now they came to whip him.

"Father," he prayed, "give me strength to bear it."

His body shook under the many and powerful strikes of the soldiers' whips.

Pilate trusted that the people's thirst for revenge would be satisfied by seeing Jesus after being whipped. So, he showed them his bloodied body and said, "Look at him. He has received his punishment."

Whipping Him Is Not Enough

But the people did not agree.

"Crucify him! Crucify him!" they shouted unceasingly.

Pilate made one last attempt to save Jesus' life; Barabbas, a dangerous murderer who had no qualms about killing anyone, was in prison. So, Pilate said to the people, "You know that there is a tradition to set a prisoner free at Passover time. Would you like me to set Jesus free or Barabbas, the criminal?"

"Barabbas! Barabbas! Let Barabbas go!"

Hearing that, Pilate was at a loss. He, who was not a Jew, was trying to save the life of a Jew, whom the rest wanted killed. So, he said, "I don't want to be responsible for Jesus' death. I wash my hands of this matter. Do with him whatever you want."

Without wasting any time, they made Jesus carry the cross to Mount Calvary, where he would be crucified.

The wood of the cross was very heavy and Jesus was already debilitated from the torture he had endured. Halfway through he could not bear it any longer, and every three steps he would fall under the weight of the cross. They forced one of the bystanders to carry the cross. His name was Simon of Cyrene.

A group of women following Jesus could not stop sobbing and lamenting over him. Jesus told them, "Women, don't weep for me. Cry rather for those around you, because if they are capable of doing this to me, who have always done good, what will they do to the rest?"

Death on the Cross

When they arrived at the execution site, they nailed Jesus to the cross. While they were doing so, Jesus prayed, "Father, forgive them, for they don't know what they are doing."

They also crucified two thieves with Jesus, one on either side. Pilate had an inscription written on the cross that read, "Jesus of Nazareth, king of the Jews."

Some of the people were laughing at him, saying, "Didn't you say you were the Messiah, the Son of God? Then save yourself. Haven't you saved others? Do the same for yourself."

One of the two thieves they had crucified with him said, "That's right. Save yourself and then save us if you are so powerful."

The other, however, chastised him, saying, "Be quiet! Aren't you going to show some respect? We deserve our punishment; he doesn't."

And, addressing Jesus, he said, "Lord, remember me when you go into your kingdom."

"You will be with me in paradise today," Jesus assured him.

John, the apostle, and Mary, Jesus' mother, stood by the foot of the cross together with other women. So that Mary would have her place secure among the apostles, Jesus looked at her and said, "Woman, there is your son."

And to the disciple, "Behold your mother."

From that time on, John welcomed her into his home as a true mother.

"I am thirsty," Jesus said from the cross.

A guard soaked a sponge in vinegar and put it to Jesus' lips. After so much suffering, Jesus exclaimed, "Everything is fulfilled."

And at that moment, he died.

A soldier who realized this proclaimed, "Truly this man was the Son of God."

After His Death

The people asked Pilate to break the legs of the crucified and remove them from their crosses so that the bodies would not stay on the cross on the Passover Sabbath. Pilate sent some soldiers to break the thieves' legs, but Jesus had already died, so they pierced his side with a spear.

One of Jesus' disciples, Joseph of Arimathea, took the body of Jesus down and, with Nicodemus' help, they embalmed it with perfume, as was the custom. Then they placed it in a new tomb, near the place of the crucifixion.

The authorities thought they had quelled the religious movement initiated by Jesus. He had died practically abandoned by all his disciples. The authorities imagined his disciples to be deathly afraid, hiding under rocks. And that was true for a couple of days after Jesus' death. Then rumors started spreading about the tomb being empty, about Jesus being alive. Both the disciples and the apostles said they had seen him and eaten with him. Their fear had turned into courage and the disciples left their hiding places and started proclaiming the teachings of Jesus and his resurrection.

The Empty Tomb

On Sunday, the first day of the week, the women went to the tomb with perfumes. They were surprised to see the guard of the tomb running toward the city. He was going there to report to the priests that the tomb was empty. The priests told the guard, "If anyone asks, you will say that the disciples came in the night and took the body."

They were trying to prevent the news of the resurrection from spreading.

When the women got to the tomb, they saw that the stone was removed from the entrance and the tomb was empty.

"They have taken away the Master," was the first thing they thought.

But the mystery was soon dispelled when two angels appeared to them and said, "Do not look inside a tomb. The living are not to be found in tombs. He is alive! He has risen on the third day such as he had announced to you."

Appearance to Mary

One of the women was Mary Magdalene. When the other women left, she stayed crying by the tomb. Then she heard a voice behind her, which said, "Why are you crying?"

"Why else? They have taken my Lord," Mary answered, convinced that she was talking to the gardener.

"Mary," she heard.

Then, she recognized the voice. "Master, you are alive!"

And, spontaneously, she hugged him.

"Of course I am alive."

"Lord . . . ," Mary was all choked up and could not get the words out.

"Go and tell the apostles: I am going up to my Father, who is also your father, to my God, who is also your God."

Mary did not waste any time. She ran and explained to the apostles what had happened, and they thought she had gone insane. Even after seeing the empty tomb, they could not believe what she was saying.

Jesus Among the Disciples

That same Sunday afternoon, the disciples were gathered together behind closed doors for fear of the people. Then Jesus appeared to them, saying, "Peace be with you."

The disciples were astonished. They thought it was a ghost.

"Don't be afraid. Look at my hands and my feet. I still have the marks of the crucifixion."

And he showed them his hands and feet. He saw that they were not convinced, so he said, "Do you have anything to eat?"

They offered him a piece of fish, and he ate it.

"Doubt no more. Touch me."

Little by little they grew used to having Jesus among them, and he said to them, "Look, I send you as the Father has sent me, to proclaim my teachings."

He gently breathed on them, saying, "Receive the Holy Spirit. Now you will have power to forgive sins or to bind them."

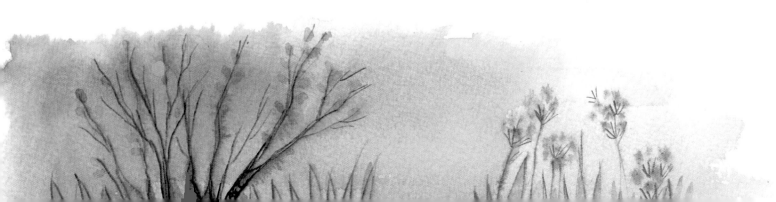

Thomas Does Not Believe It

They talked about the days they had been apart. However, there was one apostle missing from this meeting: Thomas.

When he arrived, they told him at once about the apparition, but he did not quite understand. When Thomas finally realized what they were talking about, he said, "Say what you will, but if I don't touch the wounds of his hands, his feet, and his side, I will not believe it is he."

No matter how many details they gave him, or how much they insisted, they could not convince him.

Eight days later, Jesus appeared again. He neared Thomas and said, "Thomas, put your hand in my side and put your fingers in my other wounds."

Jesus had not finished speaking when Thomas said, "My Lord and my God!"

"Did you have to see me to believe? It would have been better if you had believed in their words."

Good Fishing! Just Like Before . . .

A few days later, a group of disciples went fishing with Peter. After laboring all night, they caught nothing. Then Jesus appeared, but they did not recognize him, and he said, "Cast your nets on both sides of the boat."

They did so, and they caught so many fish that the nets almost broke. Just then they remembered the many times they had gone fishing with Jesus and they recognized him. When Peter realized, he could not wait for the boat to reach the other shore; he jumped in the water to run and see Jesus.

When the other disciples arrived with the full nets, they found a fire already started so they could cook the fish. After eating, Jesus asked Peter, "Peter, do you love me more than these?"

"Yes, Lord, you know I love you."

"Watch over my sheep."

A little later, Jesus asked Peter again, "Peter, do you love me?"

"Yes, Master."

"Keep my sheep."

A third time Jesus asked, "Peter, son of John, do you love me?"

"Lord, you know everything. Why do you ask me again?"

Peter was sad that Jesus asked him the question so many times.

"Tend my sheep. When you were young, you tied your belt, but when you grow old, someone else will tie it and take you where perhaps you do not want to go. Get up and follow me," Jesus said.

Last Piece of Advice

While the two were taking a walk, the apostle John was following them. Peter complained and Jesus said, "Let him be. If I want him to stay until I come back, what difference does that make to you?"

These words of Jesus were misinterpreted by the apostles, who concluded falsely that John would not die.

When they returned to where the others were staying, Jesus said, "All power has been given to me over heaven and earth. Go to all the world and make disciples. Baptize them in the name of the Father, the Son, and the Holy Spirit, and explain my teachings to them. Remember that I will be with you until the end of time."

They were near Bethany. Then Jesus blessed them and rose to heaven until they could no longer see him. The disciples prostrated themselves. They then went to Jerusalem where they waited for the fulfillment of Jesus' words.

8.
The Apostles Proclaim Jesus' Death and Resurrection

The Holy Spirit

When the disciples were in Jerusalem, Peter suggested, "The time has come for someone to replace Judas the betrayer. There are two men who, because of their exemplary behavior, could aspire to take that place: Joseph and Matthias. We will cast lots. In this way, God can indicate to us which one is the more adequate."

Matthias was chosen. Henceforth he joined the group of the twelve as one more apostle.

A few days later was the celebration of Pentecost—the completion of the Passover. A new harvest was celebrated and the Jewish people thanked God for the Law Moses had received at Mount Sinai.

The apostles were together when a great noise and a stormy wind left them speechless. At that instant, they were filled with the Holy Spirit. Then they started to speak in foreign languages as if they had always known them. During that time of the year there were many foreigners in Jerusalem and they were dumbfounded when they saw these men speaking in their own tongues, even though they came from different countries. Of course, there were some others who wanted the people to believe that the apostles had had too much wine.

Then Peter spoke to the crowds, saying, "Do I look drunk? No one among us has drunk anything. What is happening is not a consequence of alcohol but of the Holy Spirit who has come down upon us.

"What do you wish now? To destroy our reputation as you did with Jesus of Nazareth? It was evident that, after all the miracles he performed, he was the one sent by God. And what did you do? Kill him by nailing him to a cross.

"But Jesus' death was known to God long before you thought of it. So, you only helped him fulfill what had been written. Jesus announced his own death many times, and we just didn't want to listen.

"However, don't think for a moment that his death has meant the end of Jesus or of his teaching, because he has power over death and has risen. We are his witnesses, we have seen him and spoken with him. His teachings will not pass away as long as we have a voice to proclaim them. The Jesus you crucified is the Jesus the Scriptures spoke of."

Many of those who were listening to Peter believed in his words and asked, "What do we have to do to join you?"

"You have to believe that Jesus is the Messiah and be baptized in his name. Everyone can become a follower of Christ, old or young, regardless of origin," Peter replied, glad that they showed interest.

As a consequence of Peter's speech many were baptized, and they joined the apostles to build the first community of followers of Jesus.

The Lame Man Walks

The persons who were part of the community went to the Temple to worship like the rest of the Jews, and in their homes they shared bread and wine as Jesus had taught them. They thus commemorated his death and resurrection. All they had they shared with one another and divided it according to the needs of each person. The most important thing for them was praying and practicing the teachings of Jesus. The number of believers grew each day.

One day John and Peter were going to the Temple to pray. Traveling there, they saw a lame man who used to sit by the Temple entrance. When he saw them, he asked for alms.

Peter surprised him by saying, "Look at us."

The man was not sure what was happening. He did not know what these men wanted and he could not run away if they attacked. He was in for a big surprise!

"We don't have any money, but we give you what we have. In the name of Jesus of Nazareth, walk," Peter said to him.

Without knowing how it happened, the man started to walk. He was not paralyzed any longer.

The news spread like wildfire. The lame man had been sitting in that same spot for so long—almost since birth—that he was like a fixture of the Temple. Soon a crowd congregated around Peter. The healed man was with them and everyone could see with their own eyes that the man who had been paralyzed since birth was no longer so. Then Peter said to those who had just come,

"Why do you look so surprised? Do you think we are magicians or witches because this man is walking? It hasn't been our power that has saved him, but rather Jesus of Nazareth who, through us, has given strength to his legs.

"Jesus of Nazareth, yes. Do you remember him? The man you sent to the cross. The one Pilate tried to liberate while you advocated for the freedom of Barabbas, the murderer. But we know you did that out of ignorance. Jesus, however, was dead only for three days. We are witnesses to his resurrection. In this way the Word of God was fulfilled where it says that the Messiah would have to suffer.

"God has sent his servant Jesus to you first so that you may believe in him and be saved. Seize this privilege and repent. Your sins will be forgiven if you stop sinning and abandon evil."

The clamor caused by the actions of the two apostles did not go unnoticed by the priests. They showed up there when Peter was still speaking, and they arrested Peter and John. They thought it insufferable that Peter and John, whom they did not control, could have the power to gather together such a crowd. It was even more unbearable that, after their preaching, the Jews would become disciples of the same Jesus the priests had sent to his death. But, in spite of the priests, Peter's words caused many conversions that day. This filled their hearts with joy, although they were in a dark dungeon, waiting for the priests to judge them for their boldness.

Peter and John Before the Priests

They did not have to wait long. The following day they appeared before the Sanhedrin—the council of priests. They asked the apostles, pointing to the healed man, "In whose name have you healed this man's legs?"

"It was Jesus of Nazareth who cured him," Peter said with a powerful voice, "the one you put to death. But he has risen. If we compared God's laws to bricks in a building, Jesus is the cornerstone of the whole building. On the other hand, you as priests should watch over these laws. You are the builders, and, instead of accepting him as the cornerstone, you have rejected him. Keep in mind that Jesus of Nazareth is salvation. He alone was given to us for our salvation. Without him we shall not enter paradise."

Peter's speech left them astounded. They had expected him to go back on his words, to apologize, or at the very least to excuse himself—even if it was only out of fear of the punishment that could come to him. He not only acknowledged the accusation, but even dared to preach to them, the priests—the know-it-alls. They were the ones who were supposed to educate, not to receive teachings from anyone.

In order to speak freely between themselves, the priests made the apostles leave.

"Aren't these people who have spoken ignorant fishermen? I'd like to know where they have learned to express themselves like this," one said.

"You can be sure they were fishermen, and also that they accompanied Jesus everywhere he went," another one stated.

"We all know well the man they have cured. This is a miracle; we cannot deny the man is healed," still another reminded them.

"We can deny whatever we please. But this time it wouldn't look right; the lame man is too well known and the entire city of Jerusalem would be on our backs," another one honestly reasoned.

"What about telling them not to do it again?" a priest ventured to ask.

"I don't think we'll get very far, but I don't see that we can do anything else," another member of the Sanhedrin resigned.

As soon as they reached an agreement, they called the apostles in.

"Although you have been disrespectful to the Sanhedrin, we will let you go without punishment so that you see we don't hold grudges. But we are giving you a warning not to speak about Jesus anymore. If so we will be forced to arrest you again to protect the people from your twisted words," the high priest warned them.

"You, who are priests, certainly won't find it difficult to understand that we listen to God before we listen to human beings. We are not willing to keep quiet about what we have seen and learned."

Challenging the Sanhedrin would have cost other people their lives, but the priests were not in any position to put them to death. The people would have rebelled against them. Therefore, they repeated their warning and let Peter and John go.

Share Everything

When the other apostles heard what had happened to Peter and John, they all agreed to pray and asked, "Lord, despite the threats of the priests, help us to be willing to proclaim your teachings with courage and firmness. Let us also perform wonders in your name so that more people will believe in you."

When they finished praying, the same flames that appeared on Pentecost appeared over their heads as a sign that the Spirit of God was upon them. And, overcoming their fear, they continued to speak about Jesus and in the name of Jesus.

After these words and the deeds of the apostles, the community of the believers began to grow. As they felt they were but one family, they wanted to share their possessions with all. Two of these new disciples were Ananias and his wife, Sapphira. They had sold some property but agreed between themselves to give the apostles less than what they had gotten. They would keep a part for themselves.

Knowing the deceit, Peter received the money from Ananias and said, "Ananias, you want to deceive God. You are free not to sell your field; no one has forced you to be part of our community. However, if you join it, it has to be without deceit."

Hearing those words, Ananias dropped dead. A little later Sapphira, his wife, arrived, unaware of what had happened.

"What price did you put on your field, Sapphira?" Peter asked.

Sapphira answered the same as her husband. Then Peter said, "Look, Sapphira. Now those who have taken away your husband's body are coming for you so that you keep him company and you won't deceive God ever again."

At that moment, Sapphira died and was buried with her husband. After this event, a great fear spread among all those who heard this story.

Threats Will Not Frighten Them

By the power of God, the apostles worked miracles. Their fame spread so fast that, when Peter walked down the street, people would take their sick loved ones out so that at least his shadow would touch them. The priests could not stand the apostles' popularity, so they put them in prison. But an angel of God took them out of prison and told them, "Go to the Temple and preach Jesus' teachings."

The following morning, when the Sanhedrin wanted to interrogate the arrested men, the soldiers answered, "We have gone to the prison looking for them. The guards were in their places and the doors were locked; but when we opened up, we did not find anyone inside. We don't know how this could have happened."

Then other soldiers came in and reported, "The men you are looking for are in the Temple, explaining their teachings to the people."

Immediately soldiers went in search of the apostles to bring them before the Sanhedrin. They did not use force so that those captivated by the apostles would not rebel. When Peter was before the Sanhedrin, they asked him, "Hadn't we forbidden you to teach and speak in the name of Jesus?"

"We must obey God before all human powers. The God of our parents has raised Jesus, whom you crucified. This Jesus has been lifted up as a Savior and has thus obtained for Israel forgiveness for its sins and conversion. We are witnesses to all this and we have to proclaim it," Peter answered resolutely.

Peter's courageous response enraged the members of the Sanhedrin, who were excitedly talking all at once trying to decide what to do with the apostles. Many were in favor of eliminating them. Then a Pharisee in the Sanhedrin named Gamaliel cut in and said, "Look, I don't see things that clearly. In any case, I would like to remind you that Jesus' case was not the only one we had in the country. Before him, there were others who would attract a following. Once the leader of the pack was dead, the group dissolved or only survived for a short time. If what they are defending is a human work, it will have the same fate: it will fall by its own weight. But if it doesn't dissolve, perhaps it is God's doing, and, if that is the case, who wants to go against God?"

This intervention calmed down the most excited ones among them. After a few more consultations, they decided to follow Gamaliel's proposal. Those most enraged were satisfied to see the apostles flogged.

The Sanhedrin saw how the apostles left grinning, happy to have suffered for Jesus Christ's cause. They were astonished to see the apostles' determination.

Stephen Preaches

Jesus' disciples were increasing. Among the converted Jews there were some Hellenists—who came from the farthest lands of Israel—and Hebrews—hailing from Jerusalem and its surrounding areas. The group of Hellenists were complaining that their widows were not cared for because the apostles did not have any time to pay attention to them.

The apostles solved the problem by addressing the assembly of all the disciples: "We think you are right, but we cannot be two places at the same time. We have to choose between one occupation and the other. We don't think we should dedicate less time to the teaching of the Word of God because of this problem. We think it would be better if, from among yourselves, you choose seven honest men to be in charge of this service. In this way, the widows will be cared for and we will be able to dedicate our efforts to spreading the Word of God."

They did so. The men elected were Stephen, Philip, Prochorus, Nicanor, Timon, Parmenas, and Nicholas of Antioch. In order to consecrate them, the apostles laid hands on them—in this way they would transmit the Holy Spirit.

Among the seven chosen ones Stephen was outstanding, and he proclaimed the Word of God when his other obligations allowed.

One day he was speaking at the synagogue of the Freedmen. Some Jews stood up to argue with him, but they did not keep it up long, because they didn't know how to continue their debates, since Stephen skillfully disarmed all their arguments with his wisdom. When they did not know what else to say, they realized they had been embarrassed before the rest, and they felt hatred toward Stephen. So they paid some people to accuse Stephen of saying something he had never said.

In order to judge him, they brought Stephen before the Sanhedrin. The false accusers said, "This man does not cease speaking against us and against our Law. He says that Jesus the Nazarene will destroy the Temple and change the traditions Moses handed down to us."

"Is that true?" the priests asked Stephen.

Will Stephen Keep Silent Before the Judges?

Stephen answered as follows:

"My brothers and fathers of my people, listen. The history of the relationship between God and our people dates back a long time. Abraham listened to the voice of God in Mesopotamia and followed. He trusted in God's promise despite all appearances to the contrary. The patriarchs, sons of Jacob, jealous of Joseph, sold him to slavery in Egypt. But Joseph went on to prosper and become general governor. Thanks to this, all his brothers and his father's family were saved from the horrible famine of that time. They established themselves in Egypt where they were appreciated.

"Once Joseph was dead, the pharaohs enslaved the Hebrew people. Then Moses, who was raised as an Egyptian, discovered he was a Hebrew, and God entrusted him with the mission of leading his people to freedom. After many plagues fell upon Egypt, Moses finally succeeded in leading them to the Promised Land. He was their intermediary and communicated what God wanted from the people, but as soon as they had a chance, they turned their backs on him and built other gods in the shape of golden calves. And they were punished for that.

"Later, God had a tent of the covenant prepared; and so it continued until the time of David, who wanted to build a Temple. It wasn't until Solomon's reign that the project was completed. The highest God, however, doesn't dwell in houses made by people but is present in heaven and on earth.

"Will you be incapable of understanding the prophets as your ancestors were? Will you also doubt and forget, as they did? Or will you kill them, as you did to John the Baptist who announced the coming of Jesus, whom you have betrayed and nailed to the cross? You have already received an explanation for salvation; so you are more to blame for not having accepted it. Look, now I see the heaven open and Jesus at the right hand of God."

They did not want to listen any longer. They kicked him out of there and began to stone him.

"Lord, do not hold them accountable for this sin; receive my spirit," were Stephen's last words before he died.

As difficult as it is to accept the death of a loved one, it is almost unbearable to accept our own. What a strong heart and spirit must Stephen have had to accept his own death without wavering and to keep faithful to his own beliefs, the teachings of Jesus!

This was what Stephen had done by speaking before the Sanhedrin without fear. And when they were killing him he followed Jesus' example—he asked God to forgive his murderers.

A young man named Saul was keeping the cloaks of those who were stoning Stephen. It was his way of collaborating in the death of someone who, in his opinion, was jeopardizing the Jewish faith.

After Stephen's death the community of believers in Jerusalem was openly persecuted. It was Saul who zealously seized the disciples of Jesus wherever they may be found. He did not hesitate to imprison women, men, or children. The flight of believers, however, helped spread the message

of Jesus to remote lands. Despite everything, Stephen's body did not remain unburied—a group of pious men took care of burying and mourning him as he deserved.

Not Everything Can Be Bought

Philip, one of the seven chosen by the community of Jerusalem, was preaching the Good News—Jesus' teachings—in Samaria. He did not object to teaching the Samaritans, although the most strict Jews did not consider them true Israelites. The Samaritans listened attentively and converted easily.

In Samaria there was a magician named Simon, who, with his tricks and spells, had captivated the Samaritans. When Simon saw the miracles Philip worked in the name of Jesus—people possessed by demons who were liberated, paralytics who were cured—he was curious and wanted to be baptized together with many people in town.

When the apostles learned that Samaria had welcomed the Word of God so enthusiastically, they sent Peter and John there. The two apostles prayed that the Holy Spirit would come upon the Samaritans. When they laid hands on the heads of the converted, the Spirit invaded them.

Simon the Magician realized that the capacity to transmit the Holy Spirit was a special power; so he went to see Peter and John and said to them, "Look, I am a magician, and my powers are not like yours. If you give me your ability to transmit the Holy Spirit, I can give you a lot of money which will probably come in handy for you—you are not exactly traveling in a gold carriage."

Simon thought that everything could be sold and bought; he did not anticipate Peter's response.

"You and your money can rot in hell. We don't have any powers. We are only carriers of the power of God and he gives this power freely to whomever he wants. Do you think we have paid for this? Were you planning to make a profit of this power? Fifty coins per pound of Spirit? It is clear your intentions are not good. Change your way of thinking and pray to the Lord to forgive you."

"I hadn't quite understood what this is all about. Please pray for me so that I don't go to hell."

Although Simon the Magician did not get what he wanted, the term "simony"—when someone offers material goods in exchange for something that is not for sale—was coined from this event.

303

Philip and the Ethiopian

After giving witness to Jesus, the apostles returned to Jerusalem. Wherever they found Samaritans they preached and baptized.

In the meantime, Philip received instructions through an angel of the Lord.

"Go south, on the road that goes from Jerusalem to Gaza."

He did so. On the way he met a carriage that transported the internal revenue minister of Ethiopia, who was Jewish by religion and black by race. This man was reading passages from the prophet Isaiah. At the angel's indication, Philip approached the carriage and said to the Ethiopian, "Good morning. I see you like Scripture. Do you understand what you are reading?"

"I try, but I have many doubts because no one explains the meaning to me. Do you, by any chance, know the Scriptures? Why don't you sit down and explain them to me?" the foreigner asked Philip.

While he was explaining the Scripture, Philip also communicated the message of Jesus of Nazareth. He did not have to do much insisting, for the Ethiopian minister said, "I believe Jesus Christ is the Son of God. I want to be baptized."

As soon as the minister received the waters of baptism, Philip disappeared from his side and the Ethiopian continued on his journey to his country, full of joy at having met Philip. In this way, the message of Jesus would reach the farthest countries known at the time, such as Ethiopia, regardless of the fact that the people there were from different races and cultures.

From Persecutor to Persecuted

In spite of all this, the persecution against the converted did not stop. Saul continued to be the main promoter of the repression. He put so much effort in his task that he even wanted to go out of the city limits of Jerusalem in order to catch Jesus' followers. So, he asked for permission to lead an expedition to Damascus, a foreign land, to arrest the Jews converted to the faith of Jesus.

When he had gotten the necessary permits, he quickly went to Damascus. He was approaching the gates of the city when lightning struck his horse.

"Saul, Saul, why do you persecute me?" he heard.

"Who are you?" asked Saul. "I don't know you."

"I am Jesus of Nazareth, whom you persecute."

The man he had persecuted so resolutely was now before him. At that moment he knew that what the apostles were proclaiming was true. He only needed an instant to realize that he had been wrong, change his attitude, and ask, "Lord, what would you have me do?"

"Go into the city and there you will receive my instructions."

The soldiers who were accompanying him helped him get up off the ground, but they also had to help him walk, because he was blinded.

"What do you want us to do, Saul?" they asked in a panic.

"Help me go into the city," Saul said with great effort.

The apparition of the Lord had moved him so much that he spent three days without eating or drinking anything. He then received the visit of Ananias, a disciple of Jesus.

"Saul, my brother. God sends me to lay hands on you, so that you gain your sight back and be filled with the Holy Spirit," he said.

When Ananias covered Saul's head with his hands, he could see again and immediately asked to be baptized. Hearing this, Ananias was relieved. He had gone to see Saul following God's instructions, but he was fearful. This was no one less than the awesome Saul, who had imprisoned thousands of Jesus' followers. Ananias was afraid that, once he had regained his sight, Saul would imprison him.

Ananias and the other disciples of Damascus were relieved when they saw Saul, after being baptized, openly preaching Jesus' doctrine in the public squares of Damascus. Neither the Jews of Damascus nor those of Jerusalem were happy, however, when they learned of the amazing conversion of Saul. There was nothing that would cause them to lose face faster than the fact that one of the most ardent persecutors of Jesus' followers was now a follower himself. So, they decided to kill Saul.

But the believers heard of the Jews' intentions and they saved Saul's life by placing him in a basket and lowering him down the city walls one night.

Saul left Damascus but did not hide from anyone. He went on his way to Jerusalem but he found it very hard to relate to the disciples there. They did not want to come in contact with him because they did not trust his conversion to be real; every time they heard Saul's name they automatically went into hiding, so great was their fear of him.

Thanks to Barnabas, who trusted in him and explained to the rest the courage with which Saul had proclaimed the name of Jesus in Damascus, he was admitted into the Church—the community of believers—of Jerusalem. But even so, he could not stay there long. Since he had been the closest friend of the high priests, he was now the most hated enemy. He had to flee Jerusalem and go to Tarsus, his hometown.

Is Peter Collaborating with the Invaders?

In the meantime the apostles were doing everything in their power to spread the teachings of Jesus. Peter decided to visit the communities of Lydda and Joppa. In Lydda he met Aeneas, who had been paralyzed for eight years.

"Come on, get up, and make your own bed," Peter said to him.

That same instant, Aeneas rose, although he did not quite understand what had happened to him. If he had not felt the strength in his legs, he would have thought he was dreaming. All those who knew him were amazed.

From Joppa they called Peter because Tabitha, a good woman of the city, had died. Peter went to her house and knelt by her body. After praying, he commanded, "Tabitha, get up!"

She opened her eyes and sat up. She presented herself alive to all those who had gone to mourn her death. Many people in the city converted when they saw this wonder. The men who had power over death must possess the truth, which dispelled the doubts in the minds of many people. Tabitha and her family were still recovering from the astonishment they felt; they did not stop expressing their joy at Tabitha's resurrection.

But Peter could not stay long in this city because some unfamiliar messengers arrived. They were messengers from Cornelius, a Roman centurion, who begged Peter to visit him in the nearby city of Caesarea. It was a double offense for Jews to go into the house of a Roman. In terms of religion, the centurion was a pagan, a worshiper of false gods, and should be pitied. Politically, however, he was an invader, who should be despised.

Peter's first reaction was to refuse, but he then remembered a vision he had had the previous day, and Cornelius' petition helped him understand it. God wanted him to forget his lifetime prejudices about the people he could and could not relate to. God wanted him to consider those ideas only in terms of whether people were willing to believe in Jesus or not. Peter surprised himself by accompanying the messengers to the centurion's house. There Peter explained Jesus' teachings. He

had not finished speaking when the Holy Spirit came upon all those who were there, regardless of whether or not they were Jewish. This confirmed that Peter had made the right decision in going to the house of the centurion. He baptized all those who wished to be baptized.

Jews or Christians?

But being in Caesarea was not the same as being in Judea. When Peter returned to Jerusalem, he had to explain to the community about his contact with the pagans. He told them about his mission, the coming of the Holy Spirit on the pagans, and the enthusiasm with which the pagans had welcomed the Good News of Jesus. Peter tried to make them understand that pagans too could receive the doctrine of Jesus.

The same thing happened in Antioch, where many disciples had gone after fleeing from Jerusalem.

In Antioch a great number of pagans became followers of Jesus without having been Jewish first. Until that moment, the disciples of Jesus were a special kind of Jews—they had a slightly different interpretation of the Scriptures, enlightened by Jesus' teachings, but they were still Jews.

Those who had been pagans before becoming followers of Jesus needed a name. They were called Christians for the first time in that city, and from there the name spread and was applied to all of Jesus' followers, Jews and non-Jews.

But Jews and Christians became alienated from one another as different communities when Herod, the king of the Jews, had James, one of the twelve apostles, beheaded. The rest of the Christians were filled with sadness at James' loss and fear that what had happened to James could happen to them, too.

Origins of the Name "Christian"

In the Acts of the Apostles we read that it was in Antioch that the disciples first received the name of Christians. It must have been the pagans who made up that name for the followers of Jesus, the Christ. Christians called each other brothers, disciples, saints, faithful, the elected, while the Jews called them Galileans, Nazarenes, and even heretics.

Antioch was the capital of the Roman province of Syria. Many Christians took refuge there after the persecution broke out right after Stephen's death. Christians found a hospitable environment in this city and one of the most important first communities was formed there. Since the Christians professed a new religion and showed a different attitude and behavior, the pagans mockingly called them Christians. However, Christians themselves soon adopted the name. Many became Christians in the Roman world; there were so many that, after three centuries, Christianity had taken roots in practically the entire Roman Empire.

Bad Blood in Jerusalem

But King Herod's persecutions did not end with Stephen. He imprisoned Peter—the head of the Church—with the intention of executing him, too. He wanted to leave Christians without their leaders so that the communities would disperse and abandon their beliefs.

Peter was sleeping on the hard, cold dungeon floor. Suddenly in his dreams he saw an angel of the Lord who loosened the chains of his hands and accompanied him, passing unnoticed by the prison guards. When they had gone through the big iron prison gate, the angel disappeared and Peter found himself in the middle of the street. But it was not a dream; it was real. God had liberated him so he could continue his mission. Immediately he went to Mary's house and found the apostles there praying. It was not easy to convince them that he was Peter and not an impostor since they thought it was impossible for him to have escaped. But Peter explained how he had been liberated by the Lord. All thanked God for this. Then they went to Caesarea so that Herod would not find them.

The following morning, no soldier dared to tell Herod that the prisoner had escaped, because they knew what their fate would be. The guards' fear was confirmed when Herod had them executed for their ineptness, which soothed the anger he felt at Peter's escape.

Herod's reign did not last long. One day a short time later, he was talking to the people dressed in his finest clothes, as if he were a god, and the Lord sent him an illness. Worms ate his insides and everyone could see that his body was only flesh, like that of all the other mortals. He soon died from that illness.

Barnabas and Saul were in Jerusalem. They had been sent from Antioch to support the Christians of the sister community of Jerusalem, which was suffering because of the persecutions.

Calm was restored to the Christian community of Jerusalem upon Herod's death. So Saul, Barnabas, and his nephew John, the apostle, returned to Antioch.

A Magician or a Demon?

They did not stay in Antioch long because their wish to spread Jesus' teaching led them to the island of Cyprus. The Roman governor Sergius listened to them very attentively. But their teaching was not very useful because Elymas, a Jewish magician who had a great influence over Sergius, ridiculed everything the apostle Saul said or did. Saul—who from that time on would take the name of Paul—grew tired and said, "Elymas, son of the devil, when will you stop mocking the teachings of the Lord? You won't feel like doing it anymore once you are blinded. Perhaps then you will regret having gone against God's action."

Immediately the false magician went blind, and the governor joined the rest of Jesus' believers. John, who had accompanied them, returned from Cyprus to Jerusalem. Paul and Barnabas went to Antioch in Pisidia—a city with the same name as the one they had just been sent to, but where they had never preached about Jesus before. But in this city, the Jews, jealous of the apostles' success and of the growing number of people converting to Christianity, succeeded in throwing the preachers out. They then went to Iconium.

There they also were very successful preaching in the synagogue. Many people, both Jews and pagans, converted. But the same thing happened as in Antioch: the Jews who did not believe influenced the minds of the pagan and Jewish leaders to persecute the Christians. The apostles also had to leave this town, although the community of believers stayed alive.

We Are Not Gods

They continued on their way to Lystra, where they preached the Word of God. Among those who were listening was a man who was paralyzed. Paul looked at him and saw he had enough faith to be cured, so Paul said to him, "Get up and straighten up!"

The man did so. When the news spread, the population of the city looked for them to offer a sacrifice, convinced that only gods in human form could perform a miracle like that. They gave them Greek names and insisted again on offering a sacrifice. The apostles did what they could to prevent this.

"Don't offer any sacrifices. We are not gods, but men like yourselves. Listen to our words and do not be so excited. We proclaim the Good News of the living God who made heaven, earth, the sea, and all that exists. Follow God's teachings and leave aside those stories about false gods."

However, a few hours later, the attitude of the citizens of Lystra changed drastically. The Jews from Antioch and Iconium arrived and won over the people. Those who had looked for the disciples to proclaim them gods wanted to kill them now. Paul could not escape and he was stoned.

The people left the apostles for dead, but Paul got up and entered the city as alive as ever. After these events, they continued on their way to Derbe, and, after their preaching, they started another Christian community. They left some leaders in charge there and returned to where they had come from: they once again visited Lystra, Iconium, and Antioch of Pisidia. With their words, inspired by God, they dispelled the doubts of the new believers and encouraged them to stand firm in their commitments as followers of Jesus.

The fact that they had had to flee these cities in the past was no reason to abandon the communities that had been created there by their preaching. It was necessary to proceed cautiously, but they did not intend to leave them to their fate.

Circumcision: Yes or No

It was time to return to Antioch, the community which had sent them to preach the Word of God to new cities and towns, and they did so.

It was evident that the account of their adventures and all the conversions made during their journeys gladdened the heart of the Christian community of Antioch.

After a time, a group of Christians from Jerusalem said to those of Antioch, "To be saved you need to be circumcised as the Law of Moses commands."

Paul and Barnabas discussed this because it was not good for members of the same Church to disagree on their teachings. Therefore a gathering of Christians from all over the world convened to deal with the issue of circumcision; it was called a council.

Barnabas and Paul were sent to the council by the community of Antioch. The council of Jerusalem started with a speech by some Christians who had been Pharisees before and who argued, "It is necessary for the pagans who have been converted to be circumcised and keep the Law of Moses."

A very heated discussion ensued. In the end of it Peter spoke and said, "You know well that some time ago by divine instruction I went to the pagans to speak to them about God. I would never have come up with such an idea by myself. While I was speaking, the Holy Spirit came upon them, those who were uncircumcised. Would the Spirit have come down upon them if they needed circumcision? Don't we agree that salvation is a free gift from God to people? Why impose requisites the Lord is not demanding from them?"

Paul and Barnabas explained the resolve with which many pagans joined the Church of Christ and faithfully practiced its teachings. Then James said, "I don't think we can ask for circumcision from those who were not Jewish before they became Christians. But it would be advisable to ask them to refrain from consuming meat offered to the gods, unclean meat, and blood, and to avoid illegitimate marriages."

This opinion was accepted, and, just as James had proposed, it was made known to the Christians of Antioch in a letter.

What a Great Deal, the Woman Possessed . . .

From this city, Paul and Barnabas thought they would continue their missionary work. But, since they could not agree on who should go with them, they went their separate ways.

Barnabas went to Cyprus with John, his nephew. Paul went with Silas to Lystra, where Timothy joined them.

But in the outskirts of Lystra there were already other communities. Paul felt the need to go to lands where no one would have heard of Jesus, so they went to Philippi of Macedonia.

His preaching in that city yielded the important conversion of Lydia, a cloth merchant, and her family. Once baptized, the family insisted that the disciples remain there for a time.

Very early one morning when they were going to pray, a woman possessed by a demon followed them and kept saying, "These men are servants of God who proclaim salvation." This slave woman was good business for her masters, for she was a fortune teller.

Paul got tired of hearing her, and said to the spirit possessing her, "In the name of Jesus Christ, I command you to come out of her."

The spirit obeyed and left the woman, but she was left without the ability to foretell anything else. For this reason her masters denounced Paul and Silas to the judges, who, after scourging them, placed them in a dark dungeon.

Why Don't They Escape?

At midnight there was an earthquake, and the gates were opened and the prisoners' chains were broken. When the jailer saw that, he took his sword out to commit suicide, for he thought the prisoners would have fled. But Paul stopped him, "Don't do that. We are here."

The guard came in with a light and saw that was true. The men who had not escaped in order to save the guard from punishment were truly extraordinary. What kind of person who had the opportunity to escape from an inhuman prison would have stayed to protect the jailer? Their behavior made him understand they had the truth. He asked them, "What should I do to be saved?"

"Believe in Jesus and you will be saved," Paul answered.

Then the guard took them to his home. He nursed their wounds, fed them, and he and his whole family were baptized.

The following morning, the guard received the order to free them. Happily, he told Paul, "They have ordered me to take you out of prison. You can go in peace."

But Paul replied, "I don't think this is any way to treat Roman citizens. They have scourged us without a trial, they have thrown us in prison, and now they want to free us quietly. If they want anything, they should come themselves to take us out of here."

When the judge heard that those people were Roman citizens, he apologized and asked them to leave the city. Paul and Silas did, after saying goodbye to Lydia and her family.

Preaching Despite All Difficulties

From Philippi they went to Thessalonica, where they found a Jewish synagogue. There they discussed Scripture for three days. Some Jews believed in their words, but others incited the people against them. They said, "These men proclaim that we have a king other than Caesar, a certain Jesus."

Upset, the people looked for the disciples but could not find them because they were already on their way to Beroea, where the Word of God was much better received. Many men and women, both of humble and high classes, became disciples of Jesus. But the Jews from Thessalonica would soon get there. These were the same people who, with their lies, had thrown them out of the city. To protect himself, Paul took a boat to Athens. Silas and Timothy stayed behind with the intention of rejoining him later.

Paul found the city of Athens full of gods. He went to the synagogue to talk with the Jews and to the public squares to talk with the Greeks. Officials at the Areopagus, the Greek court, called Paul in to ask him, "What is this new doctrine you are proclaiming? We had never heard things like that. We want to know what they mean."

And Paul explained the basics of Christianity. All listened attentively, except when he started speaking about the resurrection. This was an absurd idea to the Greeks. Even so, some people were baptized by Paul, who then continued on his journey to Corinth.

There he met Aquila and Priscilla, a married couple who were tent makers like Paul, and he worked with them. A few days later, Silas and Timothy arrived. Then Paul concentrated on explaining the teachings of Christ to the Jews of the city. But they did not want to hear of Jesus, so Paul addressed the pagans. Many Corinthians who heard, believed and were baptized. But Paul thought this whole thing was going very slowly.

Then, in a vision, God told him, "Don't grow discouraged. You will make many disciples in this city. I am with you and will protect you."

And he stayed there for about a year and a half.

He was still in Corinth when he got news that in the city of Thessalonica, where he had already preached, there was some confusion within the community of Christians that had been formed there. In order to help them, Paul wrote the following:

"I have heard that some of you have stopped working while waiting for the coming of the Lord. This is not what I taught you. When I was among you, I worked so as not to be a burden to anyone. Everybody in the community has to work to be able to eat. If someone wants to go on without working because he or she expects the immediate coming of the Lord, he or she should not eat. You will soon see how it feels to be in need."

Once his stay in Corinth was over, Paul started on his way back to Antioch, where he arrived after a few stops.

Paul, the Tireless Apostle

He stayed in Antioch and the surrounding areas for a short time, just long enough to greet the communities, and once he saw believers thriving, he planned a journey to areas more in need of his presence.

He had heard that a certain Apollo had preached in Ephesus. Paul was not sure that the doctrine proclaimed was the right one. To clear his doubts, he went there.

When he arrived he asked the Christians, "What kind of baptism have you received?"

"We were baptized by John," they answered.

"John's was only a preparation for the important one that was to come: the baptism of Jesus," he clarified.

Once they had been instructed, he baptized them in the name of Jesus Christ and laid hands on them to transmit the Holy Spirit, whom they had not heard of until that time. All together there were twelve people.

He also spoke in the synagogue, but the Jews did not listen to him. After three months of trying in vain, he took the teaching of the word of Jesus to the school of Tyrannus, where he stayed for two years.

From there, Paul received news of the different Christian communities. At that moment, in Ephesus, he was concerned about the Corinthian community. Since he could not go there, he wrote to them to guide them, answering the doubts the Corinthians had presented.

Love Is the Most Important Thing

Many wise men from our city ridicule our beliefs; they say it is absurd to follow a crucified man.

"Look, brothers and sisters, God has called few powerful and influential people and very few noble families to be part of his people. God has often chosen what is considered insignificant. You don't have to waste your energy on those worldly issues. Your nobility comes from being followers of Christ; that's your pride and your satisfaction," Paul clarified for them.

Some of us have been taught by Apollo and some by you. We do not always agree among ourselves and we don't know who is right, Apollo or you.

"What are the jealousies and fights among you? There are some who have been taught by Apollo and some by Paul. Both are mere messengers of the Word. You have to say: we share the same beliefs and for that reason feel like brothers and sisters. You are like the field God tills or the building God builds. What difference does it make who waters or sows, who prepares the mortar or the bricks? The workers are only instruments. God is the one who joins us all together, the one from whom all teachings come."

But if we don't know which of the two is more important, how will we know whose teachings to follow when we are in doubt?

"You want to know who is more important? Don't be judges. The Lord, who knows the intentions of the heart, will judge; that is God's role. I am not superior to Apollo, and no one grants me superiority over others. Both of us are servants of Christ. If I apply that to myself, you should do the same and not say: I am superior because I am Apollo's, or I am superior because I am Paul's."

To Respond with Love

But somehow we must respond to the contempt and insults of the most important people in the city.

"Of course! When they insult us, let us bless them. If they speak ill of us, let us answer with sweetness. And, if they insist, let us take it patiently. This has to be our answer. Those who are truly wise will understand it," Peter affirmed.

But responding to aggression is human. It is impossible to always react calmly.

"If we want to get them to understand us and to one day accept the teachings of Christ, we must react with love. Only love is constructive; anger and hatred destroy. If we react as they would, they can despise us with good reason because then we are no better than they."

What is that kind of love that forces us to allow people to mistreat us?

"Love is long-suffering; love is helpful; it doesn't know jealousy. Love is not proud or selfish, it forgets and forgives wrongdoing; love is just; truth is its joy. Love excuses everything, gives trust and trusts others. It never loses hope; it bears everything. Love is more important than anything else. It is more important than all knowledge, than wisdom, than science. I might have all those things; I might have hope and faith, but if I have no love, I am nothing."

That is a difficult kind of love. Is it worthwhile to look like a fool in the eyes of important people?

"Those important people don't want to accept our position as real, because they are incapable of following our way. They don't want to give up their injustice. What do you want? To be as unjust as they are? Don't you know that those who are unjust will not have a place in the reign of God? Many of you were also unjust before accepting the teachings of God. The sacrifice of Jesus and the Spirit of God have made you God's friends. You will see the expression on the faces of those who now torment you when they are not admitted into God's kingdom. Try not to be excluded from the kingdom yourselves."

United as Members of One Body

How is it possible for us, who are not important at all in this society, to be considered important by God?

"Look at your body. Is there any organ that is not important? You have one body and many parts. All are necessary and important. Likewise, when we were baptized with the Spirit, we became part of one single body, the body of Christ; each one with his or her function. Sometimes the members thought to be the least important are the most necessary, those without whom the body would not function. What makes you important is that you are part of the body."

Yes, but there are some members who always carry the weight, and others never do.

"Although members of the body are all different, they all depend on one another. If one is sick, all of them feel it. Because of their relation, they are concerned about each other. When a member suffers, the others feel the suffering as their own. This same communication must exist among those who form the body of Christ. The stronger members must give strength and consolation to those who are more tired or weak."

We often discuss among ourselves whether one should marry or stay single.

"Those who get married have to be concerned about their spouses and about supporting their families. Getting married carries with it a series of responsibilities that need attention. If you are married, you cannot be fully dedicated to the Lord because you have other things to attend to. Whoever is single and can stay single should do so. He or she will have more time to take care of the needs of the Church of God. Widows and single people who don't think they can remain celibate, they should get married."

The resurrection is another topic we don't quite understand. How can we rise once we die and our bodies rot?

"When we sow seeds, they must rot so that they can later create new life in a new plant. The same will happen with the resurrection of the dead; our body will have disappeared but another purer and nobler life will come from us."

Does that have something to do with that saying about reaping what you sowed?

"Well, it is clear that those who sowed little will reap little and those who sowed abundantly will have an abundant harvest. That is, those who are generous will receive generosity in the measure in which they have given. Each must have a measure of generosity; the point is to give with joy, not reluctantly, but willingly. That way giving will be a source of happiness."

This Is Not Magic

God performed wonderful miracles through Paul, to the point that, to be cured, a sick person only had to come in contact with a piece of cloth Paul had touched.

The sons of Sceva, a Jewish high priest, wanted to imitate Paul by performing miracles. They tried to do it with a man who was possessed by an evil spirit, saying to him, "In the name of the Jesus that Paul preaches we command you to leave this man."

The evil spirit answered, "I know Jesus and I also know Paul, but who are you?"

And he jumped on them so furiously that they had to flee wounded and half naked.

In the meantime, Paul was writing some instructions to the community of Philippi:

"I know you are concerned with knowing to what extent you should devote yourselves to human affairs so that they don't take you away from God. If you have learned the teachings, you will know which human activities befit you and which ones do not. Do what is noble, true, and just, the things you consider to be good according to our ideals. Not only should you not reject them, but you must work to accomplish them enthusiastically, because everything human and noble is part of the Christian duties. Keep this in mind and act accordingly."

The Galatians also wanted to receive Paul's guidance. Paul wrote to them to make up for not being able to see them personally.

If It Is Not by Word of Mouth, at Least in Writing

"Is faith in the Law of Moses different from faith in Jesus Christ?" the Galatians asked.

"In the era before Jesus Christ we were like minors. We were enslaved to the Law because, since we were underage, we could not decide for ourselves. When Jesus Christ came, he rescued us from that slavery and lifted us up to the category of children of God. The Law of Moses was like a tutor, accompanying us in everything and everywhere, but faith in Jesus Christ has liberated us from the authority of that tutor. Now we are children of God because we form one single body, one person in Christ; since he is the Son of God, we become God's children too. What more could we ask for? There is no dignity higher than ours nor generosity greater than God's."

Does that freedom allow us to forget abiding by the Law of God?

"If Jesus Christ gave his life for our freedom, to liberate us from the old slavery, and you now turn your freedom into selfishness, you are exchanging one slavery for another. Freedom will only be true freedom if it is based on love. Any thought or act coming from you must be formed by love and in accordance to the teachings of Christ. Do you wish to fulfill all the precepts of the Law? I will make it simple for you. Love your neighbor as yourself, then you will know what you love. This is a guide telling you to what extent you must love one another: as much as you love yourselves."

And if we see a friend doing something bad, what should we do? Keep quiet so that he or she does not get mad?

"It is not necessary for you to be watching to see when your friend does something bad. But if we realize something, we don't have to accuse him or her as if it were irreparable. We have to correct our friends with gentleness and help them not to do it again. Showing gentleness and sharing some part of the responsibility will help them straighten up and choose the correct behavior. This is the best way to convince someone. You could find yourselves in the same situation at one point, and you would probably like to be treated gently."

And if we do it that way so that they later can do the same with us, isn't that a form of selfishness?

"It would be selfishness if that were the only reason you did it; the true reason must be that you feel good doing it because you are helping the other person and following Jesus' teachings. Jesus loves you and does not suggest that you do anything that will bring you harm. Although this is not your only motivation, you can neither forget nor ignore the fact that whatever you do will provoke reactions toward you that will be positive or negative in direct proportion to your pleasant or unpleasant behavior."

No Kidding with Real Business

There was a great temple in Ephesus dedicated to the goddess Artemis. Silver craftsmanship was linked to that temple. The craftsmen sold miniature replicas of the chapel to Artemis. Demetrius controlled the business of the reproductions, and he realized that the sales had gone down greatly since Paul began preaching there. He told his coworkers, "Since Paul started preaching that 'those made with human hands are not gods,' sales have gone down. If this trend continues we will have to close the business down. We must stop those Christians, especially Paul. The great temple could suffer if we can't get those madmen to stop preaching here."

All the workers related to the silversmith trade started shouting out in defense of their work, "Long live Ephesus' Artemis!" They went throughout the city seeking out Christians and threatening them, but they only found Gaius and Aristarchus, Paul's traveling companions, whom they dragged to the theater.

Paul wanted to come before the crowds, but the Christians convinced him not to do it. When everyone was present in the theater, the city leader spoke to them, saying, "Citizens, you have brought me some men who have not blasphemed against our goddess or been disrespectful to her. There is not a single city in the whole empire that does not know that Ephesus is the keeper of the great temple of Artemis. What do you then fear? You have let yourselves be driven by passion. Today's clamoring is not at all justified. Release these men and go on with your work."

With these words, the assembly dispersed.

When the noise of the tumult had calmed down, Paul informed them, "I have to go to Macedonia to help and expand the communities there."

During his three months in Greece and Macedonia he raised the spirits of the Christians and increased the number of communities.

He stayed in Gaius' house in Corinth, encouraging the community there. In addition to the work he did, he took care of other communities he wished he could visit, but his mission in Greece did not allow it. During those days he wrote a meaningful letter to the Christian community in Rome. Paul realized how much Rome meant, since it was the capital of the Roman Empire and influenced the rest of the Empire in every cultural, social, and religious aspect. If Christianity took root in Rome, sooner or later it would spread throughout the whole Empire—which was like saying the whole world. This was Paul's greatest wish. It is not strange then, that he painstakingly and enthusiastically prepared his explanations to the Christians of Rome.

Is Being a Christian Profitable?

Do you have to be a Jew before being a Christian, or can pagans convert straight to Christianity?

"I am a slave of Jesus Christ. He has chosen me to bring the Good News to all, Jews and pagans. Pagans can embrace the teachings of Christ because God loves all human beings tenderly and calls them to be part of his people. The sacrifice of Jesus Christ was meant to save all men and women, Jews or pagans. God's call is for everyone, provided they want to follow the teachings of Christ and become part of the community of Christians."

Can any pagan be a Christian, or is a special behavior required?

"God does not demand anything special from people. People come in all shapes and sizes, so there is no prerequisite for becoming a Christian; a person only needs to believe in Jesus Christ and accept his teachings. God invites people to his friendship, and faith is the only condition; you don't need to be wise or well educated. Any person with faith becomes a friend of God and therefore part of God's people."

But if, as a pagan, you profited from your self-centered life, as a Christian what reward is there in caring for others?

"Jesus Christ did not need to become a man, go through the difficulties he went through, and die on the cross for us. He gave everything up, even his life. Regardless of how much we give, we will never give as much as he did. Everything depends on the standards we set for our lives: if the standard is selfishness, anything will seem difficult; anything you have to do, no matter how small, will represent an effort. This is not a generous attitude. But if the Holy Spirit is the one inspiring your action, each thing you do for others will give you gladness, and you will do it effortlessly because you will think it is totally normal; you will do it almost spontaneously. You asked about rewards, and I speak to you of happiness, the happiness granted by the great and small satisfactions of giving of yourselves to others."

At any rate, it is difficult to always respect God's Law; evil has some very attractive aspects.

"If you hate evil, it would be difficult for you to see its attraction. If you cling to goodness it will seem natural to you to cease doing evil, although it sometimes may seem attractive. If your love is sincere, you will share cordially and with tenderness, and you will receive as much back. This will reaffirm you in your resolve, and the attractiveness of evil will lose its strength and will not be able to convince you to follow it."

How can we tell that our love is truly sincere?

"The teachings of Christ are the rules that ensure our love. But there is a simple and easy way to remember. Love your neighbor as yourselves, do unto others as you would have them do unto you. We sometimes make mistakes that are only unintentional misunderstandings. Keep in mind the rules you apply to yourselves when others sin against you. Treat others as you would want to be treated. You are the reference point. It is easy to remember and test this, although it is not easy to do: that's the challenge of being a Christian."

Authority Is Important

And if we do all that, will we be important?

"Don't have delusions of grandeur. Don't act like know-it-alls in front of other people; rather, share in their feelings. Cry when they cry and laugh when they laugh. You will be great, but not as society defines greatness. Your greatness will consist of mixing in with simple people and sharing plans and concerns with them. Explain your own concerns, listen to theirs, and there will be harmony among you that will make you happy."

But if someone does something very bad to us, can't we get even?

"In those cases you can show how much you love people. It is not easy when something like that happens. Loving means doing no harm; you are not justified in doing something just because someone does it to you first. In that way you will prove that you are different. Do not return evil for evil, because you would do nothing more than lose your dignity. Do good to all people, even in cases such as you are talking about, and both of you will benefit."

Should the wrong that others do then go unpunished?

"You must try to live in peace with all people. Whoever does something wrong will receive punishment, but not from you. Punishment does not belong to you, but to the Lord; God rewards and punishes those who deserve it. Leave everything in God's hands. You must control your thirst for revenge because you do not get anything from it. On the contrary, you would lose out because that would mean evil has triumphed. Do it differently; do good to your enemies, feed them if they are hungry, and when they see you are repaying with goodness, they will be greatly ashamed."

If they have done something very serious, can't we punish them, even after a trial?

"If you judge them, they can judge you too. Haven't you ever been wrongly judged because people did not know your true intentions? The intentions, the motivations, the thoughts can remain inside each person. Do you know the inside of your enemies? Then you are not in any position to judge them. Only God knows. That's why God has reserved justice and punishment, when necessary. If anything, try not to bother your rival, but rather to help him or her."

We submit to the authority of God. But do we have to do the same with civil authority?

"There is no authority that is not subordinate to God's authority. So each person has to submit to the authorities who hold power. That is, obedience to the authorities is your duty. You must not just be afraid of the punishment you could receive if you rebel against it, but you have to think it is your moral obligation to submit without resistance."

So, God places each one in the right place, whether or not it is a place of authority?

"That's right. And it is not our place to criticize. Can you imagine the clay vessel saying to the potter: 'Why have you made me like this?' That's unthinkable. The potter is the one to decide what to make of the clay, not the clay itself. God is free to use one kind of clay for a vessel that will be considered noble and another for one that will be considered ordinary. We are the clay, would we dare ask for a change in God's plans? That would be as absurd as if the clay decided what it would become. On the other hand, if we trust God's decision sooner or later we will be glad."

Paul, Before Going to Jerusalem

On his return, Paul stopped in Troas and celebrated the breaking of the bread, or Eucharist. While he was celebrating, a boy fell asleep on a window sill and fell from the third floor. No matter how hard they tried, they could not revive him. The mother was crying desperately; the father did not react: he was numb, as if his soul had been sucked out of him.

As soon as he found out, Paul stood by the body of the child, brought him back to life, and said, "Don't be alarmed; the child is alive."

When the boy got up and embraced his family, everyone broke out in cries of gladness.

Paul was in such a hurry to get to Jerusalem that he could not stop at Ephesus. For this reason, during his stop over in Miletus, he met with the elders of Ephesus whom he had convened. He said to them, "I only want to bid farewell to you because we won't see each other again. I am going to Jerusalem and I know what awaits me there. I only want to encourage you to stand firmly in the faith I have taught you. Goodbye, my friends!"

At that time, everyone was moved by profound emotion. They would never again see the person who had given them the teachings of Jesus Christ.

"Goodbye, my friends!" were Paul's last words to them.

On his journey to Jerusalem, he went through Caesarea, where he visited Philip. A prophet who had just arrived from Judea came to Philip's house, and, after fastening Paul's belt around his waist, he said, "This is how the Jews in Jerusalem will tie up the man who owns this belt; they will leave him at the mercy of the pagans."

All pleaded with Paul not to go to Jerusalem, but he said to them, "I am not only willing to go to Jerusalem, but to die for the name of Jesus."

They could not say anything else, and they let God's will be done. When they got to Jerusalem, they went to the house of James, who had written some recommendations for the Christian communities who were in need of advice. This is what James' letter said:

Irritation, Riches: Difficulties

Why do we, Christians, meet with so many difficulties everywhere?

"When you encounter all sorts of problems, your faith is strengthened and it gives you perseverance. It is in contact with people who are not Christian that you can strengthen your resolve to continue on the way of Jesus Christ because you believe in his teachings. So you will see how trials help you to keep up your faith. You should be happy for all the past difficulties. Although you are faithful, know that you should show your faithfulness by doing things well. This faithfulness will make sense if you eagerly do whatever work is entrusted to you; it will be reflected in your life."

Why do we have to renounce wealth in order to follow Jesus?

"You sound as if you want riches. Many rich people are fooled into thinking their possessions depend on them because they are their property. That makes them feel superior to those who are not rich. This feeling prevents them from listening to, helping, and sharing with others, and they easily stray from the way of Jesus. It is difficult for them to consider their wealth as something passing, something that has been given to them and could easily disappear. They find it hard to think of wealth as something accidental; instead they believe it is a central part of their lives. A rich person who doesn't know how to be humble and dedicates all of his or her time to business is certain to wither away.

The Word of God tells us that we should treat rich and poor alike. How can we do that if the poor only bring us burdens and the rich give us profits? It seems more logical to be more considerate toward those who give us donations, right?

"Think of the people God has chosen. Many are poor and others are despised by people. Do you think Jesus has looked at the material riches? All people deserve your kindness, regardless of their material possessions. Faith in Jesus demands that you do not discriminate among people. Don't you see that a poor person might possess a great richness in spiritual values? What good would your favoritism be? Those who contribute something to the community should do it out of generosity and not to receive a better treatment from you. You would also like to be treated well for who you are and not for what you have, since you could lose what you have, but you would continue to be the same person. Do the same, then, for others."

So, we shouldn't be looking at what other people have, but we should treat them as we would like to be treated?

"Now you are talking! If you practice the Law of God, fulfill the main rule: love your neighbor as yourself. So, if you discriminate in your dealings with people, you will not be fulfilling the law, you will be sinning. And don't say, 'I don't keep this teaching, but I keep all the others,' since rules are different aspects of the same Law. This won't be any excuse when they judge you. If you never want to transgress, always treat others as you would yourself."

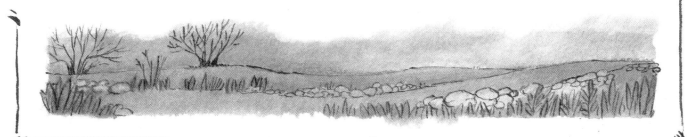

Faith, Criticism

In our community, some say that the most important thing is to have faith, and others that it is to fulfill the Law. Who is right?

"Faith, believing in Jesus Christ, is very important. But faith must be accompanied by works; faith without action is worth nothing. If a naked and hungry person would come before you and you would say, 'I see you don't have anything to wear or eat; go on, don't be cold or hungry,' what good is your observance to the person? You have to give him or her clothes and food; then it makes sense that you believe in his or her situation. The same happens with faith; if it is not expressed in action, it is dead in itself, and a dead faith is good for nothing. The demons, who only practice evil, also believe in Jesus, and they will not be saved by doing evil."

Some of our brothers and sisters criticize each other. What should we do about that?

"Ah, the tongue! It is the hardest organ to control; it is small in size but great in power. It is like the steering wheel of a ship that, although it is small, guides the ship wherever it goes. Or like a spark, insignificant in size, but with enough power to burn a whole forest. With ingenuity, human beings have domesticated many wild animals, but no one seems able to tame the tongue. It should be easier than controlling animals, but it isn't so. The tongue can praise or speak ill. When we pray, we use it to speak to God with respect and tenderness; but it is full of bitterness when we speak ill of others. Don't you see what a contradiction it is to speak sweetly to God, but bitterly to someone who has been created by God? Do you know of any fountain that alternately gives sweet and bitter water? There is none. Let us control our tongues so they don't produce bitter words when we talk about others, and then we will be able to pray in peace."

Does this advice about prudence in words go for swearing too? Can we swear when someone questions the truth in our words?

"Why would you need to swear? If people don't believe you, that's too bad for them! Sooner or later they will realize their position. If they don't believe you, who is to lose? They are. Do you think that those who are not willing to accept your words will change their minds just because you say it in the name of heaven or God? The truthfulness of your words will be proven later, and they will realize they have behaved like children. Say yes when you mean yes, and no when you mean no. You don't need to swear; the name of God should never be used lightly."

Going back to speaking evil of someone, can we criticize someone's actions when we think it is evident they are doing wrong?

"What a desire to act as judges! It is God who has the right to judge us and our brothers and sisters. We must be concerned about abiding by the Law, not about whether or not other people

abide by it. If we busy ourselves with criticizing the behavior of others, we will be doing something that does not befit us. Has someone appointed you to be the judges of others? Leave it in the hands of God, who will do whatever is more appropriate."

Law, Patience

Some of us devote a great amount of time to studying the Old Law in order to get more wisdom. Is this the right thing to do?

Studying the Law is good, but the wisdom that comes from repeating formulas is not as important as the one shown in works performed with simplicity. Humble behavior is the basis for true wisdom. If your heart is full of jealousy, resentments, or greed, no matter how well you recite or interpret, your wisdom does not come from heaven. It will help you to show off and receive the admiration of your companions. Such wisdom will bring disorder and confusion.

However, the wisdom that comes from heaven is peaceful and does not seek confrontation; it is friendly, seeks agreement; it is tolerant, agrees with the position of others whenever possible. Working for peace is a sign of true wisdom; whoever does so leads a life according to God's will."

We have always heard that patience is a virtue we must have. To what extent do we need to be patient?

"If your love for others were as it should be, you wouldn't be asking that. If you forgive the wrongs done to you, resentment won't pile up inside and put your patience in jeopardy. Do not complain; others could also complain about you. How patient should you be? As much as possible, be strong. Look at the patience of the farmer who waits as long as necessary for the rains to make the crops grow. What would you think of a farmer who could not wait for a plant to sprout and instead took the seed from the ground? The seed would only dry up and die. Or what would you think of one who pulled the plant up so that it grew faster? He would pull it out and not get any fruits. These are foolish ways to behave. Don't do the same; wait patiently and the fruits will come."

Some people in our community say that we shouldn't make plans for tomorrow, and others say we need to plan so that everything goes better.

"We are not like a cloud that forms here and dissolves there, or a breath of smoke that can vanish at any instant. Keep this in mind when you plan things like, 'Tomorrow we will go out to the field, or we will go on a 15-day trip . . .' Who is to say that you will be alive tomorrow? Do you perhaps know with such certainty that you can act as if you don't need to depend on anything or anyone? Say, 'God willing,' and then make your plans, but keep in mind that your lives depend on God and do not presume that you are totally independent, as if you were untouchable."

When he felt it was necessary, James also wrote letters like this one to help the most distant communities. After greeting Paul and telling him about what had gone on in Jerusalem during his absence, James informed him of the rumors going around in Jerusalem.

"The Jews of the city are upset with you because they have heard false reports that you are recommending that Jews from outside Jerusalem not be circumcised. To clear up this rumor you should go to the Temple tomorrow with four of the disciples who are going for their purification. You should do the same so that they see you have not forgotten the Law of Moses."

Paul followed James' advice, but when the Jews realized he was there, they did not bother to find out what he was doing. They only cared about inciting people against him so that, before he knew it, Paul was surrounded by Jews who were beating him up and insulting him.

A group of soldiers saved him from the crowd's blows—which could have killed him—and arrested him. Before going into the fortress, Paul wanted to speak to the people who were there, but his words were to no avail because people were out of control. Not willing to listen to him, they kept on insulting him.

"Take him inside and whip him until he confesses what he has done to these people who want him dead," the Roman governor said.

"You cannot whip a Roman citizen without a trial," Paul defended himself.

"You are a Roman citizen? I paid a lot of money for my citizenship."

"I didn't have to pay one penny. I am a citizen by birth."

At the end of the night, the governor convened the Sanhedrin to find out what the accusations against Paul were. When Paul was before the council, he said, "I have acted in good conscience, in accordance to the Law of God."

Paul realized that the Sanhedrin was not about to judge him in good faith. Therefore, he decided to confuse them. He knew that in the tribunal there were Pharisees, who accepted the idea of resurrection, and Sadducees, who absolutely rejected it. So he said to them, "Brothers, I am a Pharisee, the son of Pharisees. I am being judged for my hope in the resurrection of the dead."

No need for anything else! The Pharisees shouted, "This man is not guilty of anything."

On the other hand, the Sadducees proclaimed, "He is guilty. Resurrection is impossible."

The disorder was such that the Roman governor had to intervene. He sent the soldiers to take Paul away, for fear that he would be harmed.

That night the Lord appeared to Paul and told him, "Have courage, Paul. You have to give witness to me in Rome as you have done in Jerusalem."

Rome was an attractive as well as a feared place for Paul. The lifestyle in Rome, based on immediate and easy pleasure, was not at all like the Christian ideals, so it would be a hard place to bring about conversions. On the other hand, he hoped that, from the core of Rome, Christianity would spread throughout the world. But it would still be sometime before he got to the city. Peter was in Rome at that time, carrying out his mission. From there, Peter felt the need to write to the Christians of the five regions of Asia Minor to help them stay on the right course. These were the issues Peter explained to the Christians in answer to their concerns:

If We Are Not Evil, People Laugh at Us

What is the way to holiness all about?

"Before you received the teachings of Jesus Christ, your desires consisted of accumulating goods, acquiring a prominent social status, and enjoying as many pleasures as possible. Perhaps the habits of your old way of life will try to make a comeback and impose themselves on you again. You must be watchful not to fall back into a pagan style. Try not to let the behaviors you practiced for so long creep back into your souls without your noticing it. Lead a balanced life; think of the price you paid for being freed from your old habits: Jesus Christ offered his life up for you even before you had heard of him. Holiness is imitating him in everything. Be obedient children of God as Jesus Christ always was. Even at the most difficult moments he did not back down. If you do so, you will attain holiness, as Jesus Christ is holy."

But evil presents itself in many different shapes and with many different faces. What can we do to always prevent it?

"Look, your spirit has to be like those of newborns, who yearn for the pure milk of their mother. You know well how eagerly they drink from their mother's breast! Your pure milk must be the Word of God. If you digest it well, if you understand it and practice it, you will grow like children; you will become adults in the Word of God. By absorbing it, it will become a part of you; then there won't be any room in your hearts for deceit, lies, or jealousy. Persevere in this conduct and you will attain salvation."

The truth is that it is difficult not to practice evil like the pagans do. Some of them laugh at us, while others speak ill of us, as if we were criminals.

"It doesn't have to be easy for you to want to do the same things they do, and yet, you have to refrain, even if it means enduring insult. Even so, do not allow human passions to settle in your souls, for you will only obtain passing pleasures. Your satisfaction must be fulfilling the Word of God and enjoying the peace that comes from it. Maintain your good behavior among the pagans and let them talk. Sometimes their mockery is self-justification for their behavior, but if they see your good works, deep down they will admire your courage, and they will end up accepting the Word of God."

So, we have to bear it when they mock us and laugh at us?

"You'd be so fortunate to be insulted for being Christians! It shouldn't be a surprise to you, for you are different from pagans. You must be glad because you share the sufferings of Christ; this is a way to thank him for the sufferings he endured for us. Do not be ashamed. If they accused you of being thieves, murderers, or any type of criminals, you would have to be ashamed. But are you criticized because you are Christians? Thank God for that."

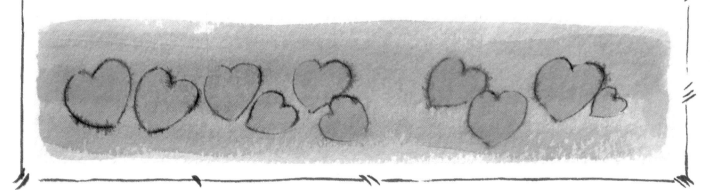

Is It Really Possible to Love So Much?

And we cannot defend ourselves from their attacks?

"Do not return evil for evil or injury for injury. Do not act as they do. As difficult as it sometimes is to love those who are part of the Christian community, loving those who are outside the community is even more difficult, especially if they continue to insult you. But you should also love them. Do not answer back. Leave if you are not able to keep quiet; that will make them wonder about your behavior, and they will be impressed."

But is it possible to love that way? Isn't this rule too demanding?

"You know how Jesus Christ loved so that you could change your lives and be saved. With him as your model, you will be able to do what you might think is impossible. If you allow love to invade you, it will be much easier. Love one another truly, because love overcomes all faults. If you love deeply, you won't feel like doing anything evil or getting even with your enemies. Jesus Christ, by being human like us, achieved much more than that. But he gave everything of himself."

Then, being a Christian means being constantly attentive, no matter where you are?

"It is total availability, as if your inner self had been transformed. Listen attentively to this: add faith to your virtue; knowledge to your faith; self-control to knowledge; perseverance to self-control; faith to perseverance; fraternal love to faith; love to fraternal love. Do all this and it won't be necessary for you to be on guard, because whatever comes from you will never be contrary to the Word of God."

There are some brothers and sisters who are beginning to think that we are just passing through this world, and so it is better to enjoy as much as possible while we are here.

"Of course we are passing through! And we have to keep this in mind, but we must not conclude that we need to turn to easy and dubious pleasures as if we are racing through life without brakes. We are people in passing, and so we need to take advantage of time as much as we can and enjoy it in the deepest sense of the word. True gladness comes from inner peace rather than from wild pleasures. I feel as if I live in a tent, which is my body; I am certain that I will soon have to leave this tent, so I intend to constantly remind you of what you already know but need to keep in mind: fulfilling the Word of God will give you the greatest and most lasting pleasure."

Are we so little a thing in this world?

"If we compare ourselves to the earth and everything in it, we cannot consider ourselves too great. If we were looking down from heaven, we could hardly see ourselves because we would seem so insignificant. The time will come when, with a great blast, heaven will disappear and the earth will be no more, undesirable people will dissolve, and a fire will swallow up everything. Where will we then be? It will depend on how we had behaved. If we had followed the teachings of Jesus, we will be welcomed in the reign of God; but if we have followed our instinct to satisfy impure desires, rejecting the Lord's power, we will disappear with the rest of the people."

The Authority, the Spouse

As Christians, should we pay attention to human authorities?

"You have to submit to human authorities because the Lord so wills it. Obey the orders of the king or his delegates like any other citizen must. To silence those who would portray you as outlaws, respect them, and they will change their minds about you. You must respect everyone, but young people must respect their parents even more so, because of their age. Exercise humility and this will allow you to serve one another."

Should a wife obey her husband?

"Wives should obey their husbands, even if some of them don't partake in the Word of God. Women must be chaste and respectful, so their behavior will win over their husbands and they, too, will share the Word of God."

There are different opinions in our community about how women should dress.

"Clothes certainly express the personality of women. One should not be concerned only with external appearances, since beautiful hairdos, precious jewels, or elegant dresses are not enough to give value to a wife. Her clothing should consist of, first of all, a deep personality, which is not noticeable at first sight, but it is the indestructible ornament of a sweet and calm spirit. A wife who has these virtues is the best dressed one, even if the clothing she wears is not the most expensive."

And the husband, how should he treat his wife?

"The husband must treat his wife with respect and shower her with all the attention she deserves as a wife. Both share the gift of Christian living. Their life together must allow them to help each other to keep ever faithful in their following of Jesus Christ."

It is difficult for such a demanding ideal to be accepted by the majority of people. Only a few will dare to accept the challenge of living according to the Word of God.

"Although the Word of God demands a lot, accepting and following it also gives great peace. Time will have to pass, but more and more people will eventually come to accept the teachings of Jesus Christ. Our hope is that one day all people will be part of God's design, having accepted the practice of his word. On that day we will have achieved a new earth and a new heaven."

Paul's Captivity

Let us return to Jerusalem: When dawn came, the Sanhedrin was dying of anger and shame for having let Paul go free the previous day—and for the embarrassing scene they had made before the Roman governor. They had sought Paul for a long time, and now he had laughed in their faces.

They wanted to get rid of the bad feelings that Paul caused them, and they planned to do so by killing him; in that way their anxiety would be gone. Forty men made a commitment not to eat or drink until Paul was dead.

This threat reached the ears of one of Paul's nephews, who informed his uncle. After pondering long and hard, the Roman governor decided to send Paul off to Caesarea to free him from the risk he was running in Jerusalem. He was sent to the house of Felix, the procurator, and almost three hundred soldiers accompanied him to protect him.

The Sanhedrin was dumbfounded. Now that they had a group of men ready to do anything to kill Paul, he had disappeared. They had no choice but to be patient. Five days later, accompanied by a lawyer so as not to embarrass themselves again, they asked the procurator Felix for an audience.

Felix asked them, "What is your accusation against this man?"

"We must warn you that this man is a real threat. He has gone throughout the world provoking confrontations in every Jewish community he has visited. Besides, he is the leader of the sect of the Nazarenes. He tried to profane our Temple when we persecuted him. If you interrogate him, you will realize what we are talking about."

Then Felix asked Paul to speak in his own defense, and Paul said, "I will speak before you with the freedom of knowing that you have been the judge of this nation for many years and, therefore, that you know what is going on. I have been in Jerusalem for only a few days. I have not had any argument or provoked any unrest among the crowd. They accuse me because it is easy to speak, but have they brought any proof of their words? None.

"I must confess, yes, that I am a Christian. The Christian movement is not a sect as they say, and I continue to accept all the laws of Moses and the prophets. Because I am a Christian, when I was in the Temple doing my purification, some Jews fell on me and started beating me up.

"If I were guilty of anything, they would have condemned me when I appeared before the Sanhedrin. The only thing they consider me guilty of—and not the whole Sanhedrin at that—is of having said that there is resurrection from the dead. Judge for yourself if that accusation is reasonable."

Felix decided, "When the governor arrives I will take care of your case."

And he left Paul in prison but allowed his family to come to help him. Paul was sorry he could not visit his dear communities. Sometimes he worried when reports about some communities were not positive. News came from Colossae that said that the faith of the community was in danger because teachings that were adverse to the teachings of Jesus Christ had surfaced. In his letter to that community, Paul tried to find the right way to strengthen the faith of the Colossians and to spread the Word of God.

Must Pleasures Be Enjoyed?

Philosophers have come to our city who say that the cravings and pleasures of the world must be enjoyed. Many people have paid attention and we feel confused.

"Your confusion does not surprise me. These philosophers propose a lifestyle like the one you had before you came to be part of the community of Christians. Do you remember what was going on with your uncontrolled desires? They led you to evil-doing. An extreme sensuality and a constant pleasure seeking led you to conflict, anger, and evil. Remember everything; not just the sensual pleasures you had, but also the quarrels and the hatred your uncontrolled desires led you to. Perhaps you are not really confused, but you are missing all that. You have been fortunate to receive the teachings of Jesus Christ. Now you know them and cannot claim ignorance. When we baptized you, your old habits and behaviors were left behind. Your human condition changed. You left behind the old person and clothed yourselves in a new person. You are different now. Do you really want to go back to what you were before?"

People think we are dumb. It seems unreasonable that we don't want to enjoy the same pleasures as our neighbors.

"There are instant pleasures and there are enduring pleasures. Before being called to Christ, the pleasures you enjoyed left you unsatisfied when they ended, which happened over and over again. Compare that with the gladness and peace you feel by following the teachings of Christ. You have clothed yourselves in a new person that appreciates the new feelings that come from patience, humility, and kindness. Do not let yourselves be taken over by the old person again. Be tolerant, forgive offenses. Hasn't the Lord forgiven all the evil actions of your past life? Do the same. Is it hard? Love. Grow in love for each other, and that will be your strongest bond. If you truly love, your desire for evil will vanish because no one wants to do harm to those one loves."

Paul Wants to Go to Rome

Two years later, Felix was replaced by Porcius Festus, but Paul was still in prison. The Sanhedrin tried to convince the new governor to transfer Paul so they could kill him en route, but Festus did not allow it.

A few days later in Caesarea, Paul and his accusers went before the governor. They accused him of everything they could think of, but they could not prove anything. Festus realized that the accusations were totally unfounded, but he wanted to ingratiate himself with the Jews. He asked Paul, "Would you like to go to Jerusalem so that I can judge you there according to the accusations presented?"

Paul answered, "By now you should know that I have not committed any fault against anyone. If you find fault in me, tell me what it is, and I will accept the verdict, even if that means death. But if I am not guilty of anything, you cannot leave me in their hands. If you transfer me from here to Jerusalem, you will hand me over so they can murder me on the way. As a Roman citizen, I appeal to Caesar."

"If you appeal to Caesar, you'll go to Caesar," Festus concluded.

But the transfer to Rome was not to happen immediately. Unconcerned about his own situation, Paul despaired over the problems of the different Christian communities whom he would have liked to comfort with his word. But his captivity prevented him from doing that, so he again took up the written word to guide the Ephesian community.

Total Transformation

Will those who behaved wrongly before becoming Christians be saved?

"Whatever you have done in your previous life doesn't have any influence on salvation. That is a gift from God who has wanted to give it to you because he loves you. All that you are asked to do is to believe in God, but believing really means wanting to imitate Jesus Christ."

Will we have more possibilities of salvation the more good works we do?

"You don't have to accumulate good deeds to show off and see who has done more; you only have to be informed by the Spirit of the Lord and live accordingly."

What if someone believes but does not live according to the teachings?

"That person does not really believe. Believing and acting according to Jesus Christ are inseparable. Really believing means accepting the person of Christ, which goes together with living according to his teachings. Those who say they believe but don't practice the Law of God are mistaken and really don't believe. Make love the foundation of life, which is the same as saying be humble in your behavior, gentle in your dealings with each other, and patient with others."

We have heard of the new life we should live as Christians. What does that mean?

"Don't you realize? Your lives have totally changed since you became Christians. You not only live a new life, but you are different people, too. You wish to leave behind the old person who behaved as a pagan; now you have a completely different role model: Jesus Christ. You must be transformed into new people. Even if you have the same face and the same body, your mind has changed under the inspiration of the Spirit of God. You have gone from a darkened understanding, which only aspired to satisfy its drives, to a life in which the only desire is the love of God and of one another."

But sometimes, even when we love one another, we do not all behave the same. What can we do?

"In the first place, reject deceit and speak truth to one another, since you must only have one word. If you get angry at someone, do not hold on to your anger; forgive or ask for forgiveness before the sunset. Do not steal; work to obtain what is necessary to live and share what you have with those in need. Let no bitterness come out of your lips; on the contrary, may your opinions help the community and one another. Cast out shouting, insults, evil. Be compassionate and kind with those down on their luck; help them as much as possible."

Social Relationships

And why can't we have more than one wife, or possess many things?

"The demand to believe in God refers to believing only in that God, and not in any other. You could tell me that you don't consider wives or possessions to be gods, but you would be wrong. If other things occupy the place in your heart that belongs to God, those objects and desires are your gods. Be it women or riches, they become your idols since everything starts revolving around how to get them. And if you give them as much importance as idols, you will have another god who will take you away from the true God and will prevent you from entering God's reign."

Does Christian marriage have to be different from the pagan one?

"The union between husband and wife must be similar to that between Christ and the community of believers, the Church. The husband is the head of the wife, as Christ is the head of the Church, which is his body. That's why the wife has to obey the husband, just as the Church obeys Christ. A husband loves his wife as his own body, because no one hates one's own body. Those who love their wives tenderly love themselves, as Christ loves his body, the Church. In short, love your wife as yourselves, and she will love and respect you."

And how must the relationship between parents and children be?

"Children must obey their parents. This is an act of justice, since parents try to do the best for their children and make an effort to give them food and a good education. Honor your father and your mother is the fourth commandment of the Law of God. Honoring means obeying them, taking care of them when they grow old, bringing joy to their lives any time you can, and saving them from worries. Parents must be good to their children; they must not be too severe with them. Follow the Lord's example when educating them. Think how many times God has not punished people even when there were good reasons to do so."

And the slaves, do they have to treat their masters as before?

"Slaves should obey their masters with respect and dedication for what they are ordered to do, doing it as well as they can, as if they did it for the Lord and not for their temporal masters. They must be watchful to the needs of their masters without being overbearing, but with a disposition to help and accomplish whatever is needed. On their part, masters must be respectful of their slaves and avoid threats or unnecessary punishments. When God judges you, he will not take into account the condition of slave or master, but only that each has fulfilled his or her mission. The individual's social status will be totally irrelevant at that point."

Paul's Explanations

A few weeks later, King Agrippa went to Caesarea to greet Festus, who took advantage of the opportunity to tell Agrippa about Paul.

"I have a Jewish prisoner that Felix left me. But, after listening to his accusers and interrogating him, I don't find him to be guilty."

"If you don't mind, I would like to listen to him."

"Very well then; let us listen to him."

King Agrippa told Paul, "You can start your defense."

"I am glad," Paul said, "to be able to defend myself before someone who not only knows the life of Jewish people, but also the Scriptures.

"My crime has been to follow the way of God as I understood it at each point. You must know that in my youth I relentlessly persecuted Christians with all my might. I did so because I considered them to be a danger to our Law and, therefore, for the people of Israel.

"After a divine vision, I realized that the followers of Jesus did not alter the Law of God, but rather improved upon it and fulfilled it. I then placed all my heart and all my strength in the service of spreading the teachings of Jesus, that all who believe in him might be saved.

"This radical change was not accepted by the priests who had placed their trust in me when I persecuted the Christians. They called my transformation treason and have sworn to revenge. The desire for revenge is burning inside them and makes them do, say, and invent anything that could serve their purpose of eliminating me.

"But I have to give myself to my mission, which is announcing that Jesus, the Messiah, suffered and was the first to rise from the dead to spread his teachings among the people of Israel and the pagans."

"I had heard that you had a lot of knowledge, but perhaps this made you delirious," Agrippa cut in.

"I am not delirious, King Agrippa. My words are sensible and truthful."

The conversation had come to an end at that point. Festus and Agrippa continued talking. The king said to the Roman procurator, "This man is not guilty of anything. If he had not appealed to the Emperor, he could have been set free already."

A Perilous Journey

Paul was sent to Rome to appeal to Caesar. They entrusted him to the care of a kindly centurion who set sail with Paul after bidding his family and friends farewell. They were sailing slowly because of the lack of wind. Several days had passed since their departure and they had advanced little. When they arrived in Crete, they considered whether it was worthwhile to continue sailing, since there was danger of a storm.

Paul thought that it would be better to stay in Crete and wait for conditions to improve before they continued on their journey. The captain of the ship, however, thought they should continue sailing and, therefore, they went out to sea.

A few days later a terrible storm came upon them. The high waves rocked the boat as if it were a nutshell. The sailors did not know what to do to control the boat; they had cast out into the sea everything that could have sunk them. There were sunless days and starless nights; they only felt the rolls of the waves and the blasts of thunder.

They had all but lost hope of being saved when Paul said, "Don't be afraid. We will lose the boat, but none of us will die. Last night an angel of the Lord appeared and revealed this to me. It won't be long before we touch land. Eat and do not give up because you will need all your strength to survive."

Fourteen days after the storm began, they saw land. The boat did not make it, but some swam and some held on to rafters and pieces of wood, and they all made it to the beach. This was the island of Malta.

The natives of the island helped them as much as possible and lit a fire so the shipwrecked could warm up. Paul joined with them, and, as he was picking up a bundle of wood, a viper bit his hand. Everyone thought his hand would swell and he would shortly die, but nothing of the sort happened. He did not even get sick.

Publius was the richest landowner on the island. For a few days, he allowed the shipwrecked to stay in his house. Publius's father was sick at the time. As a reward for his generosity, Paul laid hands on the man, and he was healed. They brought all the other sick people in the island before Paul, and he cured them all.

Three months later they left the island. The people of the island had provided them with everything they could possibly need for their journey. This time they would reach Rome without any problems.

Making Christians in Rome

In Rome, Paul was allowed to live without the supervision of a guard.

Paul had wanted to go to Rome because he knew that if he could make converts out of the majority of people, all the known world could also be converted. He had arrived as a prisoner and after a horrible shipwreck, but to him they were just incidents of little importance. Now he could devote himself to making contact with the Jews, and later with everyone who wished to proclaim the Good News.

He did so. He got in touch with the Jewish community and explained to them, "Brothers and sisters, I come as a prisoner from Jerusalem. When the Romans judged me, they wanted to set me free, but the Sanhedrin was opposed. For this reason, I have been a prisoner for several years now, and, because of the priests' intentions to kill me, I was forced to appeal to Caesar. I don't have any accusations against my people. All I want is to defend myself."

The Jewish people in Rome answered, "We don't have any information about you. We haven't received any letters. Therefore, explain yourself so that we can decide for ourselves."

Then the Jewish people allowed Paul to explain his beliefs to them. Paul did so by saying that Jesus' work was a continuation of the Scriptures and added meaning to them.

Many meetings were necessary for a sector of the Jewish people from Rome to be convinced that Paul was bringing a message of truth. Those that converted to Christianity detached themselves from those who continued being Jews.

A significant core of people faithful to Jesus was established in the center of the empire. In this way it would soon expand. Paul started preaching to the pagans and many of them received Jesus' message with open hearts.

For two years Paul lived in his house in Rome, explaining the teachings of Jesus to all those who wanted to listen to them. It is obvious that, thanks to him, the community of Christians in Rome increased in number. They became so established that Christianity began to impact the whole known world, which was Paul's main goal.

At the end of this process, and seeing that things were taking a turn for the worse, people did not want to risk their lives by supporting Paul, and he found himself alone. He was condemned to be beheaded. It was the spring of the year 67 when Paul fulfilled his resolution to give up his life for his beliefs: Jesus Christ and the spread of Christianity throughout the world.

But his influence on the Christian movement did not end with his death. He had created a school, and his disciples developed teachings started by Paul. They also helped others understand Paul's doctrine. During this process, an important letter to the Hebrews was developed, clarifying the following issues:

About Jesus Christ

What need did Jesus have to become a human and to die, since he was God?

"Jesus wanted to adopt the human condition to share the same nature with us and to live the same life as we do. He was in solidarity with us. In this way, as our older brother and Son of God, he was granting us the dignity of being children of God. He did so to serve as a role model so that we may be able to fulfill the will of God; that the suffering he freely accepted and endured would encourage us to accept the effort and acts of generosity that the will of God sometimes requires. He wanted to offer us the greatest possession that a person can have: his own life. He accepted his physical death to free us from the fear of spiritual death. This fear had made us slaves during our whole lives. Having gone through the harshness of trial, he could help those who endure trials."

Why do we call Christ the high priest?

"Because the priests' work is to offer sacrifices for their own sins and the sins of the people. It wasn't necessary for him to offer sacrifices every day; once was enough. He offered himself up as a victim, not for his sins, for he had none, but for the sins of the people, to obtain forgiveness. Has there ever been a greater sacrifice or a more generous victim? With his action he surpassed all the previous priests and became the greatest of all."

Then has God's Old Covenant with the people ceased to be valuable?

"He has renewed the covenant of old. Christ died to free people from the infidelities committed under the first covenant. He is the intermediary of this New Covenant. He has left us the New Covenant as a testament, and a testament does not have any validity if the leader is not dead. With the death of the leader the testament acquires all its value and has the power of a rule."

What should we do when we grow discouraged because we can't seem to manage to leave sin behind?

"God outlines a path for us that requires effort. If our focus is Jesus, we will find strength in times of discouragement. Let us think that we have to free ourselves from our sins, our bad habits. Jesus did not need to do that. He left the glory he had with God, his Father, to come and die on a cross—in the same way that the worst criminals are executed—and to endure the spite of people. Let us keep in mind that Christ gave the most, even to death, without gaining any profit from it, only to give us strength when we are discouraged in our struggle against evil. Let us then reject sin with the power that his free generosity affords us."

Advice for Life

How should we treat others?

"Try to live in peace with everyone. Yield when necessary, avoid conflict, forgive faults, and treat everyone with kindness. May no one be misled by lack of control, because that would be like a bitter root in the midst of the community. For their own sake and for the bad influence they might exert on their brothers and sisters, you must avoid this."

What recommendations could we follow to stay on the straight path?

"Love one another always as good brothers and sisters. Practice love among yourselves and with people outside the community. You must be hospitable and kind. Welcome all those who visit you, and you will receive their gratitude. Visit the prisoners and comfort them as much as possible; encourage them as if you yourselves were the ones imprisoned. Help those who are abused in any way: care for them, speak to them, and try to find a solution to that abuse; listen to them and give them advice. If you were in their place, you would also want help and support."

Does possession of money harm Christian living?

"Money could be a form of slavery. We must be freed from the greed for money and possessions. If you don't do that, all your interests will revolve around money. The center of your life would no longer be God; you would have substituted what is necessary to preach the Word of God for what you need to do to acquire more money, more possessions. Why do you want to accumulate money if God has promised not to abandon you if you follow God's teachings?"

What should we do when people explain to us theories contrary to Christian teachings?

"Do not get entangled in strange theories. Jesus Christ did not die so that you would lose your salvation, but so that you could enjoy the fruits of his sacrifice. If you forsake the Word of God and follow others, you will be devaluing the death of Christ. Take Christ as your first example, and then follow the example of your teachers who have explained the Word of God. Consider how they have lived and died and imitate their faith. Isn't the inner peace that the Word of God gives you a sign that you must leave all other theories aside?"

Must we obey our leaders?

"It is your duty to obey your leaders. They will give an account for your actions, for themselves, and for what they have ordered you to do. So all the worries rest on them. The more power or responsibility they have, the more careful they should be because they are as responsible for what they ordered as if they themselves had done it. You may think they are taking advantage of you, but they really are doing you a favor because they take responsibility away from you. They will have to be accountable before God."

Are There Any Writings by Other Apostles?

Paul was not the only one to write to the Christians. After his martyrdom, inspired by his actions and examples, his disciples continued his work. In a similar way, upon the apostle John's death, his disciples wrote some letters addressed to the Christians of that time. These are still important for today's Christians. Although it was not John himself who wrote them, these writings are known as John's letters because they contain his thoughts and teachings as explained by those who could do it, his disciples, who had known him personally. Read these questions in the letters of John:

The Things of This World

Could someone be totally sinless?

"Those who say they are sinless deceive themselves and try to deceive others. God does, however, forgive our sins if we repent. What fear could there be in recognizing our sins? Before Jesus' coming that could have made sense, but not anymore."

What does it mean to say that Jesus has brought us light?

"Sometimes we believe that we live in the light when we really are in darkness, or vice versa. Jesus Christ has given us the commandment to love one another, and he has given us light and shown us the sign so that we can know whether we live in darkness or in light. If you love your brothers and sisters, then you live in the light. If you don't love, even if you say you live in the light, you are in darkness. There is a great difference between loving and not loving, as big as day and night, light and darkness. Everything changes when you love. You accept more readily what people say and do to you, you excuse the mistakes and faults of others."

Can we really call ourselves children of God?

"Of course we can! The love of the Father has given us this gift. Although our body is the same, we are God's children, because God's love has transformed us into different people with the same body. Who will do what God does, forgiving our sins if we repent and love? God sends us his only son, allows him to go through death for us, so we can be children of God. Only the best father would do such a thing."

Why are there people who rebel against God, who has done all this?

"You speak about pagans who don't want to listen to the Word of God, but apply this question to yourselves. Whoever commits a fault, whoever sins, rebels against God. Consider it then, and don't behave carelessly. Make sure that what you are about to do is in accordance with the Christian spirit. Check that whatever you do is inspired by love and then you can be certain not to offend God, our Father."

But if someone commits a sin, he or she does not intend to rebel against God . . .

"God asks for full faithfulness. You cannot be with God and sin at the same time. Those who commit sin belong to the devil; you cannot sin and still believe that you are on the path of Christ; it is contradictory. Children of God do not continue to sin: they have the Word of God inside. Perhaps they haven't fully assimilated it, perhaps they don't truly love, because if they really loved, they couldn't bear to sin. They would not separate themselves from God's way."

A Mature Love

Does that mean that loving God is enough?

"Loving God is basic, but how would you know you truly love God? Think of something easier to check: Do you love the person next to you, no matter who he or she is? Then you can be sure that you love God. What do you say? You don't love those people next to you? You don't even know them? Then you lie when you say you love God. How can you love God, whom you have never seen, if you don't love those who are before your very eyes? Do you want me to tell you that if you don't love enough, if you don't love everyone, you will receive the punishment you deserve? If necessary, I will tell you that, because that is the truth. But that is a childish way to think of love. Is it necessary to scare you into loving truly? The time has come for us to behave like adults and overcome fear, because fear has nothing to do with a mature love. Some need fear and that is a sign that their love is still far from reaching maturity."

And how can you love an unknown person? Or someone we have just met? That isn't easy.

"Nor is it that difficult. We can speak well of an unknown person or criticize that person. We can address them in a gentle or in an abrupt way; we can see their faults or their virtues. We can welcome affectionately or ridicule those we have just met; value their strengths or be jealous of them, pay attention to them, or pretend we don't see them. What does all this have to do with love? All that is love. Is an attraction necessary to make the other person appealing to us? It's better if there is. But what really counts is facts, the things we can touch and see. It is better if there are pleasant words and positive feelings, but not only that: action gives meaning to love."

When strangers come, do we have to go out of our way to welcome and help them?

"That would be a good course of action. You must behave according to your faith in all you do. You have a good example in Jesus Christ. Did he know all the people for whom he was sacrificed? And God did not hesitate to send his son to death so that all people could be saved, people from all over, known or unknown. If you act this way, you will create a current of communication and warmth that will satisfy you."

Another writing with thoughts and reflections by the apostle appeared at the end of the first century. Its name is Revelation and it addresses the following issues:

Whatever You Do, Do It Wholeheartedly

We always try not to fall into sin. Is this the right attitude?

"Watchfulness is very necessary. But your love has changed; you don't love as before. You have gotten used to doing a series of things you repeat over and over again in a mechanical way. You must do things in a reflective way, being aware that you are doing something good for the other person as well as for yourselves. You have to renew the intensity of your love to find satisfaction and encouragement in what you do. You have fallen into monotony in the accomplishment of routine actions. Place your heart in those same actions and they will take on another nature."

But aren't actions more important than feelings?

"Of course actions are most important. But remember the excitement you first placed in your actions. They made you feel fulfilled and you saw the meaning in all of your works. But you must know why you are doing them and what your intentions are. You must remember this at all times. You have to appreciate the satisfaction of others, their gratefulness, the good you are doing them. This will keep your enthusiasm alive and you will not lose your energy. This activity must be inspired by the Word of God, which is not something so tired that it has lost its power and cannot prod you on to any new things. You must find a practical application for your everyday life, and that is always new."

Some of our companions have been imprisoned; we can't help feeling afraid.

"I have received the news of your sufferings, the slanders you have to endure for being Christians, and your material poverty, which is spiritual wealth. What you suffer, both those in prison and those who are free, is a trial. Cling to the example of Christ and be faithful to him until death. Hold on to the certainty that you are not guilty of their accusations and that you are on the way to eternal life. I know that it is hard to accept this. However, if you have a tragic end, your executors will only have quickened your passing to eternal life. As human beings, this is hard to swallow. Keep this reality in mind, and it will console you and encourage you to face whatever comes your way."

Integrity, Faithfulness

We are in the midst of pagans, people who practice other religions that have a negative influence on the new Christians; we are besieged on all sides. What can we do?

"What must we do with those who do things contrary to the teachings of Jesus? They must change their minds. We have too many examples in the history of the covenant with God of situations such as these. Those who have gone astray have always ended up either in repentance and conversion, or with God's punishment. Think of this. I know that keeping faithful in everything is not easy, surrounded as you are by strange ideas, contrary to the Word of God. Even so, you must make an effort. Repent for ever having gone astray from the teachings of Jesus, but don't ever yield; don't give up. The Word of God and your relationships will give you strength for this."

There is a woman in our community who does not quite fulfill the Word of God and has some misleading interpretations, far from the true spirit. But she has such a great influence on the majority of the community that, if we leave her out of things, or confront her openly, we risk losing the community. What can we do?

"That woman is misleading the servants of the Lord by teaching them practices reserved for idols. Let us give her some time to change her attitude and repent. But if she doesn't want to do it, she will in due time be punished, then everyone will realize that the security of that woman did not come from God but from alien idols. Remain loyal in love, faith, the spirit of service, and, above all, in perseverance, and that crisis will pass and you will forget it."

There are so few of us in comparison to the pagans. How can we make any inroads in spreading the message of Jesus Christ?

"The essential thing is to keep the Word of God and not contradict yourselves in any situation—that's always more effective than words. I know that there are liars, both Jews and pagans, who pretend to be Christian in order to make you fall into their trap. Be constant in imitating Christ and you will have nothing to fear. They will become convinced when you do the right thing, you will be earning a crown in heaven. Let them be; if they don't want to believe now, they will eventually see everything when God puts the inhabitants of this earth to the test. Perhaps they will want to react then, but it will be too late and they will regret not having accepted what they had before their eyes for so long."

Is Wealth Everything?

If we are rich, what need do we have for anything else?

"Those of you who are rich have everything already? Perhaps you are rich, but by speaking in that way, you only prove that you are blind because you only look one way. You only see your own needs and wants. There are blind people who are so because their eyes don't see, but they realize the needs of those around them and help in any way they can; they can see better than you. You dress in very expensive clothes, and I see that you are naked, because clothes are only a cover-up. The important clothing is solidarity with others. Your spirit is miserable and that makes you miserable and poor—much poorer than those who have absolutely nothing to wear or eat. But, since you are blind, you must not see all this. And I am telling you this because I love you. And who else loves you? You, not your riches. Do you know what loving means? Think about it. Material wealth comes and goes—now you have it; now you don't. It would be better if you felt rich in spirit, and you could find the peace you lack. How will you achieve this? I am telling you all this for free: follow the Word of God, fill yourselves with love for others, and then you will feel and be truly rich."

What is the fate that awaits those who, in spite of difficulties, have been faithful to the Word of God until the end?

"They have already gone through the great trial. The blood of Christ, who was sacrificed as the lambs of the Old Testament were offered in sacrifice, has helped them be saved. They will be forever before the throne of God, and they will serve God day and night under his protection. Do not spare any effort to proclaim and follow the teachings of Christ in everything. You will obtain happiness in this life and eternal bliss in the reign of God."

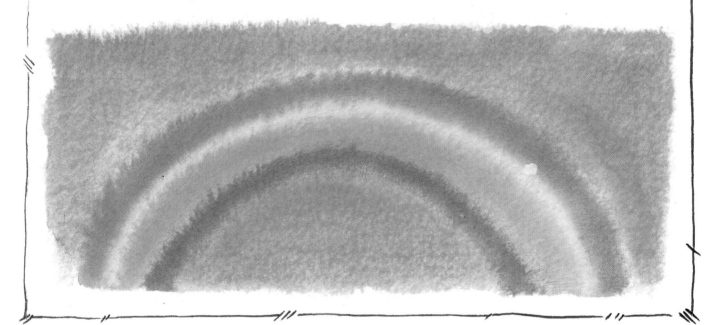

The Bible is the story of a dialogue between God and humanity. Speaking to the people of Israel, God addresses all peoples and invites them to live together with God. Those who pay attention listen and respond to God by leading the life God wills.

This dialogue is the Word of God—Sacred Scripture—manifested with human words: the biblical books, inspired by God, were written in the language and words of a down-to-earth people—with their mind and feelings, their flaws and faults.

The Bible: A People Listen to God is a summation of the Scripture texts, along with some explanation of the culture of the biblical peoples. Understanding this culture is a first step toward reading the Bible.

The story of the people who have been listening to the Word of God is the story of Israel. It is also the story of the Church—the new People of God. And so, it is our own history, the story of the men and women who want to carry out the plan that the Bible offers: a world of brothers and sisters living as God wills.

The text of the Bible has been translated (partially or in full) into about eleven hundred languages. There are different versions in English to choose from, which can be found in a bookstore or library.

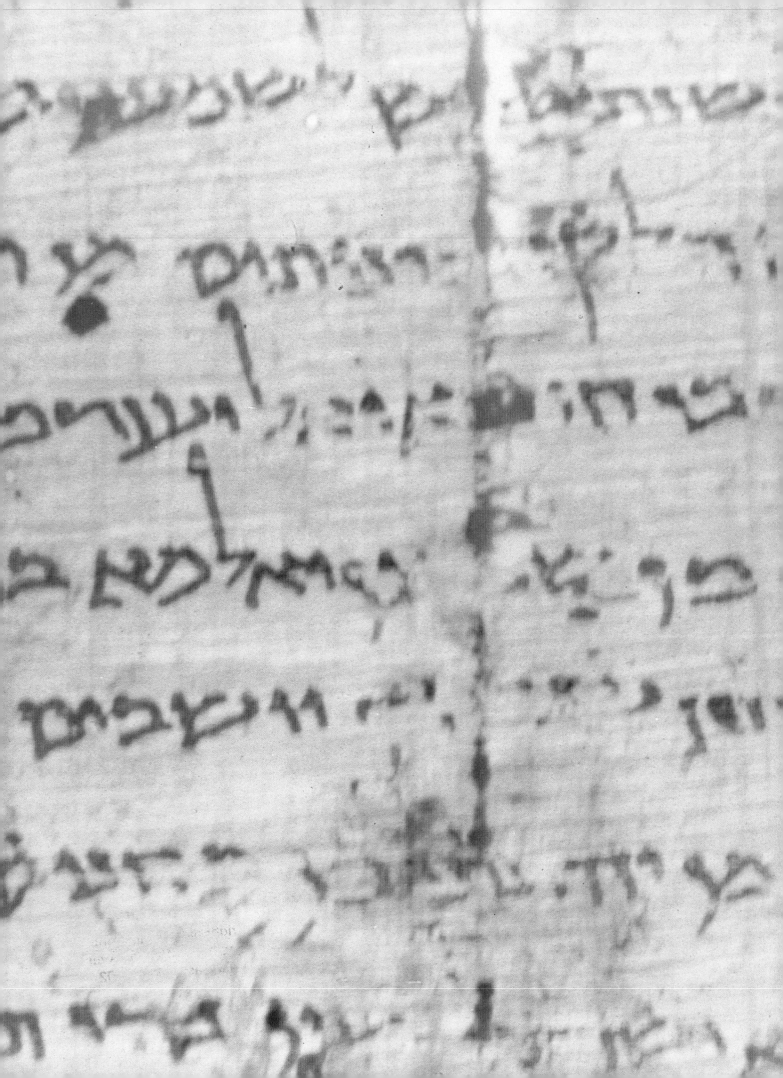